ENFORCING THE WORK ETHIC

SUNY Series in the Sociology of Work
Richard H. Hall, Editor

ENFORCING THE WORK ETHIC

Rhetoric and Everyday Life in a
Work Incentive Program

Gale Miller

State University of New York Press

Published by
State University of New York Press, Albany

Printed in the United States of America

For information, address the State University of New York Press,
State University Plaza, Albany, NY 12246

Library of Congress Cataloging-in-Publication Data

Miller, Gale.
   Enforcing the work ethic : rhetoric and everyday life in a work
incentive program / Gale Miller.
       p.   cm. — (SUNY series in the sociology of work)
   Includes bibliographical references.
   ISBN 0-7914-0423-4. — ISBN 0-7914-0424-2 (pbk.)
   1. Human services personnel—United States.   2. Work ethic—United
States.   3. Work Incentive Program (U.S.)   I. Title.   II. Series.
   HV40.8.U6M55   1991
   362.5′84′0973–dc20   89–26319
                                                                    CIP

10 9 8 7 6 5 4 3 2 1

For
my parents — Delmar and Eleanor Miller
and
parents-in-law — Henry and Jeanne Dress

Contents

Figures and Tables

Preface

One of the aspects of the contemporary sociology of work and organizations that I find both perplexing and troublesome is sociologists' general lack of interest in analyzing how work is done. As Schwartz and Jacobs (1979) note, sociologists study virtually all aspects of the social organization of contemporary work except for this issue. Too often, the work process (as it is concretely done) is treated as a mere epiphenomenon of "larger" social structures and processes, such as the division of labor. This orientation to the analysis of work differs markedly from that espoused by Everett Hughes and his students who taught us to formulate and seek the answers to sociological questions by looking directly at the mundane events and relationships of everyday life. While it is different from Hughes' approach, the same commitment to directly studying and analyzing everyday life is central to ethnomethodology, a sociological theory that seems to have had virtually no impact on the sociology of work and organizations.

This book is partly intended to show how sociologists of work and organizations might analyze work process as rhetoric. It is part of a larger project that I share with several present and former colleagues in the Department of Social and Cultural Sciences at Marquette University. They are Dave Buckholdt, Jay Gubrium and Jim Holstein. Although we have studied different types of institutions, our work is tied together by a concern for analyzing language use and social process in contemporary human service organizations. As Gubrium (1988) states, our various studies are *practical ethnographies* because they focus on the practical ways in which human service professionals and others in their work worlds make sense of aspects of their everyday lives.

In part, I note these continuities to highlight the ways in which Dave, Jay and Jim have contributed (in witting and unwitting ways) to this study. I am especially indebted to Jim who is always available to counsel me on the various practical and theoretical "troubles" that emerge when one does this type of research and analysis. I appreciate the intellectual help that they have given me as well as their friendship. Although they have never been affiliated with Marquette University, I should also mention the influences of Bob Emerson and Doni Loseke on this project. I appreciate the criticisms and advice that they have given me over the years as well as the substantial contributions that they have both made to the discipline through their research. I also must note the contributions made by Judith Blau who initially suggested and encouraged me to do this book for the SUNY Press Series in the Sociology of Work, Dick Hall (the current editor of the series), and Rosalie Robertson (the editor at SUNY Press).

Finally, I would like to thank my wife Diane for her patience and encouragement during this process. Qualitative research is a time consuming and difficult activity that has implications for one's family and family life. Thus, whatever merit there is in this book should be shared with Diane.

Aspects of the research were supported through funds provided by the Institute for Family Studies of Marquette University. I have discussed some of the issues analyzed in this book in other outlets. Of special relevance and note are the following:

"Holding Clients Accountable," *Social Problems* 31 (1983): 139–151.

"Client Attitude and Organizational Process," *Urban Life* 13 (1985): 367–394.

"Unemployment as a Dramaturgical Problem," *Sociological Quarterly* 17 (1985): 479–493.

"Defining Proper Work Performance," *Journal of Contemporary Ethnography* 18 (1989): 30–49.

"Negotiating Labor Market Effects," *Symbolic Interaction* 12 (1989): 30–49.

"Social Problems Work in Street-Level Bureaucracies," (with James A. Holstein) *Studies in Organizational Sociology* (Gale Miller, editor), Greenwich, CT: JAI Press, in press.

1

Human Service Work as Rhetoric

This book is about the everyday activities and relationships making up the social world of a Work Incentive Program (WIN) located in a small city in the Midwest. WIN's purpose is to help persons receiving Aid to Families with Dependent Children (AFDC) in finding jobs and getting off of welfare (Coudroglou, 1982; Johnson, 1973; Segalman and Basu, 1981; Stein, 1976). The program was organized to impose a variety of work norms on persons receiving such aid. Most clients were required to look for jobs and regularly report to the WIN staff on their job seeking activities. Clients assessed by the WIN staff as inadequately fulfilling program requirements were removed from WIN and, depending on the clients' AFDC statuses, lost all or a significant portion of their welfare grants.

WIN as a Street-Level Bureaucracy

Looked at one way, WIN is a "street-level bureaucracy" because it is a public agency which provides direct services to the public and its staff enjoys a relatively high degree of discretion in providing benefits and imposing sanctions on its clients (Lipsky, 1980). Analyzed as a street-level bureaucracy, WIN has much in common with public schools, hospitals, police departments, welfare agencies, low-level courts, and legal services offices. All such organizations involve applying general public policies to the concrete circumstances of persons' lives. In doing so, street-level bureaucrats give practical meaning to the policies. As Lipsky (1980: xii) states,

> the decisions of street-level bureaucrats, the routines they
> establish, and the devices they invent to cope with uncertain-

ties and work pressures, effectively *become* the public policies they carry out...public policy is not best understood as made in legislatures or top-floor suites of high-ranking administrators, because in important ways it is actually made in crowded offices and daily encounters of street-level workers...policy conflict is not only expressed as the contention of interest groups but is also located in the struggles between individual workers and citizens who challenge or submit to client-processing.

Lipsky analyzes street-level bureaucracies as filled with tensions, dilemmas and uncertainties emanating from workers' relationships with high-level policy-makers, clients and the public. He emphasizes three major sources of problems in such work. First, street-level bureaucrats are expected to provide services to all persons in need while also processing clients in efficient and effective ways, two goals that are not always compatible. A related source of work problems involves street-level bureaucrats' management of limited resources. The difficulty is partly a matter of adjusting to frequent changes in resources provided by legislatures and other funding sources. But, even when relatively high levels of resources are provided, street-level bureaucrats are never given sufficient resources to fully address all of their clients' problems.

A third set of problems involve street-level bureaucrats' relationships with clients and the public. Although they vary across institutions, Lipsky states that street-level bureaucrats are frequently alienated from their clients and the public because they perceive clients and the public as unsympathetic to their problems and overly demanding of scarce organizational resources. Problems in street-level bureaucrat-client relationships are most obviously seen in the angry exchanges which sometimes follow the announcement of street-level bureaucrats' decisions. The exchanges often turn on the clients' claims that street-level bureaucrats are arbitrary and unfair. Street-level bureaucrats frequently counter such claims by portraying their decisions as mandated by the facts under consideration or organizational policies. According to Lipsky, the long-term effect of such exchanges is an atmosphere of distrust and tension in street-level bureaucrats' interactions with clients and members of the public.

Basic to Lipsky's analysis of work and social relations in street-level bureaucracies, then, is an image of street-level bureaucrats' development of *coping strategies and practices* which are useful in managing troublesome aspects of their work. They include unofficial work routines, schemes for classifying clients and others, and methods of rationing services. According to Lipsky, such strategies are rational responses to working conditions that make the achievement of public policy goals problematic, if not impossible.

Lipsky's study is an important contribution to the sociological analysis of human service professionals and their work problems. He provides a sympathetic account of the practical constraints faced by street-level bureaucrats in attempting to fulfill their professional obligations, constraints that are not always appreciated by others. Although it is based on a different theoretical perspective, this analysis is also concerned with the practical problems associated with street-level bureaucrats' work and the ways in which they seek to manage them. It is similar to Lipsky's analysis in, at least, three ways.

First, this study is concerned with the ways in which WIN staff members dealt with problematic aspects of their work, including those emphasized by Lipsky. Second, the analysis treats the WIN staff as rational persons who sought to properly fulfill their professional obligations while working under difficult circumstances. Finally, the study emphasizes the ways that WIN staff members and others in their work world gave practical meaning to general and abstract public policies by interpreting and applying them to the diverse and concrete circumstances of everyday life. The interpretive activities are analyzed as central features of the WIN staff's work and, through them, staff members sought to fulfill their professional responsibilities and achieve organizational goals.

Despite these similarities, this study differs from Lipsky's in several important ways. The differences are discussed in the next section which also considers the general perspective and concerns of the study.

Descriptive Practice in Street-Level Bureaucracies

Basic to Lipsky's approach is an image of street-level bureaucrats as coping with problems created by others and over which they have little or no control. In a sense, the approach treats street-level bureaucrats as victims; that is, they are described as persons who are unjustly harmed or damaged by external forces (Holstein and Miller, 1990), Their responses are also described as victimlike. Like other victims, Lipsky states that street-level bureaucrats can only react to the problems brought on them by others. He further states that in coping with their work problems, street-level bureaucrats create other problems for themselves and their clients. Thus, a vicious cycle emerges in which street-level bureaucrats' attempts to manage problems created by others become the basis for further problems and injustices.

There is, however, another way of analyzing this aspect of street-level bureaucrats' work. It focuses on the ways in which street-level bureaucrats portray aspects of their work as problems and actions as coping strategies and tactics. The approach centers in treating street-level bureaucrats' portrayals of their work as descriptive practices. On the surface, descriptive practices are nothing more than reports about observable and/or factual qualities of objects or events. But they are more than this. Descriptive practices are ways of assigning meaning to aspects of everyday life and expressing persons' orientations to them. For example, when street-level bureaucrats portray their work worlds as filled with problems and their actions as professionally responsible efforts to cope with the problems, they simultaneously highlight aspects of their work circumstances and express an attitude toward them. They also de-emphasize other aspects of their work worlds that might be used to describe their work circumstances as unproblematic.

The "human service work as filled with problems" description (and orientation) is similar to that expressed by Lipsky in analyzing street-level bureaucrats' work, because it emphasizes the ways in which street-level bureaucrats are constrained and sometimes victimized by forces beyond their control. Consider, for example, the following statement made by a human service worker about the amount of paperwork that she is required to do.

> There is a lot of paper work in this job.... There is a lot of accountability, and I'm not sure that it is worth all the effort that we put into it. It just takes away a lot of my time and energy that I need to be doing other things with the [clients].... Obviously there is a balance, and obviously you can't have programs unless you can verify that they are doing

something to the funding sources.... But there's a point where it gets out of control and off balance. (Dressel, 1984: 33–34)

Looked at one way, the human service worker's portrayal of the paperwork requirements of her job is a common-sense version of Lipsky's approach to street-level bureaucracies. Specifically, she portrays paperwork as a problem that is externally imposed by funding sources who seek verification that programs are being properly implemented. She also portrays paperwork as a constraint that limits her choices and actions and takes time away from other, more important activities. In highlighting and portraying paperwork as a problem, then, the human service worker casts her actions as efforts to cope with troublesome conditions that are beyond her control.

Although street-level bureaucrats frequently portray their work in ways similar to Lipsky's and other social scientists' analyses, they are not the same. There are two major ways in which street-level bureaucrats' common-sense portrayals and orientations differ from those of social scientists. First, street-level bureaucrats' portrayals of their work are expressed as practical orientations to situationally emergent problems and concerns. They are not intended as enduring analyses, but are inextricably tied to the practical issues at hand. The portrayals are procedures for making sense of the issues and taking action toward them. Thus, street-level bureaucrats' portrayals of themselves and their work may change as they deal with different practical problems in different situations. Street-level bureaucrats portray themselves as constrained and coping on some occasions, but not on all. Indeed, on some occasions they portray themselves as having considerable discretion in responding to their work problems.

Second, street-level bureaucrats' portrayals and orientations to social reality are expressed in different social contexts than those of social scientists. Street-level bureaucrats are involved in a variety of relationships and interactions that include persons who are assumed to hold different (frequently opposed) perspectives on issues of interest to them. Such persons may include organizational superiors, clients, and even colleagues who are sometimes portrayed as having different perspectives on the purposes of their work. Whoever they are, street-level bureaucrats orient to other persons as potential sources of trouble, because they are potential sources of resistance to street-level bureaucrats' attempts to "properly" do their jobs.

One way in which street-level bureaucrats attempt to manage potentially "troublesome" others is through their portrayals (descriptions) of the practical issues which emerge in their work. The portrayals are definitions of the issues and justifications of street-level bureaucrats' preferred responses to them (Emerson and Messinger, 1977). For example, in describing clients' troubles as physical or mental disorders, street-level bureaucrats justify responses involving medical intervention and treatment. The medical portrayal is also a way of countering alternative descriptions involving dispreferred responses, such as legal and punative responses. Street-level bureaucrats' portrayals of practical issues, then, are ways of producing social conditions (understandings and orientations) making it likely that potentially troublesome others will act in preferred ways. Further, one reason why street-level bureaucrats' descriptive practices may change across situations is because the troubles and troublesome others which their portrayals are intended to manage also change.

In sum, analysis of street-level bureaucrats' descriptive practices emphasizes their active construction of their work worlds. Street-level bureaucrats do so by interpreting the practical meanings of others' decisions and actions for their choices and actions. The interpretations are more than simple reactions to the constraints imposed by others; they involve taking account of others by assigning meanings to their decisions and actions. Street-level bureaucrats use meanings assigned in this way to anticipate others' responses to practical issues and justify actions intended to avoid (or minimize) troubles resulting from their anticipated responses. Such descriptive and interpretive practices are aspects of virtually all of street-level bureaucrats' work, particularly their efforts to effectively and properly respond to their clients' troubles.

Further, street-level bureaucrats' descriptions are frequently expressed as rhetoric. Although it is used in a variety of ways by contemporary social scientists, the term *rhetoric* is used here to refer to any communication that is intended to persuade others (Burke, 1950).[1] It is one way in which persons assign identities to themselves and others. For example, the above statement portraying paperwork as a problem with which the human service worker must cope may be analyzed as rhetoric. It is an effort to persuade others that the paperwork requirements of the speaker's job are excessive, clients' needs are not being fully met because of the requirements, and she is a frustrated human service professional. The human service worker also used the latter claim to assign a preferred identity to herself and deflect whatever blame others might ascribe to her based on the amount of time she spends on paperwork.

Taken together, these aspects of the human service worker's portrayal are rhetorical procedures for producing preferred understandings of her work. The understandings have practical implications because they are used to justify a sympathetic orientation by others to her professional activity and counter alternative and dispreferred orientations. The portrayal might also be used to justify changes in the human service worker's work activities, such as reducing the amount of paperwork required of her and emphasizing other activities involving direct contact with clients which the worker portrayed as more important. More generally, rhetorical analysis of this and similar statements made by street-level bureaucrats emphasizes their political use of language. We further consider this issue in the next section.

Rhetoric as Political Discourse

Street-level bureaucrats' rhetoric is political because it is expressed as arguments. Arguments differ from other types of social interaction because the participants take partisan positions on the issues at hand. The positions are often expressed as quasi-theories which are rationales for explaining and justifying persons' preferred solutions to practical problems (Hall and Hewitt, 1970; Hewitt and Hall, 1973). Because the conclusions of quasi-theories are foregone, quasi-theorizers' major concern is with identifying "facts" which others will treat as convincing evidence for their conclusions. Hewitt and Hall (1973: 370) state, "What is essential to the quasi-theory is its logic, which is one of cause and effect, though quite disarranged temporally if viewed from a scientific standpoint. The use of quasi-theories involves the postulation of a cure, followed by an analysis of cause and effect that supports the cure."

Arguments are also organized to produce winners and losers. Street-level bureaucrats "win" their arguments when others acquiesce to their positions. Depending on the circumstances of an argument, acquiescence might involve explicit statements of agreement with street-level bureaucrats' claims and recommendations, implicit agreement that is expressed through others' actions that conform with street-level bureaucrats' recommendations, or others' withdrawal of criticisms of street-level bureaucrats' claims and recommendations. Through rhetoric, street-level bureaucrats also cast others' acquiescence as voluntary actions based on rational assessments of the issues at hand and their options in responding to them. That is, street-level bureaucrats cast others' acquiescence as based on the persuasiveness of their arguments, not coercion.

Further, rhetorically produced and justified acquiescence is situationally contingent. It must be reproduced in subsequent interactions with potentially "troublesome" others (Paine, 1981). The process of rhetorically producing and reproducing acquiescence is similar to that analyzed by Goffman (1959) as the definition of the situation. It centers in producing a working consensus which is a short-term, practical and shared orientation to issues of mutual concern. He further states that a working consensus

> involves not so much a real agreement as to what exists but rather a real agreement as to whose claims concerning what issues will be temporarily honored. (Goffman, 1959: 9–10)

Put differently, rhetorical analysis of everyday life in street-level bureaucracies challenges many of the assumptions that underlie common-sense and most social scientific understandings of organizational process. One such challenge involves the assumption that there is one enduring social reality within which we all live (Schutz, 1970). The approach taken here emphasizes the variety of ways in which social reality may be described (constructed) across situations. It also focuses on the ways in which descriptions of social reality change as the practical circumstances of everyday life change. Further, because street-level bureaucrats and others in their work worlds orient to some descriptions (definitions) of social reality as more preferable than others, their social interactions are political encounters centered in rhetoric and argumentation.

The encounters may be analyzed as reality contests because they are organized as arguments about two or more competing reality descriptions having different consequences for the interactants. The contests turn on the competing parties' (arguers') abilities to sustain their claims and recommendations in light of others' criticisms and counter claims. As with other contests, rhetorical competitors do not always have equal access to resources that might be used to advance their arguments nor are they all equally adept in argumentation. For example, street-level bureaucrats often have access to organizational records and other documents that are not available to their clients. The documents are rhetorically useful because street-level bureaucrats cite them as objective evidence of the accuracy of their claims. Clients are at a disadvantage in such interactions because they seldom have access to alternative documents which they might cite as objective evidence supporting their claims.

This approach to language and social reality is similar to that taken by Potter and Wetherell (1987). They describe their approach as discourse analysis and show how it is based on many of the concerns and assumptions of speech act theory (Austin, 1962; Searle, et al., 1979), ethnomethodology (Garfinkel, 1967; Heritage, 1984; Pollner, 1987; Zimmerman and Pollner, 1971) and semiology (Saussure, 1974; Barthes, 1964; Manning, 1987). Although different in some ways, each of these influences on Potter and Wetherell's perspective treat language and its use as consequential and a topic for systematic study. As Potter and Wetherell (1987: 35) state, speech act theorists, ethnomethodologists and semiologists

> are not trying to recover events, beliefs and cognitive processes from participants' discourses, or treat language as an indicator or signpost to some other state of affairs but are looking at the analytically prior question of how discourse or accounts of these things are manufactured.

Although the term *discourse* is used in diverse ways by contemporary social scientists, I will follow Potter and Wetherell's lead by using it to refer to the ways in which street-level bureaucrats and others in their work worlds produce accounts of practical issues.[2] The accounts are expressed as descriptions of practical issues and interactants' options in responding to them. Through their descriptions, street-level bureaucrats and others construct versions of social reality that, on occasion, become matters of negotiation. It is in such negotiations that the rhetorical aspects of street-level bureaucrats' and others' descriptions of social reality are most easily seen, including the ways in which their interactions are organized as reality contests. Study of such interactions is also a source of insight about the ways in which working consensuses and acquiescence are rhetorically produced in street-level bureaucracies. They are produced as short-term agreements to honor some versions of social reality over others.

Central to the rhetorical analysis of street-level bureaucrats' discourse is a concern for the ways in which they justify their preferred versions of social reality. Justifications are significant for street-level bureaucrats for, a least, two reasons. First, street-level bureaucrats use justifications to counter criticisms from others advocating alternative versions of social reality. Indeed, street-level bureaucrats sometimes anticipate and respond to others' criticisms by justifying their claims and recommendations before they are voiced. It is a rhetorical strategy and tactic for managing potentially troublesome others.

Second, street-level bureaucrats use justifications to cast acquiescence to their positions as a realistic response to their disagreements with others. Such justifications make it possible for others to honor street-level bureaucrats' reality descriptions while saving face; that is, while allowing others to maintain identities as competent, thoughtful and well-meaning persons. Street-level bureaucrats partly do so by portraying their potential and actual critics as reasonable and well-intentioned persons who are overlooking important aspects of the issues at hand. Street-level bureaucrats use this portrayal of others to cast acquiescence to their arguments as evidence of others' reasonable attitudes and proper intentions.

Finally, this analysis of rhetoric in street-level bureaucracies is similar to Potter and Wetherell's (1987) discourse analysis in treating reality descriptions as partial and biased renderings of everyday life. Street-level bureaucrats and others construct and justify their reality descriptions by emphasizing some aspects of everyday life and glossing over others. This statement is not intended to suggest that there is a single comprehensive or correct reality description against which other descriptions can be judged. Rather, it is intended to highlight a practical problem encountered by street-level bureaucrats in justifying their positions in social interactions with potentially troublesome others. The problem involves others' abilities to counter street-level bureaucrats' descriptions by pointing to aspects of everyday life that are de-emphasized and left out of their descriptions. Such criticisms may be further developed to justify alternative reality descriptions and orientations to practical issues.

The latter possibility is significant for street-level bureau-crats because it is a major, ongoing source of potential trouble in their relationships with others. Others' criticisms are never fully or ultimately countered; rather, they are a potential aspect of all street-level bureaucrats' interactions. This prac-tical circumstance is a major reason why rhetoric must be treated as a significant and pervasive work activity of street-level bureaucrats. It is central to their implementation of public policies and achievement of organizational goals. We next consider other practical circumstances associated with street-level bureaucrats' use of rhetoric.

Rhetoric and the Practicalities of Street-Level Bureaucrats' Work

There are at least three practical circumstances that are related to street-level bureaucrats' use of rhetoric. They involve defining and remedying social problems, formulating and justifying decisions, and claiming professional status. The rest of this section is concerned with the ways in which street-level bureaucrats' use of rhetoric is related to these aspects of their work. They are discussed in turn.

The Rhetoric of Problems and Remedies

As Lipsky (1980) states, a major issue in street-level bureau-crats' relations with their clients involves many clients' unwill-ingness to acquiesce to street-level bureaucrats' claims and recommendations about the clients' problems. The issue is made more complex by the fact that street-level bureaucrats are frequently reluctant to compel acquiescence by using legal, professional and organizational resources which might be used to impose their orientations on others. Street-level bureaucrats' inability or reluctance to compel acquiescence through coercion is perhaps best addressed in Emerson and Messinger's (1977) and Emerson's (1981) analyses of the micro-politics of trouble. They analyze human service and social con-trol organizations as hierarchies of remedies or responses to the reported troubles of clients.

According to Emerson and Messinger (1977), organiza-tional remedies to persons' troubles range from first-resort (or preferred) to last-resort decisions and responses. As Emerson (1981: 4) states,

...first resorts represent the best way to manage a particular sort of trouble. First-resort decisions are typically presented as what *should* or *ought* to be done, regardless of practical contingencies and local limitations: Given the efficacy of "moral treatment," for example, each and every person found insane should be sent for cure to the asylum. In contrast, last-resort decisions are typically framed in an idiom of *necessity*: The claim is that "we *have* to hospitalize," that there is no alternative but to turn to this particular response

Thus, a basic feature of street-level bureaucrats' work involves categorizing persons and troubles in relation to available remedies which range from those treated as most preferred (and typically used) to last-resort (least preferred and used) responses. The latter responses are typically portrayed as the most severe and coercive available. In portraying some responses as last resorts, street-level bureaucrats cast the responses as inappropriate and, therefore, unavailable to them in dealing with most of the persons and troubles that come to their attention. Further, many (if not most) of the responses treated as appropriate for dealing with "normal" persons and troubles involve efforts to persuade others. For example, rhetoric is basic to police officers' handling of "typical" family disputes, nursing home professionals' and patients' development of mutually agreeable treatment plans, and family therapists' framing of their clients' troubles so that they will choose to remedy them in preferred ways (Gubrium, 1980; Ker Muir, 1977; Miller, 1987).

Indeed, rhetoric is a pervasive aspect of criminal justice organizations and the work of legal professionals. Not only do legal professionals try to persuade adversaries and judicial decision-makers, but much of their work involves persuading their own clients and others whom they wish to help. For example, public defenders frequently represent clients who resist plea bargaining proposals that the attorneys believe to be in their clients' best interest (Maynard, 1984; Sudnow, 1965). When clients resist public defenders' recommendations, they respond with persuasion. It becomes their work. Consider, for example, the following statement made by a public defender to a client who was reluctant to acquiesce to a recommended plea bargain.

Look, you know as well as I do that with your prior conviction and this charge now that you could go away from here [to prison] for five years or so. So just calm down a minute and let's look at this thing reasonably. If you go to trial and lose the trial, you're stuck. You'll be in the joint [prison] until you're 28 years old. If you plead this one charge without the priors [prior convictions] then we can get you into jail maybe, a year or two at the most in the joint. If you wait until the preliminary hearing and they charge the priors, boy you've had it, it's too late. (Sudnow, 1965: 267)

In sum, rhetoric is a pervasive and practical aspect of street-level bureaucrats' work. Through rhetoric, they fulfill their professional obligations (including gaining client or public cooperation) without "unwarranted" recourse to last-resort responses.

Rhetoric and Organizational Decision-Making

Rhetoric is basic to, at least, two general features of intra- and inter-organizational decision-making in street-level bureaucracies. First, it is an aspect of staff meetings, which are recurring events in street-level bureaucracies. Although the meetings are partly occasions for sharing information about issues of practical concern, they also frequently involve negotiations about how to respond to the issues. Such negotiations are facilitated by the frequent requirement that professionals having quite different interests in the issues develop mutually agreeable responses to them. Rhetoric is a primary medium through which participants in such meetings seek their practical interests, including their interest in fulfilling their responsibilities to clients, colleagues and the public.

Consider, for example, the following statement made in a staff meeting in a residential treatment center serving children diagnosed as emotionally disturbed (Buckholdt and Gubrium, 1979). The meeting involved assessing the children's special problems, needs and abilities as well as making treatment recommendations. The assessments were simultaneously diagnostic and rhetorical because the meeting participants formulated and advocated for their preferred understandings of the children's problems and responses to the problems in their interactions. A related aspect of their rhetoric was the discrediting of other understandings of the children's problems.

This is your classic emotionally disturbed kid: acting out, swearing, on medication, causes trouble....And swearing! It

[the client's record] says he's been saying all kinds of juicy
things since kindergarten. You should see the teachers' com-
ments....I wouldn't say he's ready for the day treatment program. I *really know* this kid from what I've read here and he
sure isn't ready for day treatment. Floyd [the program's
education supervisor] agrees with me. Whoever recommended day treatment probably doesn't really know him in
the school...(Buckholdt and Gubrium, 1979: 192–193)

In the final analysis, then, street-level bureaucrats' rhetorical formulation of cases and remedies is as important as the
facts in shaping the development of mutually agreeable decisions. Equally important, the rationales offered by street-level
bureaucrats to justify their recommendations may involve a
wide variety of factors, some of which might be used in other
situations to justify quite different conclusions.

The second way in which rhetoric is a part of decision-
making in and between street-level bureaucracies involves
their hierarchical arrangement of case evaluation. Specifically,
actions taken by street-level bureaucrats are often routinely
assessed by higher level agency officials and/or officials of
other organizations who then support, modify or reject the
bureaucrats' recommendations. In describing their actions,
street-level bureaucrats anticipate and counter possible challenges by potentially troublesome others by treating record-
keeping and related descriptive practices as rhetorical activities.
That is, they are partly recorded with an eye to persuading others that the decisions and actions in question where
justified.

Such rhetoric is perhaps most obvious in criminal justice
organizations where actions taken by police officers are
routinely assessed by district attorneys, judges and juries.
Thus, police officers' presentations of criminal cases are partly
intended to persuade others to acquiesce to their portrayals of
events as crimes (Sanders, 1977). In processing sexual assault
cases, for example, police officers typically consider how
district attorneys will evaluate and respond to the cases
(Sanders, 1980). Because police officers frequently assume
that district attorneys are mostly concerned with the convicta-
bility of cases and not with issues of truth or justice, they try
to produce reports that provide clear, legal bases for con-
cluding that the reported sexual assaults have taken place, the
true perpetrators have been arrested, and the arrested parties

can be convicted. Although expressed in a dispassionate and legalistic language, such reports are implicitly persuasive.

Rhetoric is also an aspect of intra- and inter-organizational case evaluation in welfare agencies, juvenile courts and other street-level bureaucracies (Emerson, 1969; Higgins, 1985; Warren, 1982). For example, involuntary mental hospitalization decisions typically turn on the ability of candidate patients and their representatives to convince judicial decision-makers that tenable living situations are available to them in their home communities (Holsten, 1984, 1987). Knowing this, many community mental health professionals who seek involuntary commitment for clients and others produce documents that describe candidate patients as both mentally ill and unable to secure appropriate living arrangements outside the hospital. The documents are rhetorical because they are descriptions of aspects of candidate patients' lives which are intended to persuade potential readers to acquiesce to recommended courses of action.

Viewed as rhetoric, then, all descriptive activity in street-level bureaucracies is political discourse because it always advocates particular understandings of social reality. One such understanding is that street-level bureaucrats are knowledgeable and caring professionals in whom clients and public should place their trust.

Professional Standing as Rhetoric

Street-level bureaucrats' concern for justifying their claims to professional standing is partly related to the public's reluctance to accord them the same deference given to physicians and others typically treated as real professionals. There are at least two practical bases for public skepticism about street-level bureaucrats' claim to professional standing. The first involves the conditions under which street-level bureaucrats come into contact with the public. The contacts are often treated as unwanted intrusions into persons' lives. Further, clients sometimes treat recommended remedies as inappropriate for their circumstances, if not harmful to them.

The second factor involves persons' assessments of the distinctiveness and value of street-level bureaucrats as possessing knowledge and skills that are widely disseminated in the society, including among clients themselves (Haug and Sussman, 1969a, 1969b). It is also claimed that street-level bureaucrats have no special insight into their clients' problems or special ability to help. A variant of this claim depicts street-level bureaucrats as possessing incorrect knowledge or, at least, incorrect perspectives on the circumstances with which they are attempting to deal. Such depictions are used to challenge street-level bureaucrats' claims to special expertise and right to intervene in other persons' lives.

Rhetoric is the major way in which street-level bureaucrats counter such challenges. They do so by emphasizing their privileged knowledge about clients' troubles and how troubles should be solved as well as their compassionate understanding of clients' perspectives and experiences. Street-level bureaucrats' efforts to persuade and justify may involve claims to characteristics associated with more prestigious occupations (such as medicine and law), the recounting of street-level bureaucrats' records of success in remedying client troubles and/or descriptions of aspects of street-level bureaucrats' lives that "show" that they can "really" understand clients' perspectives and concerns. However it is expressed, such rhetoric justifies street-level bureaucrats' intervention in other persons' lives.

It may also be used to cast clients' responses to street-level bureaucrats' claims to professional knowledge and standing as tests of their commitment and/or ability to remedy the clients' troubles. That is, clients' who challenge street-level bureaucrats' claims may be assessed as uncommitted to "really" solving their troubles or unable to do so without professional guidance. Clients so assessed may be assigned "uncooperative or "troublemaker" identities and treated differently than other clients assigned "normal" identities. For example, a frequent aspect of street-level bureaucrats' justifications of last-resort responses to some clients' troubles involves portraying the clients as uncooperative and, therefore, deserving more severe responses than other clients.

Although their studies are about two very different street-level bureaucracies (a working-class school in England and alcohol treatment facilities in the United States), both Willis (1977) and Wisemann (1979) note and analyze the practical importance of street-level bureaucrats' assessments of clients' responses to their claims to professional expertise and authority.[3] The teachers used assessments of students' attitudes toward school to explain their students' academic failures (they weren't trying) and predict their futures. The teachers predicted that students with bad attitudes toward school would fail to achieve occupational success because they did not use their school years to acquire the knowledge, skills and attitudes toward authority needed for success in the work world. The alcohol treatment professionals used assessments of clients' attitudes toward treatment to justify their selective placement of clients in therapy programs. They stated that clients who refused to take responsibility for their problems as they were advised to do by the alcohol treatment professionals were unlikely to benefit from therapy.

Gubrium (1980) also analyzes how human service professionals in geriatric organizations manage meetings with "troublesome" clients. Clients become troublesome when they object to the staff members' orientations to their troubles. Gubrium states that staff members treat such objections as challenges to their efforts to present themselves as competent and caring professionals. Initially, staff members attempt to manage clients' objections by ignoring or glossing over them.

> This occurs so long as the patient's objections are not too loud nor persistent enough to make the briefing inaudible or otherwise undeliverable. Should patients' disagreement grow beyond what is taken to be routinely acceptable, they are reminded that their behavior is "inappropriate. They may even be told, with patronizing firmness, "Adults simply don't act that way," or "We mustn't be so childish," or "Let's try to be calm and more reasonable about this." With the patient's persistence, the interaction of the patient becomes increasingly enraged with staffers' diversion from what is the patient takes to be the issue at hand and where staffers, in turn, increasingly become irritated by what they believe to be the patient's unrealistic, immature conduct. Should the patient refuse to calm down and cooperate in decorously completing the routine, the patient is led from the meeting, whereupon the staffing is completed. (Gubrium, 1980: 340)

In sum, rhetoric is a basic and practical aspect of street-level bureaucrats' work. Through rhetoric, street-level bureaucrats express and justify their orientations to practical matters and manage troublesome others. The rhetoric centers in explanations and justifications of organizationally approved understandings and orientations to clients' troubles and other practical issues. One consequence of street-level bureaucrats' rhetoric and others' acquiescence to their claims and recommendations is the perpetuation of organizational routines and relationships. Thus, street-level bureaucrats' efforts to persuade have implications that go beyond the diverse and concrete problems that their rhetoric is intended to remedy. Rhetoric is a major way in which street-level bureaucracies are legitimized and maintained in everyday life. We next consider the social organization of rhetoric in street-level bureaucracies.

Social Organization of Rhetoric in Street-Level Bureaucracies

Street-Level bureaucrats' rhetoric centers in formulating arguments which justify their orientations to practical issues and to which others are likely to accede. The arguments are generally expressed as conclusions (declarations of preferred responses to practical issues) and rationales (justifications of the conclusions). In the abstract, such arguments may be endlessly negotiated and elaborated. In practice, however, arguments were situationally resolved and terminated, although they are always potentially open to reconsideration and renegotiation in subsequent interactions. Street-level bureaucrats' arguments turn on anticipated or stated criticisms of others to their claims about practical issues and recommendations for managing these issues (Perelman, 1979). Their arguments are intended to justify their claims and recommendations.

Street-Level Bureaucrats' Justifications

Street-Level bureaucrats justify their claims and recommendations by specifying the conditions to which they apply and/or the authority on which they are made (Toulmin, 1958). Street-level bureaucrats sometimes portray the conditions associated with their claims and recommendations as general, perhaps even universal, circumstances which everyone must accept. In this way, street-level bureaucrats portray the circumstances associated with their arguments as facts of life and cast their claims and recommendations as generally valid for a wide variety of practical issues. For example, street-level bureaucrats make such claims and justifications in interviews concerned with the general conditions and problems of their work world. In doing so, they gloss over the practical contingencies associated with concrete situations which might be cited to counter their claims and justifications.

As with the following response by a prison correctional officer to an interviewer's question, street-level bureaucrats also use general claims about their work circumstances and problems to assign preferred identities to themselves and others. The correctional officer also uses his portrayal of the prison system to explain why correctional officers act in officially disapproved ways.

> We are Indians in the correctional system. Everyone shits on us. We have no togetherness in this place [prison]....We are the screws no one really cares about...we are shipwrecked in the society and are always labelled as the bad guys...they [prison administrators] treat us like assholes and we will eventually become nothing but assholes. (Stojkovic, 1990:215)

Most of the time, however, street-level bureaucrats justify their claims and recommendations by portraying aspects of concrete situations and the issues at hand as conditions making their claims valid and recommendations appropriate. This practice is partly related to the organization of many street-level bureaucrats' work which centers in the management of cases. Although they are sometimes classified into general types, street-level bureaucrats treat most cases as somewhat unique and, therefore, requiring individualized attention. In social interactions concerned with cases, then, street-level bureaucrats seek acquiescence from others by portraying their claims and recommendations as responsive to the unique needs and/or best interests of the client at hand.

Consider, for example, the following argument reported by Holstein (1987) which involves a county attorney's recommendation that a woman (candidate patient) by involuntary committed to a mental hospital. The candidate patient stated that she wanted to live in a cardboard box located below a set of railroad tracks and justified her preference by favorably comparing the box to subsidized public housing.

> Now I know Miss Wells claims that this [cardboard box] is as good as the subsidized public housing programs the DSS [Department of Social Services] has suggested she look into, but we have to consider more than its construction aspects. ...You can't allow a woman to be exposed to all the other things that go on out there under the [railroad] tracks. Many of those men have lived like that for years, but we're talking about a woman here. A sick and confused woman who

doesn't realize the trouble she's asking for. She simply cannot live like that. That's no place for a woman, especially after dark.... She's not taking it [being a woman in the midst of men] into account. She doesn't realize how dangerous it is for her. It's up to the court to protect her...(Holstein, 1987: 315)

The county attorney's argument is an example of how street-level bureaucrats sometimes use images of gender to justify their recommendations and actions. Specifically, the attorney contrasted the candidate patient's status as a woman with that of men and used the contrast to justify different responses to otherwise similar troubles experienced by men and women. Different treatment of women was further justified by reference to the court's obligation to protect those who cannot protect themselves. Thus, the county attorney's argument involved both a specification of the conditions to which her recommendations applied (they applied to women because women are uniquely vulnerable to physical assault) and the authority on which the recommendation was made (it was warranted because the court has a responsibility to protect those who cannot protect themselves).

The conclusions and rationales that make up street-level bureaucrats' arguments are interrelated because each is used as a background for assessing the other. Specifically, street-level bureaucrats and others use rationales as interpretive frameworks for assessing the appropriateness of recommendations and conclusions. The assessments focus on the grounds for street-level bureaucrats' conclusions. They might involve one or more of the following questions: what are the empirical bases for the conclusions; what are the "real" motives underlying the conclusions and rationales; and do the persons making recommendations have adequate professional expertise and authority?

For example, the above recommendation of hospitalization might be challenged by asking for evidence that the patient is uniquely vulnerable to assault, questioning the county attorney's motives in justifying her recommendation based on the candidate patient's gender, or arguing that the court is required to disregard gender in making decisions about candidate patients. In negotiating such issues, street-level bureaucrats simultaneously produce mutually agreeable conclusions and rationales for their actions. Such negotiations are frequently an aspect of social interactions concerned with the appropriateness of typical remedies for clients' troubles and circumstances. As in the following exchange involving a district attorney and public defender engaged in a plea bargaining negotiation, a major way in which street-level bureaucrats justify typical remedies is by challenging the rationales offered by others arguing for the appropriateness of atypical responses.

The exchange is concerned with the best way to handle a shoplifting case in which the defendant is a first offender who has stolen a jar of soap. The public defender cites these aspects of the case to justify a recommendation that the defendant be treated less severely than most shoplifters. The district attorney rejects the public defender's conclusion and recommendation by challenging the rationale offered to justify it. In doing so, the district attorney also offers an alternative rationale for assessing the appropriateness of cases for atypical responses, a rationale that emphasizes social conditions that are absent from the case under consideration.

> [District Attorney]: I have difficulty making this other than the standard disposition
> [Public Defender]: For a dollar and some odd cents worth of Mini-wash?
> [District Attorney]: Yeah I mean I — I can BUY the logic within the limits of the — you know the items of necessity by somebody very poor but a — ....cosmetic item by a young um lady who's just uh in too much of a hurry to go pay for it. Uh I can't buy that (Maynard, 1984: 124).

Also, conclusions are used as grounds for assessing the plausibility of the various rationales that street-level bureaucrats use to justify their conclusions. This aspect of street-level bureaucrats' rhetoric is perhaps most obvious when their arguments are organized as quasi-theories (Hall and Hewitt, 1970; Hewitt and Hall, 1973). In such arguments, street-level bureaucrats' conclusions are foregone and, consequently, not matters for independent assessment or negotiation. Rather, street-level bureaucrats' major concern in such interactions is with assessing the appropriateness of available rationales for sustaining their conclusions. In the abstract, such assessments focus on whether street-level bureaucrats' justifications are consistent with their conclusions.

In practice, however, plausible rationales are treated as explanations and justifications that others treat as persuasive. Producing such rationales is a practical solution to the problem of managing potentially troublesome others. The rationales usually emphasize how street-level bureaucrats' conclusions are logical, if not necessary, responses to social conditions. Street-level bureaucrats also use rationales to portray acquiescence to their recommendations and conclusions as realistic. In doing so, street-level bureaucrats establish congruency between their conclusions and rationales, cast their recommendations as derived from rational assessments of the real world, and gloss over the ways in which their conclusions and rationales are interactively produced.

Rhetoric as Practical Activity

In sum, street-level bureaucrats use rhetoric to define and manage troubles emergent in their relations with others. Rhetoric is partly a solution to such troubles, but it is also a strategy and tactic for anticipating and identifying "troubled" relationships. Troubles are anticipated by treating others' past responses to claims and issues as indicative of their future responses. In so orienting toward others, street-level bureaucrats assign others to communities of orientation and justify the development of standardized arguments intended to counter others' criticisms before they are expressed. In part, then, rhetoric is a procedure for eliminating disputes before they emerge.

Although it is based on a different perspective, Stanton's (1970) analysis of the ways in which staff members in a welfare organization managed volunteers illustrates how troubles may be anticipated and rhetorically handled by street-level bureaucrats. A major practical problem for staff members was the requirement that volunteers determine major organizational policies and activities, a responsibility that the staff described as beyond the expertise of the volunteers. Staff members partly responded to this problem by organizing meetings with volunteers as ritualized interactions intended to persuade the volunteers that staff members were concerned about their ideas and wished to work with them. The meeetings were also scripted to gloss over the ways in which staff members determined organizational policies and activities and, in some cases, had implemented them prior to consulting with the volunteers.

Despite their efforts to anticipate and manage problematic relationships through standardized arguments, however, street-level bureaucrats' rhetoric is situationally contingent. It is partly contingent because street-level bureaucrats must continuously assess their critics' motives and interests in practical issues. It is not enough to generally classify and orient to others as sources of trouble. In anticipating and countering others' criticisms, street-level bureaucrats must also assess the specific ways in which others are troublesome, and how best to respond to them. Such assessments are made in each encounter with potentially troublesome others. Street-level bureaucrats' rhetoric is also contingent because critics' orientations to practical issues may change as well as the rhetorics that critics use to justify their positions.

Such contingencies make street-level bureaucrats' work complex and the development of argumentation skills central to their efforts to fulfill organizational goals. Billig (1987) analyzes such skills as *witcraft*. He states that witcraft centers in persons' abilities to define practical issues in preferred ways and effectively express and justify their preferred definitions. More generally, witcraft is a type of social invention and thought. It is invention because it involves the creation and negotiation of rationales for action. Witcraft and argumentation are also cognitive processes, but, as Billig (1987: 82) states, a person engaged in rhetoric is not a

> contemplative thinker, the Rodin figure who sits alone with hand on brow. The thinker of rhetorical theory is much more active, selecting and adapting thoughts, mutating and creating them, in the continual struggle for argumentative victory against rival thinkers.

One aspect of argumentation involves the strategic use of interactional turns and formulation of issues. These aspects of argumentation are discussed in the next section which considers how social competence and acquiescence are interactionally produced in street-level bureaucracies.

Competence and Acquiescence as Interactionally Produced

A fundamental aspect of all social interactions (including potential and actual arguments) is their sequential organization which centers in the ways in which speaking turns and conversational topics are allocated to interactants. Indeed, one way in which social interactions can be classified, compared and contrasted is by analyzing their sequential organizations. For example, ordinary conversations are partly distinctive because they do not involve formal agreements about the allocation of speaking turns or conversational topics. As Sacks, et al. (1978: 45) state, however,

> In debates...the ordering of all turns is preallocated, by for-mula, by reference to "pro" and "con" positions. In contrast to both debates and conversation, meetings that have a chair-person partially preallocate turns, and provide for the alloca-tion of unallocated turns via the use of the preallocated turns. Thus, the chairperson has rights to talk first, and to talk after each other speaker, and can use each such turn to allocate next speakership.

This aspect of social interaction is significant because, although potential and actual arguments are organized around pro and con positions, interactants in street-level bureau-cracies do not have equal access to or control over speaking turns in conversational topics. They are usually preallocated in ways that allow one or a few participants to allocate them. For example, a frequent form of interaction in street-level bureau-cracies involves question-answer sequences in which street-level bureaucrats ask the questions and others answer them. While this arrangement may serve street-level bureaucrats' interest in efficiently collecting information and processing cases, it also restricts clients' and others' abilities to inde-pendently raise issues of their own.

Further, although clients and others may independently raise issues by interrupting ongoing interactional sequences, doing so often involves social risks. For example, others may treat the interruptions as attempts to control (if not sabotage) the interaction or as signs of the interrupter's social incom-petence. The social risks of interrupting typical interactional sequences in street-level bureaucracies, then, partly involve persons' identities as competent and cooperative interactional partners. On some occasions, however, the risks go beyond threats to identity because interactional interruptions may be treated as signs of intentional uncooperativeness or serious social incompetence calling for official responses.

Social interactions in street-level bureaucracies may also become risky when street-level bureaucrats alter their approaches to otherwise routine and expected interactional sequences. For example, they may refuse to take their interactional turns, such as failing to respond to clients' answers to their questions. In this case, the full responsibility for sustaining interactions is placed on others, who normally respond by continuing to talk. Clients and others who fail to respond to street-level bureaucrats' refusal to take their interactional turns face the possibility of being assessed as sullen, uncooperative and/or secretive. However, as Holstein (1988) shows in his study of involuntary commitment hearings, the consequences of continuing to talk are sometimes worse than remaining silent.

Specifically, Holstein analyzes how district attorneys strategically refused to take their interactional turns in cross-examining candidate patients. The attorneys referred to their tactic as "letting them [candidate patients] hang themselves," meaning that if allowed to talk long enough the candidate patients would reveal their mental illnesses to court officials. Although it did not involve direct appeals to court officials, the "let them hang themselves" tactic was a rhetorical procedure intended to persuade others to support the district attorneys' recommendations that candidate patients be hospitalized. Consider, for example, the following exchange. The occasions when the district attorney refused to take an interactional turn are indicated with "((Silence))."

[Attorney]: How long have you lived here?
[Candidate Patient]: Since I moved from Houston?
((Silence))
[Candidate Patient]: About three years ago.
[Attorney]: Tell me about why you came here.
[Candidate Patient]: I just came.
((Silence))
[Candidate Patient]: You know, I wanted to see the stars, Hollywood.
((Silence))
[Attorney]: Uh huh
[Candidate Patient]: I'd like to get a good place to live.
((Silence...))
[Attorney]: Go on ((spoken simultaneously with onset of next utterance))
[Candidate Patient]: There was some nice things I brought.
((Silence))
[Attorney]: Uh huh
[Candidate Patient]: Brought them from the rocketship.

[Attorney]: From the rocketship?
[Candidate Patient]: Right.
[Attorney]: Were you on it?
[Candidate Patient]: Yeah.
[Attorney]: Tell me about this rocketship...(Holstein, 1988: 467)

The Interactional Production of Competence and Incompetence

Social competence and effectiveness involve more than knowledge about the topics at hand in social interactions. They also involve knowing how, when and to whom to express one's knowledge about the topics. Further, social competence and effectiveness are related to interactants' abilities to anticipate others' claims and conclusions and, where possible, to counter those that are problematic before they are voiced. For example, Atkinson and Drew (1976) analyze how witnesses in court proceedings display their understandings of and competence in the interactions by, first, recognizing that many questions asked by attorneys are intended to establish their legal culpability (blame ascriptions) and, then, by offering rebuttals to the blame ascriptions before they are explicitly made. In doing so, witnesses manage problematic interactions and attempt to achieve their interests in them, including their interest in appearing to others as honest, competent and believable witnesses.

Specifically, social competence is coproduced as speakers use their speaking turns to advance their positions and others respond in ways that sustain the speakers' claims to competence. The response is one way in which respondents contribute to the production of working consensuses. For example, Strong (1979) analyzes how middle-class parents were interactionally produced as competent and well-intentioned in his study of pediatric clinics in England and the United States. He analyzes the interactions as polite, friendly encounters in which the pediatricians helped the parents sustain an image of themselves as good parents by glossing over potentially contradictory (discrediting) information during examinations and offering explanations for past missed appointments and parents' inability to provide all of the information about their children requested by physicians.

On the other hand, the physicians refused to help coproduce an image of poor parents as competent and well-intentioned. Their refusal was related to the physicians' general orientation to poor parents as irrational and untrustworthy, a conclusion that the physicians portrayed as confirmed in their interactions with poor parents. In the interactions, the physicians took an accusatory tone and treated the parents' descriptions of their children and home lives as signs of bad parenting. Consider for example, the following parent-physician exchange which began with the mother's statement that she washed her baby's diapers in Ivory Snow detergent because it makes them soft.

> Dr S: How do you know Ivory Snow makes nappies [diapers] softer?
> Mother: (shrugs awkwardly) Well, um...(she mumbles something about her mother and advertisements).
> Dr S: You don't want to believe everything you see in the adverts [advertisements]. It's a business. That's *their* business. *Your* business is your baby. (Strong, 1979: 43)

This exchange shows how street-level bureaucrats may cast an otherwise insignificant client statement as a sign of an improper orientation and social incompetence. The pediatrician did so by questioning the parent's knowledge about Ivory Snow and then instructing her on how to properly orient to advertising about laundry detergents and her responsibilities as a mother. Another procedure for casting parents as socially incompetent involves treating aspects of their demeanor as signs of improper orientations to parenthood. Consider, for example, the following parent-pediatrician exchange reported by Strong (1979: 44):

> Dr S: Are there any other problems?
> Mother: Well, he chews cigarette ends...(laughs)...It's very difficult to stop him.
> Dr S: Why are you laughing? Do you think it's funny?
> Mother: No, I don't think it's funny.
> Dr S: Well, why did you laugh then; do you always laugh at this?

In orienting to some of their clients as socially incompetent, street-level bureaucrats produce social conditions that make their mutual interactions problematic. Such conditions and interactions call for rhetorical responses intended to persuade potentially troublesome clients to acquiesce to street-level bureaucrats' recommendations. As the above exchanges show, one way in which street-level bureaucrats attempt to persuade such clients is by, first, challenging their claims to social competence and other preferred identities and, then, instructing them on how to "properly" orient to the issues at hand. Another tactic involves emphasizing aspects of clients' orientations and actions that street-level bureaucrats find appropriate and wish to encourage.

Whatever their rhetorical strategies and tactics, street-level bureaucrats' efforts to persuade potentially troublesome others are contingent on others' willingness and ability to acquiesce to the bureaucrats' recommendations. Just as social competence and incompetence are interactionally produced, so is acquiescence.

The Interactional Production of Acquiescence

Respondents signal their willingness and ability to acquiesce to others' claims and recommendations through their uses of interactional turns. They generally do so by expressing agreement with speakers' claims and recommendations or by ceasing to question the claims and recommendations. The latter response is treated as a tacit agreement about how interactants will respond to the issues at hand. Acquiescence to speakers' arguments is not always readily granted by respondents in street-level bureaucracies, however. It may follow extended negotiations in which respondents persist in challenging and criticizing speakers' claims and recommendations. In doing so, respondents produce social conditions that make it necessary for speakers to modify, if not radically change, their arguments. Such negotiations are also occasions for defining the terms of respondents' acquiescence, terms that may not be preferred by speakers.

The ability of respondents to resist speakers' claims and recommendations should not be overstated, however, because speakers are also able to influence the terms of their interactions and respondents' choices within them. One way in which they do so is by restricting the interactional options available to respondents in presenting and justifying their orientations to issues. For example, street-level bureaucrat-client interactions that are organized as question-answer sequences restrict clients' abilities to explain and justify their orientations to practical issues.

A second way in which speakers attempt to restrict respondents' options in responding to their arguments is by formulating the issues at hand in ways that encourage respondents to acquiesce to their claims and recommendations. The rhetorical procedure of most importance for this study involves formulating issues as dichotomous choices. Such choices are mutually exclusive and opposed understandings of and responses to practical issues. They are formulated as contrastive pairs which are opposed cultural categories and distinctions that speakers use to organize and simplify issues (Atkinson, 1984a, 1984b). Frequently used constrastive pairs include right-wrong, we-they, true-false and objective-subjective.

Speakers use such distinctions to portray issues as dichotomous choices involving two opposed orientations, only one of which is true, right or otherwise proper. In doing so, speakers cast all but their preferred responses to practical issues as unacceptable and, therefore, unavailable to interactants in choosing how to manage practical problems. For example, Atkinson (1984a, 1984b) analyzes how contrastive pairs are aspects of politicians' speech-making and rhetoric. Politicians used contrastive pairs to simplify issues, cast their positions as more reasonable and/or moral than their opponents', and elicit applause from audience members. Applause is significant because it is usually treated as a sign that audiences agree with speech-makers. Put differently, audience's applause is treated as an expression of their choice on the issues at hand.

Street-level bureaucrats also use contrastive pairs to produce dichotomous choices and advance their positions in actual and potential arguments. A major way in which they do so is by distinguishing between "we" and "they." Street-level bureaucrats use the distinction to cast themselves and others into communities of orientation and justify different responses to persons classified in each community. They also use dichotomous choices to portray acquiesence to their arguments as the only realistic choice available to others. The portrayal involves assigning positive and negative identities to the choices. Under such circumstances, persons who do not acquiesce to street-level bureaucrats' arguments risk having dispreferred identities assigned to themselves.

Street-level bureaucrats also use their formulation of issues as dichotomous choices to justify their acquiescence to others' arguments. Consider, for example, the following probation officer's explanation of why he has stopped fighting with other probation officers who orient to their work in ways that the speaker considers improper.

> [The office supervisor] laid it out this way. If we fight each other, we're going to bring heat down on the branch office. That means we're going to have to stop cheating on office hours, start observing the grooming and dress code in the office — all that stuff, so we buried the hatchet. I admit that I go out of my way to piss those old dudes [other probation officers] off and I get a kick out of it when they blow their cool. But I'm going to stop that stuff now because it's not worth it. We're all going to mind our own business, and if some beef comes up, we're going to take it to [the office supervisor]. (McCleary, 1979: 70).

This statement is significant because it shows how street-level bureaucrats use portrayals of the practical circumstances of their work to cast themselves and others as having dichtomous choices. Specifically, the probation officer states that the ongoing disagreements between staff members was likely to result in the intervention of organizational superiors into the probation officers' everyday work lives. One consequence of such intervention would be the elimination of officially disapproved practices which all staff members wished to keep. Although staff members could continue to fight, it would be an unrealistic and counterproductive response to the situation. In this way, the probation officer casts his changed behavior and acquiescence to his supervisor's recommendation as a rational act. He also uses the explanation to assign a preferred identity to himself and others.

In sum, argumentation (or witcraft) in street-level bureaucracies is a complex process involving a variety of aspects and contingencies. It is not enough to note that social relations in street-level bureaucracies are often organized as conflicts of interests. It is also necessary to consider how such conflicts are formulated and expressed in concrete social interactions. It is within such interactions that we can see how street-level bureaucrats and others use their interactional turns to explain and justify their positions on practical issues and coproduce acquiescence.

Conclusion and Organization of the Book

Looked at one way, the rhetorical approach is a critical and unsympathetic perspective on the WIN staff's and other street-level bureaucrats' work. It may be further portrayed as intended to make such professionals look foolish, insincere or crassly self-interested. That is not the intent of the analysis. Indeed, I have no reason to doubt the WIN staff's claims to being sincerely concerned about the issues emergent in their everyday work lives, especially about helping their clients find jobs and get off of welfare. Certainly, they faced many serious and complex problems in fulfilling their professional responsibilities. Thus the analysis is not intended as an assessment of the WIN staff's sincerity and commitment in helping their clients or to the purposes of the program.

Rather, it is concerned with the social organization and practical uses of rhetoric in the WIN staff's relations with others. Most generally the staff members used rhetoric to assign meanings to aspects of their work world and identities to themselves and others. Staff members also rhetorically justified actions having serious and sometimes fateful consequences for their clients. Although critics of the WIN program and staff might portray the staff's actions as manipulative, the staff members (like other street-level bureaucrats) used rhetoric to organize and accomplish their practical interests in situations. Indeed, rhetoric was such a pervasive aspect of the WIN staff's work that it is difficult to imagine everyday life in this social world without it.

The chapters that follow apply and develop the issues raised here to the organizational world of a WIN office. The next chapter considers WIN as a public policy intended to remedy the employment problems of the "hard-core" unemployed and as an organization intended to implement the policies. We consider how WIN was made up of interrelated roles and activities, staff members' concerns about others' motives and actions, the staff's professional responsibilities in implementing WIN policies, and factors which staff members stated that they could not control but which constrained their choices and actions. The third chapter considers how the WIN staff oriented toward their verbal encounters with others as potential arguments. In doing so, the staff members emphasized the ways in which their interests and concerns were opposed to those of others in their work world. Further, in emphasizing the argumentative aspects of their interactions with clients, the WIN staff members produced social conditions that justified their use of rhetoric to manage these potentially troublesome persons.

The next three chapters consider the major ways in which WIN staff members used rhetoric to manage problems in their relationships with clients, other staff members and state WIN officials. The first problems involved WIN participants' obligations to fulfill organizational expectations and demands. Negotiations concerned about this matter focused on the reasonableness of organizational expectations and demands, motives of organizational superiors in making demands on others, and aspects of people's lives which undermined their abilities to fully comply with typical organizational expectations and demands. The negotiations were important partly because they were occasions for developing practical understanding of WIN staff members' and state officials' right to compel acquiescence from others.

The second problem was concerned with defining the causes of clients' and other persons' troubles. For the most part, the staff emphasized how persons' troubles were based on their own choices and actions, but they also stated that persons were not always to blame for their troubles. Thus, the WIN staff members' efforts to rhetorically define the sources of troubles in their work world turned on the question of culpability; that is, who and/or what social conditions are responsible for the troubles? Finally, a major professional concern of the WIN staff and others in their work world involved justifying organizationally preferred solutions to clients' and others' troubles. Negotiations about the proper solution to persons' troubles centered in two related questions: (1) Who or what is responsible for the troubles at hand and (2) How can troubled persons most effectively take responsibility for the solution of their troubles?

The book concludes by considering some of the general themes and implications of the findings for analyzing rhetoric and everyday life in WIN and other street-level bureaucracies. Four major themes and issues are discussed. We first consider the practical circumstances associated with WIN staff members' and others' emphasis on rhetoric in managing their work problems. Second, we consider how rhetoric and argumentation were organized as work activities in WIN. The third issue discussed in the chapter involves the social organization of rhetoric and acquiescence in WIN. Finally, the WIN staff members' and others' use of rhetoric is placed in a larger social and political context by considering how rhetoric and argumentation in WIN is similar to the political language of politicians and others who seek to influence general public policies.

2

The Work Incentive Program

This study is based on thirteen months of field work in a local office of the Work Incentive Program (WIN). The office was located in a small city in the midwestern section of the United States. The city was located in the geographical center of an urban-industrial complex extending roughly one hundred miles. WIN clients were encouraged to look for jobs throughout the area. The majority of employed persons in the city worked in factories producing durable goods, such as motorized vehicles, metal products, clothing, tools, musical instruments, books and manufacturing equipment. Other area cities were also highly industrialized and offered employment opportunities similar to those in the city studied.

The research involved extensive observation of WIN staff members' routine interactions with each other, clients, organizational superiors and other persons in their work world. Formal meetings with such persons were observed as well as informal conversations between staff members concerning treatment of clients and the practical meaning of WIN policies. I was allowed to observe any and all staff interactions that I wished. These observations were supplemented with informal interviews with the WIN staff, clients and others associated with the WIN program. Some of the data were also collected from WIN case files which included demographic information on clients, staff members' descriptions of clients' WIN activities, and explanations of staff members' decisions about the management of clients' problems.

I presented myself in the WIN office and was treated as an independent and naive observer seeking to learn about how the WIN program worked. Usually, I observed during the entire work day by moving from meeting to meeting, accompanying staff to their occasional meetings out of the WIN office, and talking with clients while they waited for appointments with staff members or looked through area telephone books and listings of area employers to identify places where they could apply for jobs. The interviews usually took place just prior to or following the activities that I observed, although they sometimes occurred during breaks in ongoing activities.

The rest of this chapter is concerned with the social organization and contexts of the WIN staff's activities and relationships. We first consider the major purposes and themes of the Work Incentive Program as a public policy. It is followed by four sections concerned with aspects of the social organization of the WIN office. We consider WIN roles and activities, staff member concerns and orientations to their work, and the practical conditions which the staff portrayed as constraints on their efforts to achieve WIN goals. These aspects of the WIN staff's work world form the organizational and political contexts for the staff members' interests in gaining acquiescence from others through rhetoric.

The Work Incentive Program as a Public Policy

WIN was initiated in 1967 and revised in 1972 and 1980 through amendments to the Social Security Act which is also the legislative source for the Aid to Families with Dependent Children (AFDC) program (U.S. Congress, 1936, 1967, 1972, 1980). The general purpose of AFDC is to provide financial aid to economically distressed families with children under the age of eighteen years. Although some adult AFDC recipients are employed in part-time or other low paying jobs, a substantial portion are unemployed persons who are totally dependent on AFDC for supporting themselves and their families. Thus, a major concern of the initiators of the WIN program was to help selected members of the AFDC population in finding employment in order to become economically self-sufficient and independent citizens (Patterson, 1981; Rein, 1974). A related concern was to control, if not significantly reduce, the amount of money spend on AFDC payments as well as the number of persons receiving them.

In part, AFDC recipients were a subject of legislative attention because they are often depicted in public discussions as an important segment of the "hard-core unemployed" and "culture of poverty" who are "overly dependent" on the government for their livelihoods (Banfield, 1968; Lewis, 1966a,

1966b). Such economic dependence is also often linked to evaluations of their moral character, psychological well-being, and respectability in the eyes of their children and others in the community. A concern for such issues was expressed in the initial WIN legislation which states:

> It is expected that the individuals participating in the program established under this part will acquire a sense of dignity, self-worth, and confidence which will flow from being recognized as a wage-earning member of society and the example of a working adult in these families will have beneficial effects on the children in such families. (U.S. Congress, 1967: 1002)

Thus, the WIN program is an aspect of a general trend in American welfare policy concerned with holding the poor accountable for their public aid by making it contingent on the recipients' passing "work tests" (Garraty, 1978; Grønjberg, Street and Suttles, 1979; Macarov, 1980; Miller, 1981; Patterson, 1981; Piven and Cloward, 1971). Such tests are institutional procedures for applying publicly preferred values and expectations about proper adult and family life to the poor and outcast. One such value and expectation is that morally worthy adults prefer to support themselves and their families through employment. The value and expectation is analyzed here as the *work ethic*.

WIN as a Work Test

As it is expressed in WIN policies, the work ethic is based on the assumption that otherwise morally worthy adults must sometimes turn to welfare to manage economic problems that are beyond their control. The policies portray such persons' welfare dependence as an unavoidable and short-term condition, not a freely chosen way of life. One purpose of WIN is to identify and eliminate clients who have chosen welfare dependence as a way of life. Thus, WIN policies also define morally worthy clients as persons who are committed to getting off of welfare and reassuming their proper roles as the sole economic providers for themselves and their families.

Clients commitments to getting off of welfare are tested by treating their willingness to seek and accept employment and, more generally, to fulfill assignments made by local WIN staff as signs of clients' moral right to receive public aid. WIN policies state that local staff members are justified in withholding public aid to clients assessed as uncooperative; that is, as unwilling to properly look for jobs or fulfill other WIN assignments intended to make them employable. Thus, clients assessed as uncooperative by local WIN staff are treated as having failed WIN work tests. In withholding public aid to such clients, the local staff enforces the work ethic and holds clients accountable for their improper actions and orientations to WIN and welfare.

WIN is a work test that a substantial number of AFDC recipients must take. Specifically, during the time of the research, all AFDC recipients were required to participate in WIN except those who met one of the following conditions of exemption:

> children under [the] age of 16 or attending school; those ill, incapacitated, or of advanced age; those so remote from a [WIN office] as to preclude participating; those caring for a member of the household who is ill or incapacitated; another in a family where the father registers; and a mother of a child under age six. (Rein, 1974: 115)

Persons required to participate in WIN had to minimally comply with the assignments made by the WIN staff. Local staff responded to clients assessed as inadequately fulfilling their assignments by making formal complaints against them and, in cases assessed as intolerable, terminating their participation in WIN. Depending on their organizational status, termination from WIN resulted in the elimination of all AFDC support to clients and their families or a substantial reduction in AFDC support.

WIN policies involved three major requirements for local staff members. First, WIN staff members were required to monitor their clients' activities to ensure that the clients were making sincere and adequate efforts to fulfill the terms of their welfare grants; staff members were required to hold accountable clients assessed as uncooperative. Second, WIN staff members were required to provide basic social services needed by their clients in seeking and finding employment. Such services included counselling for family and personal problems, help in obtaining needed medical services, and providing information about educational and vocational training programs. The WIN staff was also required to provide services that directly aided clients' job seeking efforts, such as making funds available for hiring baby sitters while clients looked for jobs, partially reimbursing travel and related job seeking expenses, and counselling on where and how to look for jobs. Finally, WIN was intended as a source for changing clients' perspectives and lifestyles. According to the framers of the WIN policy, obtaining employment is a major source for transforming the lives and attitudes of the poor. They further stated that WIN staff may facilitate change in clients' perspectives and lifestyles by teaching the clients organizationally approved understandings of their problems, including how their perspectives and lifestyles contribute to their employment problems.

According to the definers and administrators of WIN, these themes are aspects of a realistic and comprehensive response to the employment problems of the hard-core unemployed. They are aspects of an orientation that treats poverty and unemployment as largely a consequence of the inadequacies of the poor and the solving of poor persons' economic problems as their own responsibility. The orientation may be enacted and applied in a variety of ways, including treating poor persons' troubles as based on their improper attitudes and lifestyles, their lack of marketable vocational skills and experiences, and their inadequate understandings of the practical realities associated with getting and keeping jobs.

This orientation to poverty and unemployment has been analyzed as an institutionalized source of "blaming the victims" of social and economic inequality for their plight (Auletta, 1982; Ryan, 1971). More specifically, the values and expectations expressed in WIN policies may be analyzed as sources for "inferiorizing" the poor and unemployed (Adam, 1978).

WIN as Inferiorization

Inferiorization refers to the ways in which outcast groups are treated as less socially worthy than others in society. Inferiorization is one way in which persons are interactionally produced as socially incompetent and undesirable. It is a practical fact of life for poor and outcast groups seeking to survive in social worlds dominated by unequal institutions and the elites who control them. It is partly a fact of life because inferiorization is frequently treated by human service professionals as a realistic and necessary solution to their clients' problems. According to Adam (1978), inferiorization centers in the ways that poor and outcast groups accommodate and subordinate themselves to the interests of institutional elites who control access to jobs and other opportunities needed by the poor and outcast to survive.

Inferiorizing practices include treating members of outcast groups as anonymous and homogeneous, and as having insignificant interests and life experiences. The latter practice involves ignoring the desires and concerns of the poor and outcast in making decisions having consequences for their lives. Inferiorizing practices are also associated with recommendations that the poor and outcast accept prevailing social relations and practices. Such persons are told that they can solve their problems by becoming like members of more powerful and highly valued groups. Put differently, inferiorization partly involves teaching the poor and outcast that they can only solve their problems by "fitting in."

Adam (1978) treats such inferiorizing practices as aspects of a general process producing (or accomplishing) inferiorized groups and classes. Further, inferiorizing practices have practical consequences. The practices promise to simultaneously remedy the most pressing troubles of the poor and outcast and perpetuate the unequal institutions and relationships that dominate their lives. Adam (1978: 1–2) states,

> To understand the production and maintenance of social order necessitates focus upon the social accomplishment of inferiorization in everyday life. Socially structured life constraints elicit behavior which adjusts, accommodates, or subordinates itself to adverse situations in the interest of survival and thereby functions to produce the constraining social order.

One way in which the poor and outcast accommodate to others is by accepting the practical limits imposed on them by dominant institutions and elites. Accepting these limits is often portrayed as a central aspect of a realistic and effective orientation to the solution of the problems of poor and outcast persons. It involves taking advantage of whatever opportunities others make available to the poor and outcast. Adam (1978) states that a second accommodative response is assimilation that is intended to integrate the poor and outcast into social worlds from which they have been excluded. Adam states that the assimilationist response is organized as an exchange because the poor and outcast are promised an opportunity to improve their life chances by becoming or appearing to become like members of superordinate groups in the society.

One way in which the poor and outcast may appear to become like others is through the strategic manipulation of images of self. The strategy is similar to that analyzed by Goffman (1959) as impression management. It involves controlling and sometimes concealing information about one's self in order to positively impress others, particularly information that might be taken by others as discrediting the image of self being projected (Goffman, 1963). Thus, the assimilationist response is a practical and self-interested strategy for dealing with problematic others. It centers in satisfying one's self-interests by anticipating and taking account of others' perspectives and concerns.

Goffman (1963) further states that when impression management strategies and tactics are taught in human service organizations, they become a professionally advocated code of conduct. The code involves both instruction on how to act in one's dealings with powerful others and how to orient to self. Goffman further analyzes such codes as recipes for defining clients' social worth. One way in which the poor and outcast demonstrate their social worth to human service professionals is by adhering to the code. Persons who do so are described by human service professionals as realistic and committed to solving their problems. On the other hand, clients who resist human service professionals' instruction are described as "self-deluded" and "misguided" (Goffman, 1963: 111).

One aspect of this analysis is a concern for the ways in which the WIN staff rhetorically assigned blame to WIN clients and cast them as inferior. Such staff member activities are treated as aspects of their orientations to their clients' economic troubles, the purposes of WIN, and the practical issues emergent in their social relations with clients and others in their work world. The staff members' inferiorizing practices were tied to their interest in responding to client troubles in organizationally approved way while working in an environment that they portrayed as uncertain and offering few options for properly responding to the troubles. But the WIN staff's work involved more than assigning blame and inferiorizing clients. For example, in some interactions staff members portrayed their clients as victims of forces beyond their control; most notably, as victims of resessionary area labor markets.

Thus, the WIN staff's work orientations were not a simple reflection of the ideological emphases of WIN policies. Rather, staff member orientations to concrete issues were formulated and expressed in relation to a variety of practical concerns and contingencies which varied across situations. The staff's practical concerns were partly related to the organization of roles and activities in the WIN office which we consider next.

WIN Roles and Activities

At the local level, WIN is administered by the district office of the State Job Service and the County Welfare Department. The Job Service is responsible for meeting the job seeking needs of clients by providing them with employment-related counselling and information as well as organizing and monitoring their job search activities. The Welfare Department is required to provide supportive social services to WIN clients. Such services include personal counselling, payment for baby sitting expenses incurred while job seeking, help in managing the family's budget, and aid in finding professional help for clients' health, family and emotional problems. In addition, representatives of the two organizations are required to engage in a variety of joint activities, including registering new clients, approving requests for enrollment in vocational training programs, and dealing with troublesome clients.

During most of the research period, the WIN staff was made up of seven WIN workers and a WIN supervisor associated with the State Job Service, and three social workers representing the County Welfare Department. Six of the seven WIN workers were assigned to the program on a full-time basis while the three social workers devoted half of their time to it. The WIN supervisor was in charge of the day-to-day operation of the office. The staff also included a WIN worker designated as the *WIN counsellor*. He was assigned clients portrayed as the most difficult and uncooperative. Another WIN worker was in charge of the *job club* which was a special job-search group meeting daily in the WIN office. She was also in charge of *conciliation sessions* which were formal meetings in which the staff made official complaints against uncooperative clients. Two of the social workers counselled WIN clients and the third devoted most of his WIN time to registering and appraising new clients. In addition, one of the social workers was a member of the *training committee* which considered client requests for training grants and another was the Welfare Department representative at conciliation sessions.

Six of the eleven persons who made up the WIN staff were women and all but one were white. Although detailed information is not available on the careers and backgrounds of the staff, their associations with WIN involved two major routes. First, the social workers were long-term employees of the County Welfare Department who had been involved with a variety of the department's programs over the years. One group of WIN workers was similar to the social workers because they were long-term members of the state civil service whose careers included assignments to many different social service programs. The other route included staff members who first became involved with WIN as clients. Indeed, they sometimes described themselves as "WIN graduates." These staff members used the resources provided by WIN and other government programs to qualify for their positions in the state civil service system and WIN.

My observations of the work activities and styles of WIN graduates and other staff members show no significant differences between them. Both groups included staff members who were described as tough on clients and others who were described as lenient. Advancement within the organization was also unrelated to persons' initial involvements with WIN. For example, the WIN supervisor was a WIN graduate, but the staff member who assisted her in administering the program (the *lead worker*) was not. Finally, staff members did not classify or orient to one another as WIN graduates or career civil servants. They treated their initial involvements in WIN and career patterns as irrelevant to their interactions and the practical issues making up their work. For these reasons, I will not differentiate between WIN graduates and other staff members in most of the rest of the analysis.

The exception to this position involves staff members' explanations of their own and others' motives in responding to clients. Staff members sometimes used the WIN graduate-nongraduate distinction to explain why they or other WIN graduates were skeptical of clients' claims and why they demanded that clients fulfill their WIN obligations. It was one of several explanations used by staff members to account for their professional orientations and actions. Consider, for example, the following WIN graduate's explanation of her orientation to clients.

A lot of these people [clients] think they can manipulate me. You know, make excuses or give me a sob story about their problems and why they can't do anything [fulfill their WIN assignments]. They don't know that I was one of them. [Describes the time and place of her WIN involvement.] I remember the first time I went to WIN, I had no intention of looking for work. I liked not doin' anything all day and I tried every trick in the book to get out of it. They're not doin' anything [that] I didn't try. They don't know it, but I know what they're thinkin' even before they say anything.

Staff members did not use this explanation all of the time, however, because they did not always portray WIN graduates as tough on clients. Also, staff members did not use the account to explain why staff members who had not been WIN clients were tough on clients. Both circumstances called for different explanations.

A general image of the types of persons enrolled in WIN may be gleaned from the records of the WIN staff. Of the 1,568 persons enrolled in the program during a 12 month period of the research, 65 percent were between the ages of 21 and 35 years and 79 percent between 21 and 40 years; 54 percent were women; 76 percent were white; 39 percent had high school diplomas or their equivalent, while 52 percent had less than 12 years of formal education. The official family size was relatively small; 59 percent were families of two to three persons and 82 percent included two to four persons. The family size was defined as the number of adults and children included in the client's AFDC grant. It did not necessarily reflect the number of persons living in clients' households.

The amount of government aid provided was $401 per month for two-person families, $473 per month for three-person families, and $563 per month for four-person families. The primary jobs held by WIN clients prior to enrollment in the program were clerical, sales and service occupations (38 percent) and industrial occupations (48 percent). Clients left the program for various reasons. The most frequently mentioned were because clients had found employment or another source of income — such as qualifying for Unemployment Compensation benefits (36 percent), clients moved out of the county (13 percent) and clients were terminated from WIN for failing to cooperate with the staff (10–11 percent). Clients who moved out of the county were terminated from WIN because AFDC eligibility and funding are county based. If they wished to receive AFDC benefits, these clients had to reapply for AFDC and register with WIN in their new counties of residence.

In general, WIN clients were processed in the manner depicted in Figure 2-1.

FIGURE 2.1
Client Processing in WIN

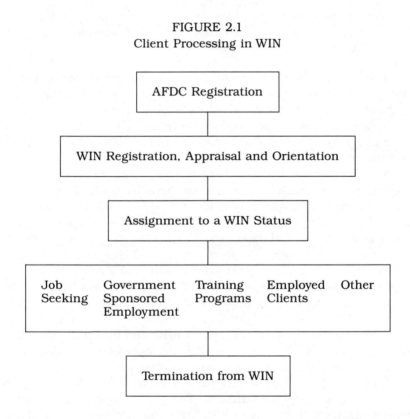

The rest of the section is organized as brief discussions of each aspect of client processing in WIN.

From AFDC to WIN

The process of becoming a WIN client began with a person's initial application and approval for AFDC. Many applicants were approved for such aid contingent on participation in WIN and others were told that they could volunteer for the program. Most of the clients studied were required to participate in WIN. Whether mandatory or voluntary participants, persons registering with WIN were first assigned to one of two welfare statuses having consequences for their participation in WIN: AFDC and AFDC-UP. The heads of single-parent households (mostly women) were assigned to the AFDC category and heads of two-parent households (mostly men) were assigned to the AFDC-UP category. Unlike persons classified as AFDC-UP, persons classified as AFDC could hold full-time jobs, continue to receive limited government aid, and remain in WIN.

The limited aid provided to persons classified as AFDC was make possible because, although their welfare grants were reduced by the amount of the wages and salaries they earned from jobs, a portion of the wages and salaries were ignored to take account of expenses associated with their employment and to offer an incentive to take employment. Persons classified as AFDC were terminated from AFDC and WIN when they earned the equivalent of their welfare grants plus the amount which was ignored. On the other hand, persons classified as AFDC-UP were terminated from AFDC and WIN when they earned the equivalent of their AFDC grants or were employed for a total of one hundred hours during a one month period. The latter grounds for termination held regardless of the wage or salary earned by the client.

Finally, the consequences of termination from WIN for failure to cooperate with the staff were different for persons assigned to the AFDC and AFDC-UP categories. AFDC clients so terminated from WIN lost the portion of their welfare grants that was assigned to them, but their children continued to receive their share of the families' grants. Clients classified as AFDC-UP who were terminated from WIN for failing to adequately cooperate with the staff lost their families' entire grants

Becoming a WIN Client

The WIN registration and appraisal process was organized around the completion of a series of forms concerned with identifying basic client characteristics (e.g., age, gender and educational background) and employment history; determination of clients' social service needs; and development of employability plans indicating the types of jobs that clients were expected to seek. New clients were also given brief introductions to the purposes and general requirements of the program. In most cases, WIN workers who registered and appraised new clients continued to supervise their subsequent activities in the program. During the latter phases of the research and in response to cuts in staff positions, new clients were registered and appraised in groups.

For some clients, the registration and appraisal session was their full introduction in WIN because they were immediately assigned to a program of activity intended to make them more employable and/or to get them a job. Most, however, were first required to attend an orientation session. The sessions were held several times a week and were intended to introduce clients to the procedures and expectations of the program. Orientation sessions included discussions of the following topics: the legal mandate of WIN; rules associated with mandatory participation in the program; forms to be maintained by clients in documenting their participation in the program (particularly those concerned with job searching); bases for partial reimbursements for travel and other job searching expenses; staff's expectations about the types of jobs that WIN clients should seek; procedures for registering a complaint about WIN workers; WIN staff's record of success at helping clients find jobs; and consequences of failing to cooperate with the staff.

WIN Programs and Remedies

One part of the registration and appraisal session was the assignment of clients to WIN statuses. Clients' initial assignments to WIN statuses were not permanent, but subject to change based on the staff's ongoing assessments of the clients' abilities, needs, desires and moral character. However, the statuses to which clients were assigned were significant indicators of their WIN activities and level of contact with the WIN staff. Clients were placed in twelve WIN statuses which are here classified and discussed as five types of remedies to client troubles: job seeking, government sponsored employment, training, clients holding jobs, and other remedies.

For the staff, the most preferred WIN statuses were those requiring that clients look for jobs. Clients assigned to such statuses were referred to by the staff as *active*, in contrast to clients assigned to other WIN statuses who were not required to engage in full-time job seeking. Some active clients were required to look for jobs individually and others as members of job seeking groups, such as the job club. Clients assigned to job seeking statuses were also more closely supervised than others. Indeed, some clients were required to report to their WIN workers everyday to show that they had made a designated number of job contacts (job inquires or applications) each day. All active clients were required to maintain job search forms listing the employers whom they had contacted for jobs.

The second set of WIN statuses involved various types of government sponsored employment programs. They included short-term work experience programs in which clients were required to do nonsalaried work for local nonprofit organizations, and subsidized employment programs which paid employers to train WIN clients and eventually hire them as regular employees. A third set of WIN statuses involved clients who were pursuing vocational training. Some clients were supported by funds provided by WIN and others by funds obtained from other sources. Whatever the funding source, clients were required to obtain permission from the WIN staff to enroll in the programs.

A fourth set of clients were assigned to statuses reserved for those who were employed, but did not made enough money from their jobs to be totally removed from their AFDC grants. Some of these clients were required to search for other jobs offering more pay and/or full-time employment, but others were not. The staff explained and justified the latter responses by portraying the clients as lacking job skills or having personal and family problems limiting their ability to get and hold better paying jobs. The staff portrayed such clients as unemployable because they were unlikely to ever by fully self-supporting. Finally, some clients were placed in various residual statuses which are here classified as *other*. Most such clients were portrayed by the staff as persons who were unable to look for and/or keep jobs. although they did not meet the standards for full exemption from the program. For example, clients reporting serious health and emotional problems were temporarily assigned to this status until their problems improved or they could be exempted from the program. Clients assigned to the latter two categories were not closely supervised by the staff or required to engage in intensive job seeking.

In sum, the WIN staff had a variety of options in classifying and processing their clients. Their options were increased when we consider that the staff did not treat WIN statuses as mutually exclusive categories; rather, clients were often required to participate in activities associated with more than one status. For example, clients who were attending school on a part-time basis were also frequently required to look for jobs during part of the day. The WIN staff used the assignments to improve clients' chances of getting jobs by helping them obtain needed vocational skills and knowledge while also enforcing the work ethic. They also treated the practice as one way of "testing" clients' moral rights to training that the staff portrayed as a special program to be reserved for clients who had shown that they were committed to getting off of welfare by finding jobs.

Thus, the staff's most preferred client statuses and remedies involved intensive job seeking. Their least preferred remedies involved terminating clients from the program based on health and family problems or clients' failure to adequately fulfill their WIN assignments. The latter responses were treated by the WIN staff as remedies of last resort. Although they were portrayed as last resorts, the staff stated that it was sometimes a professionally and organizationally necessary and responsible act to terminate "uncooperative" clients from the program. According to the staff, such terminations ensured that only persons committed to getting off welfare by finding jobs remained as WIN clients. The staff assigned varying degrees of preference to other statuses and remedies, depending on their assessments of clients' abilities and circumstances and the practical options available to them in dealing with clients.

Leaving WIN

Clients left WIN in a variety of ways. The staff preferred that clients leave by getting full-time jobs that paid enough that the client no longer qualified for AFDC. Many clients did leave in this way. Others, however, left for reasons that were less preferred by the staff, such as giving birth to a child, developing a serious medical incapacity that limited their abilities to hold jobs, having their oldest children reach the age of majority, or being terminated for "uncooperativeness." Clients who left because they found employment were counted as organizational successes if they remained employed for thirty days. Unless they re-enrolled in WIN or appealed their involuntary terminations from WIN and AFDC, the WIN staff had no further contact with clients subsequent to their leaving the program.

A related aspect of the social organization of the WIN staff's work involved their concerns in implementing program policies, which we consider in the next three sections. We begin with the staff's concern for assessing clients' orientations to WIN, welfare and employment.

Staff Concern for Client Orientations

Although they sometimes disagreed about the practical meaning and implications of WIN policies, the WIN staff members
expressed general agreement with the legislative intent of the
program. They portrayed the major purpose of the program as
to help clients find jobs and get off of welfare. They also stated
that a basic part of achieving organizational goals involved
changing clients' orientations to adult and family roles and
lifestyles as well as to welfare and employment. The staff portrayed clients' "improper" orientations as signs and causes of
their employment problems. In so attending to clients and
their troubles, staff members treated their interactions with
clients in the WIN office as occasions for assessing clients'
underlying attitudinal and behavioral orientations. They stated
that clients' underlying orientations had consequences for
clients' willingness and abilities to fulfill their WIN assignments and find employment.

Consider, for example, the following staff members' explanations for their clients' employment troubles.

> I talked to a [client] the other day. She said her son comes
> home for supper between four and ten [o'clock] every night.
> [She said,] "It's hard to keep his meal warm." I said, "My God,
> can't he come at a certain time?" She said, "No boys and men
> are like that. There's nothing you can do." Well, it's obvious
> what an attitude like that means for work. They don't care

> There are some general groups of people that we deal with.
> Well, they're all individuals, you know, but you could put a lot
> of them into types.... Well, a lot of them are, it's not a popular
> term, but character disorders. They're immature. A lot of
> immaturity. They just don't act like adults. A lot of people in
> their late twenties who can't act like adults.

> [We] deal with those who won't take care of themselves. Not
> like those upstairs [clients of the State Job Service] who can't
> [take care of themselves] now because of [economic] conditions.

Thus, the WIN staff members' interest in assessing their
clients' orientations to employment and welfare was related to
their assumption that many clients were socially incompetent.
They assumed that poor and unemployed persons possess personal and cultural traits which keep them from properly fulfill-

ing their social obligations, the most important being finding and keeping jobs. As the above statements indicate, one aspect of the WIN staff members' everyday rhetorical work involved developing and sometimes negotiating explanations for client's social incompetence. Although the explanations focused on different causes for clients' employment troubles and social incompetence, staff members used all such explanations to justify their practices of assessing clients' orientations and citing the assessments in defining appropriate responses to clients' troubles.

In assessing clients' orientations, WIN staff sought to identify factors keeping clients from getting and keeping jobs. One part of the staff's assessments involved treating clients' dress, grooming and demeanor in the WIN office as signs of their improper orientations and causes of their employment troubles. According to staff members, clients' appearances and actions in the WIN office were reflections of general patterns of inappropriate understandings and actions which reduced their chances of getting jobs. The explanation was central to the staff's claim that bad WIN clients were also likely to be bad job seekers. The staff also stated that in taking actions intended to improve clients' performances in WIN (including their dress and grooming), they were improving clients' chances of getting jobs. Consider, for example, the following staff member portrayal of the causes of clients' employment troubles.

> Look at these people [nods in the direction of a group of clients in the office] when they come in here. They have to come here but I think they go to employers [looking] that way too. A lot go from here to job apps [applications]. They haven't shaved or changed their jeans in a month. They [men] wear ponytails. That's okay at a beach but not a work. They don't know that a lot of getting hired is subjective. Employers are subjective as hell. You don't know what they look at [in making hiring decisions]. Maybe you haven't brushed your teeth and someone else gets the job. If two people are equally qualified, appearance makes the difference, grooming, demeanor, how you present yourself. It's no wonder these people don't get jobs.

Looked at one way, staff members' assessments of clients' underlying orientations were similar to their assessments of clients' health, family circumstances, levels of educational achievement, and other aspects of their lives which the staff treated as factors influencing their employability. When the staff assessed such factors as having negative influences on clients' employability, the staff portrayed them as *job barriers.* The staff stated that one part of their professional responsibility in WIN involved helping clients manage, if not overcome, such barriers. In general, WIN staff portrayed clients assessed as having medical, educational, family related job barriers as suffering from conditions for which they were not culpable. The staff sought to remedy such barriers by utilizing resources available within the WIN program and seeking specialized help from other community organizations. For example, clients assessed as having health barriers were required to seek medical or psychotherapeutic services.

Although the WIN staff treated improper client orientations to employment, welfare and family roles as somewhat like other job barriers, they did not treat them as exactly the same. Specifically, the staff treated client orientations as matters for which clients were responsible and should be held accountable. The staff members partly justified their different attitude toward client orientations by stating that many clients were intent on avoiding their responsibilities to their families and the government. They added that one purpose of WIN is to identify such clients, give them a chance to change their orientations and ways of life, and, if they did not make the required changes, to eliminate them from the welfare rolls. But the staff did not portray all clients assessed as having improper orientations in this way. They stated that some clients' improper orientations were the result of two other factors.

First, the staff stated that some clients had developed their improper orientations to employment, welfare and family based on experiences in local social service institutions which are organized around policies and practices that unintentionally encourage persons to be dependent and avoid their responsibilities as adults. The three institutions that staff members most frequently portrayed in this way were area schools which were said to pass students without regard to their abilities or efforts to learn, welfare agencies that provide aid without demanding that clients make an effort to solve their troubles, and psychotherapeutic programs which teach clients that their troubles are a result of emotional problems for which they are not responsible. They explained that a major undesirable consequence of the policies and practices of such organizations is that students and clients are not given needed opportunities to learn about the expectations that prevail in most work places or the consequences that are associated with persons' failure to meet expectations. The staff added that one source for clients' employment troubles was their unrealistic understanding of what is required in getting and keeping jobs as well as their value in area labor markets.

Second, the staff stated that continuing failure at finding jobs may be a source of improper orientations because clients become frustrated and depressed and, ultimately, lose their desire to find jobs. The staff portrayed such clients as coming to accept continuing dependence on welfare as a fact of life and preferable to the frustrations of job seeking. They further portrayed this pattern of accommodation to failure as a natural and understandable response which is observable in the reactions of many persons to unemployment, not just WIN clients. For example, the staff members explained the response of one of their colleagues to being laid off from WIN (due to funding cuts) in this way. They stated that the former staff member's difficulties in finding a new job were based on his inability to handle the frustrations that accompany being rejected for job openings. As one staff member stated, "He's acting just like one of our clients."

One staff member explained the WIN staff's concern for countering client frustration and depression by linking Maslow's theory of human needs to WIN's emphasis on job seeking as the preferred solution to client troubles. She stated that Maslow's theory involves a

> triangle where you [people] have to take care of basic needs like shelter before you can worry about other things like love. Well, we're [WIN staff] dealing with *the* basic problem. These people are worrying about shelter and food. It's a very delicate situation. We [people] say that we don't care about money and clothes and so on, but we do and these people are losing them. Our identities get connected to them. Plus working is basic to our identities. When you go someplace, people ask "What do you do for a living?" and, if you're unemployed, well it's depressing...Looking [for jobs] on their own helps them save face, a little. [It] gives them a feeling they are in control. It helps to protect their identities.

Thus, staff members' interest in and assessments of clients' orientations to WIN, welfare and employment were complex.

They were also central to staff members' portrayals of their major professional responsibilities in implementing WIN policies, to which we turn next.

Staff Responsibilities and WIN Policies

No matter how they assessed the sources of clients' "improper" orientations, the staff stated that clients would not change their perspectives and behavior unless they were held responsible for them and made to change by WIN officials. Staff members added that one of their major professional responsibilities in WIN was to help and, if necessary, force changes in the perspectives and behavior of clients assessed as holding improper orientations. The staff sought to achieve this goal by treating clients' acceptance of personal responsibility for their employment troubles as a major part of remedying them. Consider, for example, the following excerpt from a conversation involving two WIN staff members.

> You know, sometimes I don't know whether these people [clients] don't think or if they're the last true Christians. [Other staff member laughs.] Well, you know, there's an element of idealistic Christian faith that Christ will provide, so you just live for the present and God'll take care of the future. It's a crude kind of Christianity, but I sometimes think that's what they believe... You just get a sense that these people feel they are totally controlled by the world out there. They don't seem to feel that they have any power or influence. We have to break through that [feeling] and make them assertive and responsible for their lives. They have to see that they can control their lives.

Staff members stated that the primary way in which they sought this goal was by enforcing organizational rules intended to make clients accept responsibility for their employment troubles. It centered in requiring that clients look for jobs or engage in other activities intended to make them more employable. Staff member also portrayed such rule enforcement as a source for forcing unwilling clients to change their behavior and attitudes by introducing them to the rules and expectations of the typical work place. In so portraying their intentions and actions, staff members cast WIN rules as sources for both controlling and helping clients. One staff member explained.

They say you can't help a person who doesn't want it, but you can. You can make 'em do it. That's what we do here.

Also, consider the following staff member explanation of the purposes of WIN and WIN's interest in clients. It was make by a staff member in accounting for the success of a program requiring that clients meet with him each morning prior to looking for jobs.

...a lot of 'em [clients] come in with a [job seeking] plan for the day already made out and they're gone [out of the WIN office] by eight o'clock. That's a lot of what this is about, getting them to plan and follow through....they need to learn how to get up early enough so that they can get cleaned up and in here on time. It's a crude form of behavior modification is what it is.... You've seen these people, how they come in here. They look at the beginning of the day the way most people look at the end of the day. It's a matter of changing behavior, that's most of what we do. You can't do it meeting with 'em once every week or two. There isn't enough control, it has to be everyday so you can see 'em. I told 'em again today, don't go to a job interview in sandals. They hafta learn these things.

They also used the portrayals to distinguish the purposes of WIN from those of other local social service agencies concerned with the poor and unemployed. Specifically, the staff stated that because they did not emphasize holding WIN clients responsible for solving their troubles, other social service agencies perpetuated clients' unemployment and welfare dependence. Consider the following staff member portrayals of WIN as a unique approach to unemployment and welfare dependence.

Staff Member 1: You see, welfare is like a dream world. These people can get along on it, but it ain't like the real world out there. They're not prepared for the real world. They're protected.

Staff Member 2: The schools too. They pass them [students] along even if they don't do the work. They [WIN clients] don't understand the natural and logical consequences of their behavior. We're trying to teach them that. Employers will fire them if they don't show up for work without calling.

Staff members further explained that differences in philosophy were a major reason why they were reluctant to work with other local agencies in offering joint services to WIN clients. According to the staff, past joint programs with local agencies implementing policies different from those of WIN had resulted in disputes which undermined the WIN staff's efforts to properly solve WIN clients' troubles.

In sum, WIN staff members portrayed their work activities and goals as consistent with the legislative policies defining the program. In doing so, they cast WIN clients as responsible for their own employment troubles and justified actions intended to hold clients responsible for remedying the troubles. Although such staff member portrayals of their work goals and activities may be treated as rationales for "blaming the victims" of economic, political and social inequality, the staff stated that only a few of their clients were clear-cut victims of social injustice. They explained that most WIN clients were responsible for their employment troubles, although few clients would admit it.

According to the staff, a major way in which clients were responsible for their employment troubles was by holding unrealistic expectations about their value in the marketplace and proper employer-employee relations. The staff stated that many WIN clients were only willing to accept relatively high paying jobs for which they were seldom qualified and were unwilling to defer to the rightful authority of employers. They further portrayed clients' improper orientations as the basis for inappropriate actions while on the job, resulting in clients' unstable job histories. For example, the staff stated that clients' improper orientations sometimes resulted in insubordination on the job as well as chronic tardiness and absenteeism. In this way, the staff cast clients' job histories as signs of their underlying orientations and causes of their employement troubles. Such portrayals of clients' orientations and troubles were also central to staff member justifications of their emphasis on holding clients responsible for remedying their employment troubles. Consider, for example, the following staff member explanation of the sources of WIN clients' troubles and the staff's professional responsibilities in remedying them.

Staff Member 1: We have to start changing these people's behavior. They've got to learn to behave like people with jobs.

[To the observer:] Aren't there some real differences between these people and those who have jobs? [The observer states that he doesn't know.] There must be differences though. When you look at how many of these people have lost good jobs. When you look at their references, there just must be some basic behavioral differences between people who can hold onto jobs and these people. We hafta get these people acting live everybody else.

Staff Member 2: Yeah, I know, but how do we get them there?...

Staff Member 1: Well, I think we should make it tough on 'em. People don't change if they don't have to, why should they? I think we should make them uncomfortable and this should be an unpleasant experience.

Through such explanations of their clients' troubles, WIN staff members justified actions which were partly intended to inferiorize clients. Specifically, they sought to teach clients realistic employment expectations by instructing them on their "true" value in area labor markets, including instruction on their subordinate position in dealing with employers. According to the WIN staff, the development of such understandings and expectations was basic to clients' taking responsibility for and, ultimately, solving their employment troubles. The orientations taught to clients emphasized clients' devalued status in the area labor markets and the importance of adapting their job seeking strategies to take account of employers' interests and concerns. Clients assessed by the staff as positively responding to the instruction were portrayed as "good" clients who were making sincere efforts to get off of welfare. They stated that it was "only a matter of time" before such clients would find jobs. In this way, the WIN staff cast actions partly intended to inferiorize clients as professionally responsible and helpful to clients.

Despite their commitment to solving client troubles in professionally responsible ways, the staff members stated that they were constrained by forces beyond their control in seeking to implement and achieve WIN goals. The constraints were portrayed as factors limiting the staff's efforts to fully enforce organizational rules as well as reducing the effectiveness of the rules in producing desired changes in clients' orientations and employment statuses. The next section considers the major conditions portrayed by the staff as constraints.

Constraints on Staff Choices and Action

The staff members stated that they were constrained by three major conditions: (1) their inability to fully monitor clients' activities outside the WIN office, (2) the recessionary area economy, and (3) state- and federal-level political changes resulting in the reduction of staff positions and resources. They stated that these practical circumstances restricted their abilities to help clients find jobs and hold uncooperative clients accountable for their actions. We begin with staff members' portrayals of the major factors limiting their abilities to monitor students.

Constraints on Monitoring Clients

Although they sometimes left the WIN office to meet with officials of other local social service agencies involved with WIN clients, most of the staff's work occurred in the WIN office. Clients required to report on their job seeking efforts came to the WIN office at designated times. Client reports consisted of verbal portrayals of their job seeking efforts and the submission of job search forms partly indicating the dates and places where they had inquired about jobs. Clients also indicated on the forms how many miles they had travelled in search of jobs. Their mileage reports were used to calculate clients' reimbursement for gasoline and related job seeking expenses.

As a practical matter, then, the staff's monitoring of clients' activities outside the WIN office consisted of reviews of their reported activities. The staff members stated that such reports must be skeptically reviewed because clients intent on avoiding their obligations to look for jobs falsify their job search forms. They stated that such clients had a special interest in inflating their mileage claims in order to increase their incomes. In general, the staff members sought to hold their clients accountable for their actions outside the office by testing and verifying their reports. Test and verification involved paying close attention to clients' claims about where and when they looked for jobs as well as their mileage claims.

The staff members justified such practices by citing occasions when they had caught clients making false claims. For example, one client claimed to have applied for several jobs on a national holiday. Also, the staff members stated that they frequently caught clients making unreasonable mileage claims, such as claiming to have travelled several hundred miles during a half day of job seeking. The staff treated such incidents as evidence supporting the appropriateness of their skeptical orientation toward client reports. They also treated the incidents as occasions to hold clients accountable for their "improper" actions. They did so by confronting clients about their mileage claims and instructing them on the importance of keeping honest and accurate WIN records.

Consider, for example, the following staff member response to a client's mileage claims.

> Hello, I'm [staff member's name], I have eight years of college and I'm the counsellor here. [The client's WIN worker] asked me to look at this [the client's mileage record] and I see four hours [of] job search each day and twelve or twenty four miles [travelled in looking for jobs.]. There's a pattern here and I don't think this is accurate. You say you went to [a local company] and that was twelve miles and four hours of job search. That's the only place you have down. Well, I know it's not twelve miles [to the company] and how can you say that you spend four hours applying for one job? You know what I'd do? I'd tear this thing up and make you start over. Now, you're gonna have to be accurate with these [mileage records]. I don't believe this [record].

However, the staff members also stated that there were practical limits on their abilities to review and monitor their clients' activities outside the WIN office. One such limit involved clients' skills in falsifying reports. According to the staff members, only their greediest and dumbest clients made claims that were obviously false. They stated that more thoughtful and competent clients could avoid their WIN obligations by making false, but realistic claims about when, where and how long they looked for jobs. They further explained that it was the clients who were most intent on avoiding their responsibilities in WIN who were most likely to sucessfully falsify their reports. Such clients were portrayed by the staff as master manipulators who long ago learned how to use welfare rules and practices to their advantage. The staff stated that one of their goals in dealing with clients was to identify such master manipulators and hold them accountable for their improper orientations to employment and WIN.

A second limitation involved the staff's inability to independently verify client claims about their job seeking activities. The staff was partly limited by large caseloads restricting the amount of time that could be devoted to any single client. In addition, the staff members stated that their ability to "check up on clients" by calling employers that clients claimed to have contacted for jobs was restricted by the practical circumstances of job seeking in the recessionary local economy. The restriction partly involved the large number of persons applying for the few job openings in the community. Employers with job openings were usually inundated with job applicants and unlikely to remember whether a particular WIN clients had applied.

The staff members stated that a related problem was that many, if not most, WIN client-employer contacts were about possible future job openings for which the clients wished to apply. However, few employers were willing to take applications for nonexistent jobs. For such client job contacts, then, there was no written record to verify their claims. One staff member explained the practical difficulties of "checking up on clients" in this way:

> [Suppose] a [client] tells me he asked [for a job] at a gas station, but they didn't take an application. What am I to do? I call the manager and he says, "I don't know. I had a hundred people ask about work last week, I don't remember this kid."

Clients assessed as possibly not fulfilling their WIN assignments outside the office were closely observed by the staff who sought to identify new signs of their "true" orientations and actions. The observations were organized as a testing process intended to confirm or deny staff members' suspicions. Such tests were sometimes augmented by requiring that clients engage in special programs and activities which the staff members stated clients would find undesirable. The staff member stated that the undesirable programs and activities were intended to produce evidence of clients' "true" orientations to employment and welfare. One such assignment and test involved holding daily meetings with clients in which they were required to report on their job seeking activities and plans. Clients who failed to keep their daily meetings were referred to conciliation meetings where they were told that they must fully comply with WIN rules and procedures or face termination from the program.

A second way in which the staff tested clients' orientations was by requiring that they do unpaid work in local social service organizations. The assignments were justified to clients as ways of gaining work experience and employment references which would make them more employable. The staff also stated that such assignments were procedures for forcing potentially uncooperative clients to look for jobs. Clients who failed to fulfill such assignments were referred to conciliation sessions. As a staff member stated about his practice of assigning "uncooperative" clients to sort clothes at a local charitable organization, "Nobody wants to do that for $22.50 a week [the clients' reimbursement for travel and food expenses]. So, they look for a job."

The staff member further stated that the practice was effective because clients assigned to such tasks got jobs. Consider, for example his explanation of a client's success in finding a job. Upon hanging up the telephone, he said, "Now, there's the good news for today. [A client] called to cancel his appointment 'cause he got a job. He got back on at [his former place of employment]. See, the work experience [assignment] works. Nobody wants to work for $4.50 a day."

Through such practices, then, the staff members sought to manage a major constraint on their efforts to achieve WIN goals.

The Area Economy as a Constraint

WIN staff members treated the area economy as a set of labor markets which they defined and classified based on two major elements. First, they portrayed labor markets as territorial units within which job opportunities were available. They classified the local labor market as a territory encompassing the city in which the WIN office was located and the surrounding countryside. Other labor markets were portrayed as extending outward from the local labor market. The most important non-local labor markets were those in nearby cities because clients were required to look for jobs in both the local labor market and those located close by. Finally, the staff members sometimes treated more distant labor markets as relevant to their work by advising clients to consider moving to other regions of the country in order to find jobs. Clients indicating an interest in relocating were given limited financial aid in seeking jobs in those areas.

Second, the WIN staff defined labor markets as contrasive pairs and classified them based on the number of jobs available within them. Specifically, they distinguished between *open labor markets* which were portrayed as offering many job opportunities and *tight labor markets* which were portrayed as offering few. The staff's interest in so classifying labor markets was pragmatic. For example, the staff members' interest in distant labor markets was based on their assessments of them as open and, therefore, offering many job opportunities to WIN clients willing and able to relocate. They contrasted distant and open labor markets with those in the vicinity of the WIN office which the WIN staff classified as tight.

The WIN staff members justified their classifications of labor markets by treating public information about economic opportunities in local and distant regions and their own experiences as signs of labor market conditions. The staff assessed distant labor markets as open based on news broadcasts reporting great economic development in some regions of the country as well as their reading of the "Want Ads" sections of major newspapers from those areas. They cited such factors in recommending that clients relocate in order to get jobs. Staff members justified their assessments of area labor markets as tight based on three factors.

First, the staff cited official reports on economic opportunities in the area. Of special concern to the staff were reports indicating that many area businesses were reducing their workforce and, in some cases, going out of business. Second, staff members cited clients' reports on their efforts to find jobs. They stated, for example, that the tightness of area labor markets was reflected in the increasing number of employers who refused to take job applications in anticipation of future job openings and unemployed persons applying for known job openings. Finally, the staff members noted changes in their work circumstances in justifying their portrayals of area labor markets as tight.

Specifically, the staff treated increases in the number of persons applying for AFDC and WIN as evidence of decreased economic opportunities in the area. Staff members also stated that the stable work histories of many new clients was evidence of a recession. According to the staff, under normal economic conditions, the typical WIN client had few marketable job skills and an unstable job history involving a variety of short-term jobs. The staff also treated the reduced number of job openings listed with the State Job Service Office and WIN as a sign of a tight area economy. Consider, for example, the following staff member comparison of his present work circumstances with those of the "old [pre-recession] days."

> It's not like the old days when we had a stack of [job openings listed with the Job Service] and could send them [clients] out on five or six [job contacts]....Now, we get them [job listings] in and [before the staff can refer clients to them] they're already filled. What can we do?

The WIN staff members' portrayal of the area economy as tight was part of their explanation of their changed relationship with clients. They stated that, unlike "the good old days" when many job openings were known to the WIN staff, they could no longer provide clients with job leads. Rather, clients were almost totally responsible for both finding and getting jobs. Thus, the staff's new relationship with clients involved increased concern for monitoring clients' job seeking efforts. The staff members portrayed their concern as partly a responsibility to make certain that clients did not become discouraged by their lack of success in finding jobs. They explained that clients who would be quite employable under other circumstances were likely to have difficulty finding jobs in the recessionary area economy. For this reason, the staff member stated that they now had to watch all of their clients for signs of frustration and discouragement about their inability to find jobs.

In general, the staff portrayed the new staff member-client relationship as one emphasizing social control over helping clients. They stated that the emphasis was not based on their preference, but on economic conditions beyond their control. In this way, the staff members justified their increasing concern for holding clients accountable to WIN rules and procedures as a reasonable and necessary response to undesirable circumstances. One staff member portrayed the new staff-client relationship in the following way:

> You see, we're the police. We can't get people jobs, but we can say, "You have to look for one." What can we do, we're [the] police, that's all.

In part, the condition of the local economy was important to the staff because they stated that clients could make sincere efforts and still not find jobs. The staff added that this circumstance meant that clients' failure to get jobs could be used as the sole criterion for determining whether the clients were fulfilling their WIN obligations. The staff assessed the practical meaning of clients' inability to get jobs by also considering aspects of the staff-client relationship. That is, staff member assessments of clients' orientations toward WIN were used as backgrounds for assessing the meaning of clients' inability to find jobs. In this way, the staff's assessment of area labor markets as tight was associated with its treatment of clients' orientations to WIN as signs of clients' abilities and willingness to find employment and as causes of their economic troubles.

In general, clients who kept their appointments with the WIN staff, made "realistic" claims about their job seeking, and stated that they were committed to getting jobs and getting off of welfare were assessed by the staff as making sincere efforts to find jobs. Their failure to find jobs was treated as evidence of the tightness of the area economy. Indeed, the staff sometimes lamented such clients' inabilities to find jobs by describing their circumstances as unfortunate, unfair and unjust. On the other hand, clients who were unsuccessful in finding jobs and assessed as uncooperative in their dealings with the WIN staff were treated as potentially uncommitted to getting jobs. Clients so assessed were closely monitored by the staff. In this way, the WIN staff sought to manage and control some of the undesired consequences of the recessionary area economy while continuing to hold uncooperative clients accountable for their actions.

Political Environment as a Constraint

The WIN staff members portrayed the political environment of their work as volatile. They stated that like other career government employees, the practical circumstances of their work (including their job security) were subject to change based on federal- and state-level political developments. One such change occurred during the latter phases of the research. It involved funding cuts affecting the number and types of services that the WIN staff could offer to clients. The cuts also resulted in a decrease in the number of staff members assigned to the program and an increase in the caseloads assigned to remaining staff members. The staff members treated the funding cuts as signs of an emerging anti-WIN political climate. Specifically, they stated that the political trends would likely result in further reductions in funding for WIN as well as increased funding for the development of competing approaches to work and welfare.

The staff cited these trends in explaining the reorganization of aspects of the local WIN program near the end of the research period. For example, staff justified the development of group approaches to registering new clients, instructing them on how to look for jobs, and monitoring their job seeking as necessary responses to funding cuts and subsequent increases in each staff members' caseloads. They also responded by redefining the practical meaning and implications of the WIN emphases on helping clients get jobs and holding uncooperative clients accountable. It involved reclassifying clients based on new criteria for assessing their levels of job readiness.

Clients were classified as job ready if they were assessed by the staff as able to get and hold jobs. Clients so assessed were assigned to WIN statuses requiring that they look for jobs. During most of the research period, the staff treated all clients as job ready unless they could provide documentary evidence of medical, emotional or family problems making it impossible for them to hold jobs. Clients assessed as "not wanting jobs" but otherwise able to accept them were required to look for employment. In doing so, the staff sought to both implement the purposes of WIN and test clients' orientations to work and WIN.

Near the end of the research period and citing funding cuts as the cause, the staff redefined job readiness to exclude clients assessed as not wanting to be in WIN and/or not wanting jobs. The staff members stated that such clients' attitudes were job barriers with which they could not deal under the changed circumstances of their work. In this way, the staff justified reclassifying clients assessed as potential troublemakers. The clients were assigned to WIN statuses requiring little staff supervision and job seeking. Although the staff members portrayed such adaptations as unfortunate and inconsistent with some of the purposes of WIN, they justified them as necessary and realistic responses to conditions beyond their control.

Conclusion

Looked at one way, the aspects of WIN discussed above were factors making the WIN staff's work complex and problematic. They were similar to those emphasized by Lipsky (1980) in analyzing the unique and problematic work circumstances of all street-level bureaucrats. The WIN staff members portrayed their work in this way in most of their interactions with clients and others in their work world. Looked at another way, however, these aspects of the WIN staff's work circumstances are rhetorical resources because the WIN staff members used them to seek their practical interests in their dealings with others. Specifically, staff used them to persuade "problematic" others to act in preferred ways and to assign preferred identities to themselves and others.

For example, in their interactions with clients, the staff members sometimes cited changing government policies and the emerging anti-WIN political climate in justifying their emphasis on job seeking as the most appropriate remedy to clients' troubles. They did so by treating the policies and climate as external forces over which they had no control and which required that they treat job seeking as clients' primary activity. In part, the staff members used such portrayals to cast themselves as organizational functionaries who were simply "doing their jobs." The staff members also used the portrayals to redirect client criticisms of their actions to state- and federal-level politicians and WIN officials who were portrayed as responsible for the constraints under which the local staff and clients worked.

In sum, rhetorical analysis of WIN staff members' work circumstances is not concerned with the truthfulness of their claims. It does not matter whether area labor markets were really constraints on the staff members' choices and actions or client orientations were the cause and solution to their employment troubles. What matters is the ways in which staff members used images of area labor markets and client orientations to organize and justify their actions. Further, rhetorical analysis of WIN emphasizes how staff members portrayals of their work circumstances changed as their interests changed.

For example, although they consistently portrayed area labor markets as tight, the staff assigned varying practical meaning to them depending on the issues at stake in their dealings with others. With clients, the staff portrayed the recessionary area economy as a hurdle which clients could overcome if they really wanted to find jobs. In their dealings with state-level WIN officials, on the other hand, the staff portrayed the area economy as a barrier that made it impossible for their clients to find jobs and themselves to meet the increased performance goals demanded by state officials. Staff members justified both portrayals of the area economy as realistic orientations to the problems at issue in their interactions with clients and state-level WIN officials. They stated that their portrayals of the area economy varied because clients and state WIN officials brought different concerns and orientations to their interactions with the staff. In other words, clients and state WIN officials were different types of problematic audiences.

We next consider how the WIN staff members oriented toward others in their work world as problematic audiences.

3

Social Relations in WIN
as Potential Arguments

Basic to the public policies that define WIN as a unique response to AFDC recipients' employment troubles are two related assumptions and claims. They were rationales justifying the intervention of WIN staff in clients' lives and idealizations which define proper relationships between WIN staff members and others in their work world. Idealizations are universal rules and rationales for proper social action and relationships (Garfinkel, 1967). They are intended to apply to all relevant circumstances and practical issues. Idealized rules and rationales gloss over the practical contingencies associated with diverse situations and practical issues with which persons in everyday life must deal. They also gloss over the variety of ways in which an organizational goal may be achieved and persons can make sense of practical circumstances and issues.

The first assumption treats welfare recipients as unlikely to solve their employment problems on their own. It involves several related assumptions about the abilities and life circumstances of welfare recipients. They include the following which are presented as policy claims.

1. Welfare recipients lack fundamental resources (such as fully operational cars, money to buy gasoline, and reliable baby sitting services) needed to look for jobs;
2. Welfare recipients suffer from medical, emotional and family problems that make job seeking impossible or diminishing their chances of getting jobs;
3. Welfare recipients lack job seeking skills and information needed to identify the full range of job open-

ings available in the community for which they are qualified and to present themselves to potential employers in effective ways; and

4. Welfare recipients hold unrealistic attitudes toward employment, their value in the labor market, and obligations as adults and parents to support themselves and their families.

The second assumption and claim involves proper relations between WIN staff and others. They are portrayed as cooperative endeavors involving mutual commitment by staff and others to finding the most effective and humane solutions to clients' troubles. For example, official portrayals of proper staff-client relations cast staff members and clients as equally committed to solving clients' economic troubles through full-time and permanent employment. They also portray proper staff-client relations as staff centered. That is, staff members are described as providing their clients with realistic understandings of their troubles as well as guiding and directing clients' efforts to remedy the troubles.

The relationship is partly justified by portraying the WIN staff as having special knowledge about the problems and needs of clients as well as job seeking. According to WIN policies, then, there are no inherent conflicts of interest between local WIN staff members and their clients. They are both trying to get clients off of welfare by finding jobs that pay enough to support clients and their families. Further, the policies deny the possibility of a conflict between clients' concern for finding jobs and WIN procedures as the best way of solving clients' troubles.

WIN policies also portray proper staff members' relations with colleagues, area employers, officials of other social service agencies, and state- and federal-level WIN officials as cooperative. WIN is described as a unique approach to welfare and unemployment because it is intended as a coordinated and cooperative program involving a variety of specialized professionals and administrators at several governmental levels. WIN staff members and other human service professionals are portrayed as having complementary skills, expertise and interests in WIN clients' troubles, making it possible for them to work together in organizationally preferred ways. Indeed, cooperation through joint decision-making is a required aspect of many staff member activities.

In sum, the idealized policies which define the general purposes of WIN involve directives and goals concerned with how the program should influence clients' lives (it should help them get jobs) and how the staff members should relate to others in solving clients' employment troubles (they should work together toward shared goals). The rest of this chapter is concerned with the WIN staff's orientations toward these directives and goals, particularly toward those defining proper social relations in WIN. The staff members sought to achieve the goals by treating their routine work relationships as potential arguments; that is, as possible disputes involving others taking opposed orientations to issues of practical concern to staff members (Willard, 1983). In doing so, staff members cast others in their work world as potential sources of trouble.

We begin by considering the staff members' reasons for treating others as potentially troublesome and idealized organizational policies and procedures as unrealistic. Later sections focus on the staff's specific concerns in orienting to their interactions with clients, other staff members, and state officials as potential arguments. The staff members treated their concerns as social conditions making rhetoric a necessary aspect of their professional relationships. It was a strategy and tactic for anticipating and managing troubles emergent in the relationships.

Argumentation as a Realistic Staff Orientation

Although the staff members treated idealized WIN policies as preferred work circumstances and goals, they also portrayed them as unrealistic standards for assessing their daily work activities and relationships. The staff stated that the policies were partly unrealistic because they did not take account of the many uncooperative aspects of the staff members' relationships with others. Specifically, they portrayed their dealings with clients, colleagues, area employers, officials of other social service agencies, and higher-level WIN officials as conflicts of interest and orientation that were ignored in WIN policies. The staff members further stated that one part of fulfilling their professional obligations in WIN involved anticipating and taking account of such conflicts. They portrayed their concern as realistic, professionally responsible, and central to the production of cooperative relationships that were truly oriented toward organizational goals.

According to the staff, WIN policies emphasizing staff members' responsibility to cooperate with clients were based on two unrealistic assumptions. First, they explained that the policies assumed that all WIN clients want to get off of welfare, an assumption the staff claimed was disconfirmed everyday in dealing with clients. They stated that although many clients were committed to finding jobs, others were equally committed to avoiding their WIN obligations. Second, the staff stated that WIN polices involved the erroneous assumption that clients were willing to treat local staff members as professionals possessing unique and useful knowledge about job seeking. Staff members explained that many clients treated their WIN assignments and meetings with the staff as obligations associated with receiving AFDC benefits and not as sources of help and support in remedying their troubles.

According to staff members, one way in which clients expressed this orientation was by adopting a sullen and unfriendly attitude toward staff members. They cited this client attitude in justifying their orientation to staff-client interactions as impersonal encounters centered in the bureaucratic processing of clients. In doing so, staff members also described clients as a source of work problems and their responses to unfriendly clients as ways of coping with problems. Consider, for example, the following staff member descriptions of clients' attitudes toward WIN and staff-client relationships in registration and appraisal meetings.

> They [clients] get passive, sit back and look around. [They] don't pay attention [to staff member's questions and instructions]. [They] act like this is a lot of bullshit and they don't care. It's all bullshit and they're not going to do it, but they have to come here to get their [AFDC] check....It's depressing work, I guess. Frustrating, after a while you learn to turn off the frustration 'cause you see it all the time. You just do it. Go through the motions, you know?

> This is real routine, processing people. We try to be human about it, not just treat them as a number. We don't everyday, depends on how you feel and how many you have to do. When it gets busy we have to move them through. We try to talk to them, be friendly. Some are real talkative, volunteer alot. Others don't say much. They don't give us shit. It's like, here I am, let's get it over with so I can get my [AFDC] check.

The staff also stated that WIN policies which emphasized cooperative relations between local staff members, officials of other social service agencies, and higher-level WIN officials were unrealistic. They portrayed the policies as naive because they ignored the variety of perspectives and practical concerns that WIN staff members and other social service professionals bring to their efforts to remedy clients' problems. Indeed, one way in which the staff distinguished WIN from other social service programs concerned with poor and unemployed persons was by noting how the WIN philosophy differed from those of other organizations. The distinction focused on the WIN emphasis on job seeking as the best solution to clients' troubles, and how it differed from the emphases of other organizations, such as training and therapy.

Consider, for example, the following staff member explanation of the sources for a dispute between WIN and another social service agency in the community which offered psychotherapeutic services to WIN clients and other welfare recipients. "We're too pragmatic [for them]. We don't believe everybody [WIN client] is pathological. They want to treat the whole person and we just want to get 'em a job. We believe they need a little work therapy."

According to the staff members, their efforts to properly implement WIN policies were also made more difficult by some area social service and medical professionals to whom they referred clients for specialized services. The staff stated that the professionals often gave bad advice to clients and the staff because they did not understand what the WIN program was intended to accomplish and/or didn't care about helping staff members respond to clients' troubles in appropriate ways. Staff members described their problems in dealing with area social service professionals in the following ways:

> We can give short-term help [to clients] and so we send people to expensive agencies sometimes. The people there say, "I think you [the client] should be a Doctor of Psychology." They don't know [what WIN is about and what is appropriate advice for WIN clients].

> We had a woman [client] who was manic-depressive-manic, at least, probably schizophrenic, couldn't do anything. I got a note from [the] psychiatrist [to whom she had been referred to get certification to exempt her from WIN participation] saying she could work, doing general office work. I couldn't believe it.

So, I got on the phone and said, "So, this woman can work, general office work, huh?" He said, "Yup." I said, "Do you know the extent of her problem?" and he said, "Yes, but she can work." [I said,] "Well, okay, we have this thing called Work Experience and I would like to make an appointment to come talk to you about placing this woman in your office. Wouldn't you like some free typing?" He goes, "Oh no, not here!" [I asked,] "Why not, what better place to put her than in a mental health clinic working for a psychiatrist?" [He said,] "Oh, but she'd cause trouble. She babbles out of control all the time. She'd be disruptive." [I replied,] "Well, you won't take her as a volunteer, doctor, what makes you think someone [else] would hire her?" [The psychiatrist said,] "Well, she'd be okay in other kinds of offices." Who would pay money for a person like this? That's the sort of problem we face. These people [area social service professionals] don't know and don't care about work.

Finally, the staff members sometimes portrayed their relationships with area employers as problematic based on the employers' inability and/or unwillingness to specify the kinds of employees they really wanted. Consider, for example, the following staff member portrayal of area employers as a source of trouble requiring the development of staff member coping strategies. The statement was made during a conversation about the WIN staff's difficulties in matching clients with available jobs.

Many [employers] call in [with announcements of job openings] and list a bunch of job skills [needed for the jobs] but they don't hire our referrals....They're like everyone else. If you ask them about their values, they say they believe [in the same values as]...everyone else, but their behavior belies that. They have hidden agendas or they don't recognize their true desires.

In so portraying their work relationships, the WIN staff members cast themselves as participants in potential arguments involving opposed orientations to practical issues. They also portrayed their positions in such interactions as attempts to properly implement WIN policies, including helping clients solve their employment troubles by establishing cooperative relationships with them and cooperating with colleagues, area employers, officials of local service agencies, and state and federal WIN officials.

Assessing Others' Orientations

According to the staff members, an important aspect of their efforts to properly implement WIN policies was their ongoing assessment of others' orientations to practical issues, which they portrayed as part of a professionally realistic and necessary attitude for coping with potentially troublesome others. Staff members' assessments were organized as *altercasting* which is a practical and goal-oriented approach to social interaction (Weinstein and Deutschberger, 1963). It is an attempt to gain interpersonal control by projecting perspectives and identities to potentially troublesome others. The projected perspectives and identities are simultaneously an expression of persons' goals in situations and one way in which they seek to achieve the goals.

Persons use the projections to formulate strategies and techniques for controlling others. For example, the WIN staff members sought to organize and control uncertain aspects of their relationships with area employers by projecting perspectives and identities to them. They did so as part of their decision-making about which clients to refer to job openings and in instructing clients on how to properly apply for jobs. Staff members used the assessments to classify clients as appropriate and inappropriate referrals, as well as to justify their instruction of clients on proper job seeking.

They also used their assessment of employers' orientations to explain aspects of clients' work histories and predict clients' orientations to WIN. For example, staff members justified their predictions that some new clients would be troublesome by noting that they had been fired by "good" employers. Staff members described such employers as reasonable and fair in their dealings with employers. On the other had, staff members used their assessments of some area employers as unreasonable and arbitrary to discount others' predictions that some clients would be troublesome. Consider, for example, the following staff member response to another staff member's prediction that a new client might be "a problem" because he was fired from a job.

> Well, I don't think so, er, I don't know. I mean, I know about this guy [former employer] and he's nuts. He's just crazy and nobody can work for him and he's involved in crime too. [Staff member describes a newspaper story reporting on the employ-

er's recent arrest.] I think we oughta give this guy [client] a chance. The rest of his record is pretty good. And I don't think this should keep him from finding a job. Everybody [area employers] knows about [the former employer]. They're not gonna put much stock in this [firing].

Although staff members' assessments of employers' orientations were partly based on their past dealings with individual employers, they also involved consideration of the motives of the "typical employer" in making hiring decisions. In general, the staff stated that employers were looking for employees who "really wanted jobs," had stable work histories, were dependable (i.e., would show up for work everyday and do as they were told), were neatly groomed and dressed, and were courteous and respectful to others. The portrayals were central to staff members' efforts to persuade clients to assess and take account of area employers' perspectives and desires in organizing their job seeking activities. The staff members stated that in taking account of employers' perspectives and desires, they could better control the clients' interactions with employers in job seeking settings and increase their chances of getting jobs.

The staff members also stated that, despite their efforts to realistically assess and respond to employers' perspectives and desires, their assessments of the "fit" between employers' desires and client characteristics were often "guesses about what they [employers] really want." In other words, there were practical limits to their altercasting. They explained that the problem was partly a result of employers' tendencies to withhold information needed by the WIN staff in making job referrals. Such portrayals were one way in which staff members cast area employers as a potential source of work problems and themselves as competent, but frustrated, social service professionals seeking to cope with problems created by the employers.

Staff members explained that they coped with such frustrations and problems by "doing the best [they] could with what [they] had to work with." Staff members portrayed their efforts to cope as partly a problem of inarticulate and indecisive clients who had no career plans or goals. As in the following statement, staff members sometimes described their problems in identifying appropriate jobs for clients as similar to those of physicians in dealing with patients.

It [matching clients and jobs] is hard. That's why we depend on self descriptions. If a person [client] really knows what he wants, then we can help. So many say that they will take anything, do anything, go anywhere. Where do you begin with them? I start with their work experience or training. If they don't have any, I go to hobbies. It's a lot like being a doctor who's dependent on the patient to report symptoms. Some patients are good and complete. Others you have to probe.

WIN staff members also portrayed their efforts to cope as based on intuitive skills that they developed over the years in trying to match clients with jobs and employers. They further stated that their intuitive skills were better predictors of clients appropriateness for jobs than aptitude and other tests that, according to the staff, reduce job matching to numbers. Staff members justified their portrayal of job matching as intuitive by citing cases in which they had referred clients for jobs even though aptitude and other tests indicated that the clients were not suited for them. Nonetheless, the clients' performances on the jobs were superior. A staff member summarizes and justifies the staff's orientation to a job matching in the following way: "It is a lot like cooking. You take a little here and a little there and make a meal. You know that some spices and foods go together and others don't.... You go to the refrigerator and use what is there. That's why [job] matching can't be reduced to numbers."

Major Sources of Trouble for WIN Staff

Although they sometimes spoke of area employers as sources of work problems, the staff members usually portrayed themselves and area employers as having common problems and perspectives. According to the WIN staff members, an important part of their professional responsibilities involved developing employer confidence in the WIN program and local staff members' judgments. They explained that the WIN program would not be effective unless area employers could depend on the WIN staff to take account of their legitimate needs and desires in preparing clients for holding jobs and referring them to known job openings. Staff members stated that they did so by advising clients on the rules and expectations of typical work places and only referring WIN clients whom they assessed as really qualified for job openings.

The staff members also portrayed their problems with clients as similar to those experienced by area employers in dealing with clients on the job. Two such problems were client-employee undependability (i.e., failure to keep WIN appointments and show up for work) and insubordination toward WIN staff and employers. Staff members cited such problems in explaining and justifying their claim that "bad" WIN clients were also "bad" employees. Indeed, the staff members stated that the refusal of some area employers to hire WIN clients was a rational and understandable act. They stated that the employers were attempting to avoid problems that often resulted from WIN clients' unrealistic expectations and orientations to employment. The staff members further stated that one of their professional obligations involved persuading clients to adopt realistic expectations and orientations to employment in order to increase clients' chances of getting jobs and to better serve area employers.

In sum, the persons whom the staff most frequently portrayed as potentially troublesome were clients, colleagues and state WIN officials. Staff members gave two reasons for their special concern for these people. First, they stated that these persons were likely to have interests and concerns that were different and often opposed to their own. According to the staff, the differing interests were expressed as competing orientations to practical issues emergent in their everyday work. In other words, the differences were recurring aspects of many issues that, from a different perspective, might be seen as unrelated to the philosophical differences that sometimes separated WIN staff members from others in their work world. Staff members assigned politically significant meanings to their interactions with others by treating otherwise mundane actions and events as signs of trouble.

Consider, for example, the following staff member portrayals of otherwise routine staff-client interactions. The first statement deals with developing appropriate job plans and goals for clients, and the second with clients' reactions to being held accountable for their failure to fulfill their WIN assignments.

The typical case [client] is a tenth-grade dropout on welfare who answers "I want to be an interior decorator" when I ask what she wants to be. I ask if she has ever hired an interior decorator? [She replies] No. [I ask] if her family has ever hired an interior decorator? [She replies] No. [I ask] if her friends have ever hired an interior decorator? [She replies] No. "Do you know how many interior decorators there are in [the area]? I can name them. I know them." [The client replies,] "I don't care, I want to be an interior decorator."

I get awfully tired of the excuses [given by clients for not fulfilling their WIN assignments] and whining. All the whining. She [the client under discussion] said, "I'm going to cry." And I said, "Go ahead." She said, "I'm so embarrassed." I said, "Don' be, crying is just the beginning of what may happen today. You think that your life is stressful now on $440 a month [her AFDC grant amount], wait 'til I cut you off your grant and you have to live on $337."

These portrayals of WIN staff-client relations are significant because they show how staff members rhetorically cast themselves and clients as acting from different interests and motives and their mutual interactions as arguments. Specifically, the staff member used the first portrayal to justify his prior claim that a major source of trouble in staff-client relationships was clients' unrealistic attitudes to job seeking. He stated that the attitudes were most problematic when clients insisted on looking for "nonexistent" jobs despite staff members' presentations of the economic "facts of life" to them.

The staff member used the second statement to portray clients' "typical" orientation to their WIN assignments. He stated that clients treat the assignments as unfair and try to get out of them by making excuses and whining. The staff members also used the portrayal of staff-client interactions to describe an "appropriate" staff member orientation to clients' excuses and whining. It centers in holding clients accountable by confronting them with the practical consequences of failing to fulfill their WIN obligations. Although the above statements deal with two major and recurring issues in staff-client interactions, virtually any client position could be taken by staff members as signs of disagreement calling for counterresponses.

The second reason given by staff members for orienting to clients, colleagues and state WIN officials as potential sources of trouble involved the importance of these people to the WIN staff's work world. The staff members stated that their interactions with these persons were central to the fulfillment of their professional responsibilities to WIN. They were, in other words, unavoidable aspects of staff members' jobs. Consider, for example, the following staff member's statement made prior to the registration of a new client. Through it, the staff member casts the task at hand as routine and a matter of personal frustration. He also anticipates and explains the sources of trouble in the pending interaction (it is caused by welfare department officials' inadequate instruction of new AFDC clients). Finally, he describes his frustration and the ensuing troubles as unavoidable because WIN staff members are not free to tell clients that they don't have to look for jobs.

> Here we go again. [To a nonexistent client,] "Do you know why you are here?" [To another staff member,] Don't you love asking that?....And they [clients] always say no. That goes to show you that they don't tell 'em anything at [the] welfare [department]. [Welfare officials say,] "You have to go over to register for WIN to get your check." They come here and we say, "Do you know why you're here?" and they [clients] go, "No, not really." [WIN officials reply,] "You gotta look for work." [Clients respond,] "Oh, but there aren't any jobs out there." [WIN officials say,] "Oh, okay, then you don't have to look for work." [To other staff member,] Wouldn't you love to say that? You don't have to look for work.

The general issues of contention between WIN staff members and these potentially troublesome others are summarized in Table 3.11

The table is discussed and elaborated upon in the following three sections. The sections consider the sources of staff members' difficulties with these potentially troublesome others and general ways in which the staff members sought to manage the troubles.

Staff-Client Relations as Potential Arguments

During their typical work days, the WIN staff members expressed most concern about their clients as potential sources of trouble. The concern was partly related to the organization of the WIN staff's work which mostly involved monitoring clients' job seeking activities. It was also related to the staff members' orientation to the purposes of WIN and their professional responsibilities in the program which, according to the staff, centered in getting clients off of welfare. For the staff members, the preferred way of fulfilling their WIN responsibilities was by helping clients get jobs, but they also stated that some clients

TABLE 3.1
Sources of Arguments in WIN

Orientations to Practical Issues

		WIN Staff Members	Troublesome Others
Trouble-some Others	Clients	Help Clients Solve Their Employment Troubles by Finding Jobs	Avoid Their Responsibilities as Welfare Recipients and Parents to Look for Jobs
	Other WIN Staff	Hold Clients Accountable to WIN Rules, Expectations and Procedures	Take Clients' Perspectives on Troubles and Advocate for Actions that Fail to Hold Them Accountable
	State WIN Officials	Realistic Implementation of WIN Rules, Expectations and Procedures	Rigid and Narrow Implementation of WIN Rules and Procedures and/or Achieving Goals Little Related to Solving Clients' Employment Troubles

deserved to be removed from welfare because they weren't cooperating with the WIN staff. Finally, the staff members stated that their orientation to staff-client relations as potential arguments was a result of their past experiences with clients who tried to manipulate welfare and WIN officials in order to avoid their responsibilities to look for jobs and support their families.

Central to the WIN staff members' orientation to their clients as potential troublemakers was the assumption that clients acted from enduring attitudes toward WIN and employment. The staff members used the assumption to justify their efforts to identify and classify their clients' attitudes.

Staff Members' Interest in Clients' Attitudes

According to the staff members, their efforts to identify clients' enduring attitudes toward WIN and employment were justified because they are basic to clients' moral character and, therefore, do not change across situations. The staff stated that once such attitudes were identified, it was possible to predict clients' future behavior, including their probable responses to assignments made by the staff. They also stated that their assessments of clients' attitudes were useful in making sense of clients' past actions, including clients' employment histories and WIN records. For example, one way that staff members explained clients' employment records made up of many short-term jobs was by treating the records as signs of clients' improper attitudes toward employment.

In orienting to staff-client interactions as potential arguments, then, the staff gave distinctive meaning to otherwise mundane aspects of clients' actions and appearances in the WIN office. The staff treated clients' actions and appearances as signs of their underlying orientations to WIN and employment. Staff member assessments of client orientations were used as interpretive backgrounds for predicting clients' probable styles of presenting themselves to employers in job seeking situations and likely responses to different types of WIN assignments. In other words, staff members treated the assessment of client orientations as a basic part of their efforts to cope with troublesome work circumstances and implement WIN policies in organizationally proper way.

One way in which staff members expressed their concern about the troubles resulting from clients' bad attitudes was by portraying some clients as distinctive because they had good attitudes. As in the following exchange, staff members used the good-bad attitude distinction (contrastive pair) to cast some clients as acting from bad attitudes and most staff-client interactions as troublesome (as potential arguments).

> Staff member: I really like your attitude, . . . You really want to get off of welfare, don't you?
>
> Client: Oh yeah, I'll take anything [any type of job]. If somebody had a baby sitting job for twelve kids, I'd take it.
>
> Staff member: You're real different from so many people [clients] we get here. They don't care, they're beaten down from looking for work. You're refreshing

Further, the staff members stated that one interpretive skill that they developed through their dealings with clients was the ability to identify potential troublemakers based on one or two interactions. Staff members stated that although they were sometimes wrong in their assessments of clients, their intuitive, first impressions of clients' intentions and moral character were usually correct. Consider, for example, the following staff member statement about his ability to identify troublesome clients.

> I hafta say that I'm usually right when I think somebody's gonna be a problem. You can tell from the first day. Like this guy on the phone,...he's a bad actor. I knew from the start. He's just gonna do enough [job seeking] to keep me off his back.

On occasion, staff members were more specific in describing the ways in which they assessed clients' appearances, demeanor or records as the most reliable signs of clients' attitudes. Consider the following staff member explanation of his prior claim that a new client was likely to be troublesome. The explanation centers in the staff member's ability to "read" the client's face. The staff member also stated that clients with bad attitudes acted like they were retarded, even if they were not technically so. That is, they were functionally retarded.

> I could tell by her face. You know, clients say that you can't read faces, but you can. They say there's no difference between the faces of normal and retarded people, bullshit. You can tell. Some of the people who look retarded aren't really, but functionally they are. You can tell by their faces, especially around their eyes.

Staff members portrayed their development of an orientation toward staff-client interactions as potential arguments as a fundamental aspect of "learning the ropes" in WIN. For example, staff members spoke of how they naively trusted clients when they first joined the agency, but quickly "wised up" when the clients did not fulfill their promises or were later shown to be lying. Experienced staff also monitored the actions of new staff members and counselled them on a proper orientation to clients. The counselling partly involved offering explanations of clients' actions which countered those expressed by clients. The alternative explanations emphasized the ways that clients might be "making excuses" or otherwise trying to manipulate new staff members to avoid their WIN responsibilities.

Teaching Attitude Assessment in WIN

Experienced staff members counselled new staff members on their obligation to properly implement policies emphasizing job seeking and holding clients accountable for their actions, including taking responsibility for solving their own employment troubles. In part, the emphasis involved "testing" clients claims that they could not fulfill their WIN assignments due to circumstances beyond their control. Consider, for example, the following statement made by the WIN supervisor to a new staff member regarding his response to a client that she should not attend the class to which she was assigned because she could not find a baby sitter.

The WIN supervisor stated that the request sounded like an excuse and, in any case, the new staff member should not accept such client claims without first verifying them. She also instructed the new staff member on how to respond to such requests in order to eliminate future client excuses based on extenuating circumstances.

> You shouldn't make these snap judgments. Go back and get all the information that you need and then think about it, consider all the information. It's her [the client's] responsibility to find child care, you know. Find out if child care is available....If she can't make it for this class, see if she can go to the next one. You could tell her that she doesn't have to go to this one, but she should use the next two weeks to find a baby sitter. Don't just let her off....You just shouldn't make snap judgments like this on the phone, though. You need to consider the facts.

New staff members used such instruction to assess clients' motives in requesting exemptions from their WIN assignments and to respond to their requests. Client motives were tested and reassessed by considering client's subsequent actions and explanations as signs of their underlying and enduring attitudes toward WIN and employment. Clients who persisted in claiming that they could not fulfill their WIN assignments were treated as making excuses and attempting to avoid their WIN responsibilities. The staff stated that subsequent events usually resulted in the disconfirmation of clients' explanations of their motives and behavior. That is, they were shown to be excuses.

The staff also stated that subsequent events usually verified the appropriateness of the WIN emphasis on holding clients responsible for their economic troubles. In the above case, for example, the new staff member and others concluded that the clients' subsequent actions confirmed the WIN supervisor's claim that he was being manipulated. Specifically, the new staff member later called the client about her efforts to find a baby sitter. The client stated that, although she had arranged for child care, she could not attend the class to which she was assigned because she had an important meeting at the same time as the class. The staff member told the client to change the time of the meeting and directed her to attend the class. The client responded by filing a complaint against the new staff member, stating that he was "rude" and "picking on her."

The WIN supervisor with whom the complaint was filed, the new staff member and other staff members treated the complaint as a sign of the client's true and original intention which was to avoid fulfilling her WIN assignment. They further explained that evidence of the client's true orientation was produced through the new staff member's directive requiring that the client attend the class. In this way, the new staff member's directive was cast as a method for forcing the client to make a choice between abiding by or opposing the purposes of WIN. Staff members also used this explanation of the client's motives in requesting exemption from her WIN assignment and filing the complaint to justify their conclusion that the WIN supervisor's initial concerns and recommendations were proper.

More generally, they justified an orientation to all staff-client interactions as potential arguments. The staff members did so by elaborating on their conclusion that the client in question was a troublemaker. Initially, the elaboration involved treating recent troubles with the client as part of a larger pattern of uncooperative and manipulative behavior by the client. For example, one staff member linked the client's complaint with a previous interaction he had with her in which the client stated that she was a writer and should not have to look for a job. The staff member portrayed the interaction in the following way:

> I said, "Look honey, I'm not gonna have you sittin' on welfare and spending all your time trying to be a writer. That's some-

thing you can do in the evenings, on your own time.... You're going to look for a job." Well [imitating and mocking the client], she just found my attitude terribly depressing.

The pattern was generalized by treating the complaining client's actions and orientation as typical of WIN clients. In doing so, the staff cast all client complaints as a result of staff member insistence that clients fulfill their WIN obligations. They also cast the filing of client complaints against new staff members as a rite of passage signifying the staff members' membership in the WIN community. Finally, the staff members used the incident to identify the major cause of WIN clients' economic troubles; they were socially incompetent. These conclusions were produced and justified in the following way:

> Staff Member 1: Well, all I can say is that [the new staff member] has his first complaint. Welcome to WIN, welcome to the group.
>
> New Staff Member: Why should she do this to me? I mean, why would anyone not want to find a job and get off of welfare. I don't understand that. And I don't understand why you'd file a complaint against somebody for doin' his job. She must be sick or something. I don't understand why she'd do this.
>
> Staff Member 2: Hey,...you don't get on welfare if you're competent. These people are here for a reason.

Thus, staff members' assessments of clients' attitudes were central to their interest in holding uncooperative clients accountable for their actions and orientations. They were also central to the staff's interest in establishing cooperative relations with clients in order to properly guide and direct their efforts to solve their employment troubles. Specifically, the staff members stated that, although their clients could be generally classified into cooperative and uncooperative types, each client was unique. They explained that this circumstances required that staff members continuously assess each clients' orientation to WIN and employment in order to identify the most appropriate response to his or her troubles. The staff members also justified their ongoing assessments of clients' attitudes by stating that their initial assessments were sometimes wrong and, occasionally, clients changed their attitudes toward WIN and employment.

Staff-Staff Relations as Potential Arguments

According to the WIN staff members, their major interests in interactions with other staff members were twofold: they wished to (1) develop mutually agreeable responses to clients' troubles and (2) properly implement WIN policies. The first interest was related to organizational rules requiring that many of the most important decisions made about clients be jointly developed and approved. For example, client requests to enter training programs and recommendations that clients be terminated from WIN required approval of two staff members. Although it also had practical implications, the staff members stated that the second interest was ideological. It involved their understanding of and commitment to WIN policies that emphasized job seeking as the best solution to clients troubles. Staff members portrayed the policies as a unique philosophy, that was also a realistic approach to clients' unemployment troubles and dependence on welfare.

The staff members stated that although the general purpose of WIN was to help clients find jobs and get off of welfare, this goal sometimes contradicted the requirement that they hold clients accountable for their actions. They further explained that both requirements were central aspects of the WIN philosophy to which they were accountable. The staff portrayed the first requirement as a mandate to help clients deal with personal, family, and medical problems impeding clients' efforts to get jobs, as well as recommending them for known job openings, informing them of job training programs, and helping them obtain financial support in order to enroll in training programs. The staff portrayed the second requirement as a mandate to make certain that clients fulfilled their obligations to the government by fully complying with their WIN assignments.

Thus, a major aspect of the WIN staff's work involved managing responsibilities to simultaneously help clients and hold them accountable.

Managing Staff Member Responsibilities

In part, the staff members managed their potentially contradictory responsibilities by treating some situations as calling for an orientation to help clients and other situations as calling for an orientation of accountability. For example, most of the time the staff treated conciliation sessions as occasions of accountability, calling for a skeptical attitude toward client claims and a primary interest in securing promises from them that they would fulfill all future WIN assignments. The staff members also managed the contradictory emphases by portraying many of their actions as intended to help clients by holding them accountable. Staff members involved with conciliation sessions frequently explained their actions and intentions in this way.

They stated that in holding clients accountable for their actions, staff members forced clients to face the practical realities of being unemployed welfare recipients. According to the staff, this practice was helpful to clients because it was a way of changing their orientations to employment and welfare and of, ultimately, getting them jobs. Consider, for example, the following staff member portrayals of conciliation sessions as sources for helping clients change their lives by forcing them to face the reality of their circumstances.

> A lot of these people [uncooperative clients] are like alcoholics. They have to hit bottom to see [that] they have a problem, to feel pain. Then they look at their lives and decide that they hafta make some changes. They'll put it off as long as they can, though. It's only when they don't have any choice that they look at themselves in the mirror. That's what we're doin' here, forcing them to look at their lives and make some changes.

> This has more clout [than other meetings in which staff made complaints against clients]. We use more muscle here, psychological muscle. How would you like to be told to cooperate or starve? It's like when a doctor says that you have six months to live. You go, "What!" You change your life, right? That's what we try to do. They have to cooperate or lose their [AFDC] grants and that means starving for most of them, unless they can eat grass.

On other occasions, however, the staff members expressed less consensus about how they should properly implement the WIN philosophy. For example, in training committee meetings, staff members sometimes expressed differing orientations to clients' troubles, the WIN philosophy and the legitimacy of training as a response to unemployment and welfare dependence. The orientations were usually expressed as opposed positions on how to solve clients' troubles, although they were sometimes expressed as abstract concerns about the relationship between vocational training and the WIN philosophy. In expressing their opposed positions on such issues, staff members emphasized different aspects of the WIN approach to solving clients' troubles.

Consider, for example, the following staff member response to another staff member's recommendation that a client be placed in a job training program. The staff member recommending the placement stated that the client deserved such special treatment and would benefit from it. The staff member opposing the recommendation justified his position by casting the issue as a matter of the WIN philosophy. He stated,

> The problem is that we [WIN] are a job search organization and not in training. I just don't see it. I mean a person is on welfare and we're puttin' 'em through school. Why don't we put everybody through college then?

The staff members stated that their disagreements about how to properly respond to their clients' problems were often based on general differences in their professional orientations to WIN. Specifically, they stated that, although the helping and accountability emphases of WIN were not inherently opposed to one another, some staff members typically emphasized one over the other. When two staff members typically emphasized different aspects of the WIN philosophy were required to make joint decisions, then, the emphases were cast as opposed orientations and became the basis for staff-staff arguments. Indeed, staff members sometimes predicted such difficulties in their future interactions. They described the predictions as honest and realistic projections of staff member's positions on practical issues.

Consider, for example, the following staff member prediction made during a meeting about how to better coordinate the activities of the social workers assigned to WIN with those of WIN staff members associated with the State Job Service.

> We're gonna have disagreements. I'll be honest with you, my philosophy is different from yours. I don't think work [clients

finding jobs] is that important. I counsel my clients in many areas and I don't always try to get them working right away.

On occasion, staff members also theorized about the sources of others' orientations to the WIN philosophy. One such theory emphasized the ways in which some staff members' experiences as WIN clients (the WIN graduates) shaped their orientations to WIN purposes and staff-client interactions. Consider the following staff member exchange concerned with why many of the women staff members emphasized client accountability in their dealings with clients.

> Staff Member 1: A lot of, I think all of the gals working here have gone through this. They all have kids and raised them on their own....They're tough too, they know what it's like. They've done it, they've sacrificed and they know it can be done.
>
> Staff Member 2: They've sacrified and they say, "If I had to do it, so can you."

The staff members generally portrayed their differing orientations as a contrastive pair made up of *strict* and *lenient* perspectives on clients' troubles and the WIN philosophy. Staff members were assigned to the strict and lenient categories in the same general way as clients were assessed and categorized as cooperative and uncooperative. The process centered in treating strict and lenient orientations as signs and causes of distinctive and opposed understandings and responses to practical issues. Further, the classifications were subject to reconsideration and change based on person's subsequent actions or the development of new understandings of the meaning of their past actions.

Staff Members as Strict and Lenient

Staff members portrayed as strict were said to be primarily committed to holding clients accountable for their actions by strictly enforcing organizational rules, particularly rules regarding clients' obligations to look for jobs and fulfill other WIN assignments. Staff members oriented in this way emphasized clients' responsibilities in solving their own troubles. They were also less likely than staff members portrayed as lenient to recommend that clients be exempted from job seeking or that they be recommended for training programs prior to having demonstrated their "deservingness" by having looked for jobs. Staff members who usually took this position justified their orientation by portraying clients as unable and/or unwilling to become self sufficient, independent adults unless forced to do so. They also portrayed holding clients strictly accountable to WIN rules as a way of helping the clients.

Staff members portrayed as lenient were said to be less concerned with holding clients strictly accountable to the rules of the program. Two explanations were given of their motives. Staff members classifying themselves as strict stated that lenient staff members were primarily interested in acting as advocates for their clients and were too little concerned with making clients find jobs by holding them accountable to organizational rules. They explained that in acting as advocates, lenient staff members were too willing to overlook clients' records of uncooperativeness in evaluating their performances in WIN. According to staff members classifying themselves as strict, lenient staff members' actions made it easy for clients to avoid their obligations to the government by not insisting that they make sincere and concerted efforts to find jobs. They stated, for example, that lenient staff members were too quick to grant clients' requests to enter training programs because they did not always first require clients to "earn" this privilege by looking for jobs or in some other way showing that they were cooperative clients.

Staff members classifying themselves as lenient stated that strict staff members were often "too tough" with clients, were unnecessarily "mean" to them, and acted from improper motives. Consider, for example, the following staff member contrast between his lenient orientation and that of strict staff members. In developing the contrast, he casts the strict orientation as based on feelings of bitterness which have resulted from strict staff members' long-term involvement in WIN.

> I'm not as bitter as some of these people [other staff]. I really think a lot of these people are bitter. 'Course, I haven't been here [in WIN] as long as they have. But they divide people [clients] into categories and I think that's wrong, you know? You're supposed to treat everybody as an individual.

Staff members classifying themselves as lenient also stated that strict staff members should "have a heart" and recognize that uncooperative clients sometimes change and deserve a second chance. They explained that strict staff members' insistence on the full enforcement of WIN rules often resulted in the punishment of clients for being poor and had counterproductive consequences. According to these staff members, rule enforcement experienced as punishment alienated clients from staff thereby undermining the staff's ability to produce cooperative staff-client relationships and the staff's interest in gaining voluntary client acquiescence to their directives and suggestions. They also portrayed the maintenance of a sympathetic orientation to clients as a professional responsibility.

As in the following statement, lenient staff members frequently described the issue as a matter of retaining one's idealism despite work circumstances which encouraged cynicism.

> Yeah, I've become cynical. I was more idealistic when I started ...
> and I've become hardened, but I try to stay idealistic. I keep
> telling myself that the client comes first.

Lenient staff members countered strict staff members' portrayals of them by stating that, although they too wished to help clients become economically self-sufficient, they tried to take account of clients' desires and place the WIN emphasis on employment within the larger context of clients' lives. For example, lenient staff members explained that they took account of clients' family obligations and needs in responding to their employment troubles, including sometimes treating clients' family concerns and troubles as more important than their employment troubles. Consider the following staff members' explanations for their lenient orientations to clients.

> You'll find out that my philosophy is a little different [from
> other staff members]. I know that work [job seeking] is impor-
> tant but I'm not sure that it is *that* important. There are other
> things, like the family. I believe that we should protect the
> family too, especially in this day and age with everything
> going on [problems with young people]. I think the mother
> should be in the home with her kids, especially in the sum-
> mer. They say that these people aren't good parents, but
> who's to say that the other [employed mothers] would be
> better?

I sympathize with these women [clients] who want to stay home with their kids. I've never been a fan of [the job seeking requirements of WIN policies] anyway. It seems to me that work is overrated. If a woman chooses to stay home and be a housewife, no matter how restricting I might think it is, I think she should be able to and I don't think we should be able to say that you hafta get out and find a job just because she doesn't have a husband. I think the family is more important than that.

Although all staff members sometimes spoke of themselves and others as acting from strict or lenient orientations, the greatest concern for assessing other staff members' orientations was expressed by persons taking a strict orientation to practical issues. They attended to others' actions as possible signs of an overly lenient orientation which they treated as a cause of trouble in the staff-staff relationship. In doing so, they treated otherwise mundane staff-staff interactions as potential arguments requiring responses intended to cope with others' improper orientations. The responses were intended to hold overly lenient staff accountable to WIN purposes and procedures. They ranged from strict staff members' refusal to support overly lenient staff members' recommendations for responding to clients' troubles to requests that the WIN supervisor take action against staff members accused of being overly lenient.

In sum, although all of the WIN staff members expressed general commitment to the purposes of WIN, they sometimes interpreted the practical meaning of the purposes in different ways. The WIN staff members used the differences to justify assigning professional identities and orientations to themselves and others. It is possible to overstate these differences, however, because each staff member sometimes expressed positions that were portrayed by themselves or others as strict and lenient. Thus, staff member portrayals of themselves and others as acting from enduring orientations to the WIN philosophy are partly over simplifications that gloss over the diverse and complex ways in which staff members sought to respond to client troubles in organizationally approved ways.

The portrayals were important, however, because the staff members used them to explain their differing positions on practical issues, justify complaints against others, and cast staff-staff interactions as potential arguments.

Local Staff–State Official Relations as Potential Arguments

According to the local WIN staff members, their major interest in their dealings with state WIN officials was to influence, if not control, the circumstances of their work. The staff members portrayed the interest as based on their more basic concern for being effective and responsible implementors of the WIN philosophy. They stated that many of the policies created and implemented by state officials and justified as proper ways of achieving WIN goals were actually impediments to the achievement of the goals. Specifically, the staff members explained that the policies encouraged work conditions that restricted their efforts to monitor clients' job seeking activities, provide needed social services to clients, and hold uncooperative clients accountable

According to the staff, the problems were created by state WIN officials because they lacked adequate understandings of, or concern for, the practical problems faced by local WIN staff in attempting to implement the purposes and spirit of the WIN philosophy. One such problem involved assessing the WIN staff's effectiveness in fulfilling organizational purposes. As in the following staff member statement, staff members often described the "real" purposes of WIN as difficult to see and measure.

> What we do is keep people [clients] out of prisons and mental hospitals. That saves money. They [state WIN officials] don't see that. We don't always know [when we've been successful]. How do you count that?

They also stated that clients' limited abilities made it necessary to define organizational success and staff member effectiveness in flexible ways. As one staff member stated,

> You have to look at success differently [when dealing with WIN clients]. I had a client whose father [while the client was a child] said he'd buy him [the client] a bike, you know, a nice new bicycle, if he stayed in school everyday for two weeks. Well, he put in four full days one week and three the next. Technically, he failed but he didn't really. He'd never been able to put in a whole day a week before. You have to take three-quarters when you can't get it all. A half a cup is better than none.

Another problem was organizational rules and procedures which were written and implemented to further the interests of state WIN officials.

Staff Members as Victims of Organizational Rules and Procedures

The staff stated that proper and effective professional practice sometimes involved taking a flexible approach to rules and procedures, especially those which restricted staff members' discretion in managing their clients and work schedules. They explained that organizational rules and procedures are best understood as general guidelines and goals which staff should take into account in making decisions and taking actions, but they are not fully achievable in the practical worlds of local WIN offices. The staff members contrasted their orientation to that of state officials whom they portrayed as taking a narrow rigid orientation to organizational rules and procedures. The staff further stated that, based on the state officials' unrealistic orientation to the circumstances of local staff members' work, state officials created rules and procedures that were unnecessary and, often counterproductive intrusions on staff members' work schedules and freedom to respond to client troubles in appropriate ways.

The major way in which the staff members justified their orientation to organizational rules and procedures was by recounting the diverse and unanticipated demand made on their time and attention during a typical work day. The demands were portrayed as continuous intrusions reducing the staff members' ability to control the circumstances of their work and fulfill their professional responsibilities in officially prescribed ways. The staff stated that, in developing organizational rules and procedures, state officials ignored these demands on local staff members' time and attention as well as related constraints on their abilities to fulfill their professional responsibilities. The staff further claimed that idealized organizational rules and procedures were often counterproductive because they constrained staff members' efforts to effectively use their time and make decisions that were appropriate for the unique circumstances of their clients' lives and troubles.

According to the staff members, state officials' lack of concern for the practical circumstances of their work was based on the state officials' assumption that local staff members' work is (or should be) organized as highly structured and recurring routines. The staff stated that the assumption was basic to state officials' concern for developing organizational plans and goals to which local staff should strive. The staff also stated that the assumption was central to the WIN emphasis on evaluating agency and staff member performances by using numbers, such as how many clients had been processed and hired during the previous month. Staff members stated that the quantitative evaluation of agency and staff performances over-simplified the complexities of implementing WIN policies and forced local staff to emphasize some organizational goals over others, even when the latter goals were more important.

Consider, for example, the following staff member explanation for why he had stopped offering specialized counselling services to clients with serious employment-related problems, even though he was trained as a counsellor and hired to provide such services to WIN clients.

> You know, I've given up on being a counsellor. They call me that, but I've never been in a position to function in that capacity. You can't do it when people [state WIN officials] think like accountants and want to know if you've gotten your 6.3 hires [this month]....I can't function as a counsellor when I can't turn off my telephone [to have an uninterrupted counselling session], when anyone [client] can walk in on a session at any time....The thing that amazes me is that they [state WIN officials] hire professional counsellors and pay them, but they won't let them do their job. They say, "How many hires do you have this month?" If I have a person in four or five times for counselling, they ask, "What is the problem? Why isn't this person working?" So, I quit doing it and I don't have those headaches anymore.

This statement shows how staff members portrayed the quantitative assessment of their work performances as improper. The staff member also describes other work conditions mandated by state officials that make it impossible for him to do his job in proper ways, such as providing confidential and uninterrupted counselling to clients. Put differently, the explanation is a rhetorical procedure for casting the staff member as a victim of state-level organizational policies which make it necessary for him to cope by not providing some services to clients. Described in this way, the staff member's actions are a realistic response to unrealistic policies and work conditions.

Staff members also cited the diverse and unanticipated demands of their typical work days in justifying their complaints about organizational rules requiring that they keep detailed records of how they spent their work time. Such record keeping rules were partly portrayed as a waste of the staff members' time, which they stated could be better spend monitoring clients. They were also portrayed as the source of a more general problem involving the maintenance of important WIN programs. The latter problem centered in the state officials' practice of using local staff reports about the amount of time spent on different activities and programs to establish future funding levels for the programs. Programs which the staff reported spending much time on were usually funded at higher levels than those that involved little staff time.

Thus, in completing their time and activity reports, the staff took account of the long-term consequences of the ways in which they depicted their work days. They did so by reporting that they spent considerable time on programs that they deemed essential to achieving WIN goals, even if they did not take much of the staff's work time. As in the following staff member statement, the staff portrayed this as both a professionally responsible action and a lie. They also assigned blame for their actions to "ignorant" and/or "uncaring" state WIN officials who created unrealistic and counterproductive rules making it necessary that local staff cope by lying.

> You see they [state WIN officials] make us lie. We have to if we're gonna have the programs that we need. The system is set up for accountants and by lawyers. They don't know anything about what really goes on or what we really need. If it's not a number it doesn't matter to them. So we hafta lie.

This statement is also an example of how the local staff members portrayed the state WIN officials as oriented toward narrow and bureaucratic goals which they associated with the professional orientations of accountants and lawyers. Staff members justified the claim by portraying state officials as politically oriented and, consequently, more concerned with satisfying politicians and federal government administrators than with meeting the needs of local staff and clients. In this way, the local staff members cast themselves and state officials as members of opposed communities of interest and orientation. The staff members sometimes used the distinction to deflect client criticism of their decisions and actions. They did so by portraying their actions as required by organizational rules and superiors to whom they were accountable.

The staff members also stated that their actions did not reflect their desires and that clients should not take their actions personally. In other words, local staff members were "only doing their jobs." Thus, the WIN staff members' portrayal of state WIN officials as members of an opposed community of orientation was partly a procedure for rhetorically casting both themselves and clients as constrained by state officials' actions. Consider, for example, the following staff-client exchange occurring during a registration and appraisal meeting and concerned with the client's request for information about training programs. In responding to the client's justification of her request, the staff member cast himself and the client as constrained by the concerns and emphases of state and federal policy-makers. He also deflected possible client criticism of the requirement that she look for jobs by casting himself as having no choice in the matter.

> Staff Member: The main aim of welfare right now is getting you jobs.
>
> Client: I know, but getting some education would give you [clients] the background to get a job, a good job. That's the way I see it.
>
> Staff Member: I know, but they're [state and federal policy-makers] not interested in the future. They want you to get a job right now. That's all they look at.

The Annual Planning Meeting as a Potential Argument

For the local staff members, a major occasion for presenting their concerns and perspectives to state WIN officials was the annual planning session, which was a time for assessing the agency's success in meeting past organizational goals and establishing new goals for the next fiscal year. The goals of most interest to state officials were quantitative indicators of agency success in enrolling new clients in the program, providing job seeking and other social services to clients, and getting clients jobs. State officials portrayed their orientation to the planning meetings as a desire to develop cooperative relations with the local staff by developing mutually agreeable assessments of the agency's past performance and establishing realistic goals for future performance. As one state official who regularly conducted such meetings stated, "It's a chance for us to really work together."

The local staff members, however, treated the planning meeting as arguments for which they needed to be prepared. For example, they held meetings prior to the planning session to discuss issues likely to be raised there and strategies to be used by local supervisor in presenting the staff's position on the issues. The central question of the meetings was, "How can we keep next year's performance goals as low as possible?" The staff members stated that their strategy-setting meetings were made necessary by the state officials' policy of always setting the next year's performance goals above the projected achievements of the current year. They explained that the policy punished local offices that regularly exceeded their performance goals and encouraged staff "to only do the minimum" in order to keep the next year's goals at realistic levels.

The WIN supervisor portrayed the staff's orientation to the planning meetings in the following way:

> I don't think [state officials] realize that when you have an outstanding staff, they'll achieve. I mean, they're competitive people who will always do better than they have to. But when you set real high goals that they have trouble reaching, then it affects morale. They don't see the point in striving for something that is unreasonable. They aren't gonna be recognized for their effort, that's for sure.

According to a state official who regularly conducted such meetings, the local staff's orientation was typical of that taken by staffs in other WIN agencies across the state. She portrayed the orientation as an unrealistic and unfortunate attitude, because the purpose of setting performance goals was to realistically increase the productivity of local agencies. She stated that increases in agencies' performance goals was one way in which state officials encouraged local staff members to become more efficient and effective professionals. She added that only under the most unusual circumstances should local agency goals be left unchanged or reduced.

The state official further stated that the purpose of the planning meeting was to identify goals to which local and state WIN officials should be mutually committed. She concluded, however, that, because of local staff members' usual orientation to the meetings as arguments, cooperative goal-setting was not the typical outcome of planning meetings. Specifically, the state official portrayed local staff members as treating the planning meetings as games and their primary interest in them as winning. She used the portrayal to explain local staff members' resistance to increasing agency performance goals to those preferred by state-level WIN officials. According to the state official, local staff members wished to set agency goals so low that they could achieve them with little effort.

The state official stated that her major professional responsibility in the planning meeting was to resist local staff members' efforts to undermine the planning process and, in doing so, to ensure that realistic performance goals were set. She defined such goals as figures that were low enough to be obtainable by local agency staff members, but high enough to require increased commitment and effort from them. Consider, for example, the following instruction given by the state official to a local WIN supervisor about the purposes of the annual planning sessions.

> You see, what we're trying to do here is to identify some reasonable goals for next year. It's not reasonable to shoot for what you're already doing. You know that you can do that. We want to set goals that are obtainable, but will make your people have to work harder or more efficiently. This is supposed to help them be better professionals. Now, I know that a lot of locals [local staff] don't like that, but setting higher goals that may hurt a little bit at first is part of becoming a better professional.

In sum, the state official portrayed her responsibilities in the annual planning meeting much as local staff members described their responsibilities in staff-client interactions. Both portrayals focused on organizational superiors' obligations to counter potentially troublesome organizational subordinates' excuses which, from the standpoint of the organizational superiors, were intended to justify the subordinates' improper avoidance of typical organizational expectations and procedures.

Although it was focused on different issues and troublesome others, the staff members orientation to the planning meeting was similar to their orientations to most of their everyday interactions with others in their work world. The staff members treated the interactions as political encounters or

contests made up of potentially opposed orientations to practical issues. In so orienting to their work relationships and
interactions, the staff members sought to achieve their practical interests while treating others' interests in the interactions as uncertain and problematic. They sought their
interest by anticipating and countering others' claims about
practical issues and recommendations for managing these
issues and by portraying their own claims and recommendations as realistic and necessary. Thus, rhetoric and argumentation were central and pervasive aspects of WIN staff members'
work activities and relationships.

Conclusion

This chapter has focused on the WIN staff members' orientations to others in their work world as potential sources of
trouble and their mutual interactions as potential arguments.
In so attending to their work world and relationships, staff
members cast others' interests, motives and actions as problematic, and rhetoric as a realistic response to problems emergent in the relationships. They also cast their otherwise mundane interactions with clients, each other and state WIN officials as politically significant, reflecting the interactants'
potentially opposed perspectives and interests. In so orienting
to their interactions with others in their work world, staff members produced politicized relationships organized as contests.

Interactional contests center in each side seeking to maxi-
mize its goals while also seeking to minimize the gains of
opposed parties. Although social interactions so organized may
become simple contests of power in which each side seeks to
unilaterally impose its will on the other, the WIN staff's relations with clients, state officials and colleagues seldom involved
such efforts. Rather, the staff sought to produce "cooperative"
relations with others and to gain voluntary acquiescence by
persuading others to act in preferred ways. In this way, staff
members sought to overcome the anticipated as well as
expressed opposition of others and produce joint actions without recourse to coercion.

One way in which staff members sought to persuade others
and gain acquiescence from them was by defining and justifying WIN as a unique and effective approach to clients' troubles.
We consider how they did so in the next chapter.

4

Defining and Justifying WIN

This chapter is concerned with the ways in which the WIN staff members rhetorically defined the purposes of WIN and justified their orientations to practical issues. Staff members did so in social interactions involving clients and each other. Staff members' definitions and justifications of WIN were intended to anticipate and/or counter others' questions and criticisms of their preferred orientations to practical issues. In part, staff members did so by instructing others on how their preferred responses to practical issues were derived from and consistent with WIN policies and purposes. Consider, for example, the following WIN staff member justification of a proposal to send selected WIN clients to an alternative Education Center where they should participate in job seeking skills workshops.

> This is better than [other agencies in the community]. They [clients] come out of there [the other agencies] wanting to be brain surgeons or something. They're told to expect four years of training. That's not possible. Here [the Alternative Education Center], they show them how to get training while they're working, even 40 hours. [He turns to the representative of the Alternative Education Center.] That's closer to the WIN philosophy.

Although staff members stated that the WIN program was based on a set of interrelated purposes (the WIN philosophy), they expressed no interest in specifying the full meaning and implications of the purposes separate from their practical dealings with clients and each other. Defining WIN was not a academic problem for the staff, but a practical one. As in the above statement, staff members defined WIN by treating practical issues emergent in their everyday work relationships as

100

matters of organizational purpose and philosophy. In doing so, staff members simultaneously defined aspects of the WIN philosophy, differentiated WIN from other organizations based on other philosophies, related the WIN philosophy to the practical issues at hand, and justified their preferred orientations to the issues.

Through these rhetorical activities, staff members and clients also produced organizational contexts for making sense of and responding to practical issues, including clients' troubles. They portrayed the contexts as interrelated sets of obligations restricting their choices in responding to practical issues. In doing so, staff members cast themselves as responsible and competent professionals who sought to cope with difficult work circumstances. According to the staff, two major sources of trouble calling for coping responses were staff-client and staff-staff interactions. They sought to anticipate and manage problems in these interactions in two major ways.

First, they treated staff-client interactions as occasions to instruct clients on the rules and expectations of WIN. In part, the instruction involved introducing clients to organizationally approved motives, justifications and facts. It was intended to explain and justify an organizationally preferred orientation to the WIN program, staff-client relations and the client role. Staff members used the instruction to produce idealized portrayals of proper client participation in WIN which centered in how cooperative staff-client relations (defined as ongoing client acquiesence to staff recommendations and demands) served clients' practical interests in finding jobs and getting off of welfare.

The second way in which staff members managed problems in staff-client and staff-staff relationships involved complaint-making. They did so by accusing others of acting in opposition to WIN purposes and procedures to which both staff and clients were accountable. According to the staff, their complaints were the first step in holding others accountable for their improper actions. The complaints were sometimes expressed as justifications for staff members' opposition to client and staff member recommendations about how to properly respond to clients' troubles and sometimes as warnings to clients and staff members that they must change their behavior. The complaints were also expressed as recommendations to other staff members that formal actions be taken against persons portrayed as acting improperly.

In sum, staff members' instructions and complaints were descriptions of legitimate staff member and client behavior and justifications of staff members' right to hold others accountable for "improper" actions. Staff members used their instructions and complaints to assign cooperative and uncooperative identities to clients or overly lenient identities to other staff members, and to cast themselves as responsible professionals. A major way in which staff members assessed their effectiveness in implementing the WIN philosophy involved others' portrayals of the program. They stated that they were doing a good job when local social services professionals who were sympathetic to the WIN philosophy praised the program and persons who were anti-WIN criticized it.

For example, one source of information used by staff members in assessing their effectiveness was new clients' reports on present and former clients' descriptions of their experiences in WIN. Consider, for example, the following response made by the WIN supervisor to a staff member's description of a registration and appraisal meeting in which a new client said that the WIN staff has a reputation for being tough. Through her response, the supervisor cast the WIN approach to clients' troubles as a message and treated the client's statement as a sign that staff members were succeeding in communicating the message to clients.

> Good, the message is getting out. You know, they [clients and others in their social worlds] talk about these things with each other. They know what to expect before they get here. They're finally learning what we're all about.

On occasion, however, staff members' descriptions and justifications of WIN become matters of negotiation between staff members and others in their work world. The negotiations turned on the implications of aspects of the WIN philosophy for the practical issues at hand. In negotiating such matters, staff members and clients produced practical understandings of organizational purposes and their rights and obligations in the program. They also justified decisions and actions having practical (sometimes fateful) consequences for their lives and careers by portraying the decisions and actions as mandated by WIN purposes and rules.

The rest of the chapter analyzes how WIN staff members and their clients rhetorically described and negotiated the organizational obligations to which they were accountable. We first consider how staff members anticipated and sought to forestall problems with clients by describing WIN procedures, expectations and roles in preferred ways. Later sections focus on the social organization of complaint-making and dispute-resolution in WIN. They analyze the ways in which staff members and clients negotiated the practical meaning and legitimacy of WIN purposes and rules.

Describing WIN to Clients

Staff members described WIN to clients as an interrelated set of requirements and constraints having implications for their own and clients' choices and actions. They portrayed the requirements and constraints as facts of life that they and clients had to accept, regardless of their individual feelings and preferences. Thus, staff members did not ask their clients to enthusiastically embrace the WIN philosophy, although they stated that clients should be realistic about their circumstances and accept the WIN program as a necessary part of being on welfare. Staff members ought to convey such an understanding and orientation to WIN in their initial encounters with clients in registration and appraisal meetings.

The meetings began with staff members asking clients if they knew why they had been sent to the WIN office by local welfare officials. Staff members then elaborated on the clients' responses and instructed them on the practical significance of WIN for their lives. The following staff-client exchanges are examples of how registration and appraisal were initiated.

Staff Member: Do you know why you are here?
Client [embarrassed laugh]: Yeah, 'cause my old lady is applyin' for welfare.
Staff Member: Yeah, well, that and because you have to look for a job. If she is gonna get welfare, then you have to look for work.

Staff Member: Do you know why you are here?
Client: Yes, I'm here in order to get approval for [welfare] funding.
Staff Member: That's right, it is condition of your [AFDC] grant to look for work and to cooperate with us. That means being on time for appointments and looking for work.

Although they were expressed as factual portrayals, staff members' initial descriptions of WIN for clients were intended to persuade clients to acquiesce to an organizationally preferred understanding of and orientation to WIN. They were rhetorical procedures for defining the central issues at stake in staff-client interactions and the salient elements of staff member and client roles. The staff did so by portraying the staff-client relationship as part of an exchange in which clients received AFDC support and help in finding jobs in exchange for participation in WIN. For example, in the above staff-client interactions, staff members portrayed the staff-client relationship as an exchange centered in the government's provision of financial aid to clients and their families. In return, the government demanded that clients cooperate with the WIN staff by looking for jobs and being prompt in keeping their WIN appointments.

Staff members also portrayed their obligation to help clients find jobs as part of the exchange linking clients to the government. Consider the following staff-client interaction which occurred during a registration and appraisal meeting. The staff member responded to the client's explanation of why she was sent to the WIN office by linking the job seeking assistance provided by the WIN staff to the clients' obligation to look for jobs.

Staff Member: Do you know why you're here...?

Client: Yeah, I hafta register here to get my [welfare] check.

Staff Member: Well, yes, we're here to assist you in finding a job. You must look for work in order to get your check. Okay?

In so portraying the practical meaning of WIN for clients, staff members explained and justified their right to intervene in clients' lives, make demands on them, and compel cooperation if necessary. Staff members used the portrayals to produce an organizational context within which their activities were reasonable and legitimate. They also used their initial descriptions of WIN to anticipate and counter clients' questions about and criticisms of the program and their actions. The descriptions were intended to forestall future staff-client arguments by introducing new clients to organizationally preferred understandings and expectations about the program. Finally, staff members' initial descriptions of WIN were further developed in orientation sessions to which most new clients were referred.

Staff members' descriptions of WIN purposes, expectations and rules were aspects of a general theme which centered in portraying WIN as a job for themselves and clients. That is, just a staff members were paid by the government to engage in prescribed activities and were accountable to their organizational superiors, so clients should view their AFDC benefits as reimbursement for fulfilling their WIN assignments and the WIN staff members as their supervisors. Staff members further stated that just as they could be fired for failing to fulfill their organizational obligations, clients could and would be terminated (fired) from WIN if they were uncooperative with staff members. In this way, staff members cast themselves and clients as participants in two separate, but related exchange relationships with the government (their mutual employer).

Further, staff members defined and justified WIN to clients by describing it as a rational and impersonal world within which staff and clients had little discretion. Staff members rhetorically produced and used the description to cast client acquiescence to staff demands and recommendations as realistic and rational. The logic of the staff members' claims may be summarized in the following way: Because clients were obligated to cooperate with the staff or risk losing AFDC benefits, it was in clients' self-interests to acquiesce to the demands and recommendations of the staff. Viewed this way, clients who treated staff-client interactions as conflicts of interest were unrealistic and did not understand their own best interests. The claim was central to staff members' responses to clients assessed as uncooperative. They sought to persuade such clients to change their orientations to WIN by portraying clients' behavior as irrational, because, if it continued, the clients and their families would lose all or a substantial portion of their incomes (AFDC benefits).

Staff members also rhetorically produced and used their description of WIN as an impersonal and rational world to cast themselves as policy-implementors, not policy-makers. They stated that the demands that they made on clients were not expressions of their personal feelings toward clients, but efforts to fulfill their obligations as representatives of the government. Specifically, staff members stated that enforcing WIN rules was their jobs. Consider, for example, the following exchange occuring in a registration and appraisal meeting. It began when the client asked, "What will I have to do here [in WIN]?" As the interaction proceeded, the staff member to whom the client was assigned described his job as closely monitoring the client's job seeking activities ("being on his ass") and affirmed the client's portrayal of the staff member's emphasis on job seeking as mandated by federal government policies. In other words, the staff member had no choice be to "be on his ass."

> Staff Member: I'll be on your ass is what I'll be. I'll be on your ass to get a job....that's my job to be on your ass all the time to find a job.
>
> Client: I understand, it has to with the Reagan thing [the political policies of the Reagan administration].
>
> Staff Member: Now you've got it. That's right.

In the next section, we further consider how staff members sought to produce client acquiescence by describing WIN as a job.

WIN as a Job

As described by the WIN staff members the major features of their own and clients' jobs were defined by the government's interest in the AFDC program. They stated that AFDC was intended to provide temporary financial help to parents who could not provide for themselves and their children. Staff members explained that part of the government's interest in the AFDC program involved its mandate to provide for the general welfare of the citizenry, particularly its obligation to make certain that the subsistence needs of children were being met and keep intact families that might otherwise be destroyed by economic hardship. The staff members also stated, however, that the government's commitment to helping poor persons was conditional and not limitless. They explained that because AFDC was intended as a temporary source of help, the government had an interest in making certain that AFDC recipients made sincere efforts to become economically self-sufficient.

According to the staff, participation in WIN was one of the conditions established by the government to protect its interests. Staff members stated that WIN participation was intended to reduce welfare dependency by making certain that clients looked for jobs and by helping them do so. Consider, for example the following staff member's description of the purposes of the WIN program, which was given to a group of new WIN clients during an orientation session.

> Well, okay, let me start with the purpose of WIN. The federal government has an interest in your children. It has an interest in seeing to it that all children have enough food and shelter and they're protected from these problems. They don't want to see children hurt when their parents are unemployed and can't take care of them. The federal government invests a lot of money in giving your kids a stable home. And most of your money is coming from the federal government, so it has an interest in you. I mean it is doing what you can't do for your kids right now. Because of that, the government has two interests in you. First, it has an interest in finding you jobs so that you won't be on welfare anymore, so you can take care of your kids on your own. Second, it has an interest in ensuring that parents do their part in looking for a job, so they won't just sit around and not do anything. Okay? [pause] This is where WIN comes in, to help with these two things, that's why it was stated in the first place. What this means is that AFDC was set up to help people, but it is also supposed to be conditional on looking for work and temporary until you find work. Does everyone understand that? Welfare is conditional and temporary, that's important and one of the conditions is being in the WIN program.

The above statement illustrates how staff members described WIN as an embodiment of the government's interest in reducing the length of time that clients needed financial help and making certain the clients did "their part" by looking for jobs. The staff member also partly justified WIN and the government's interest in these matters by portraying AFDC benefits as an investment made by the government in clients' children and families. The investment was made necessary by clients' inability to fulfill their social obligation to support themselves and their families. Finally, the staff member's portrayal was a rhetorical procedure for constructing a social context that clients could use in assessing staff members' motives in their mutual interactions. The portrayal highlights staff members' interest in fulfilling their obligations to make certain that clients look for jobs.

Staff members elaborated on their portrayals of the government's interests in clients by describing WIN as a surrogate employer. According to staff members, WIN was partly a surrogate employer because clients earned their AFDC benefits by participating in WIN, much as employees earn their wages and salaries by doing their jobs. They also stated that WIN rules, procedures and expectations were similar to those in the typical employment setting. Staff members generally explained that WIN was similar to employment settings because they expected clients to take responsibility for fulfilling their WIN obligations, just as employers expected their employees to be responsible for fulfilling their work assignments. Staff members also stated that, like employers, they would hold irresponsible clients accountable for their actions.

In so portraying WIN rules, procedures and expectations, staff members sought to impress upon clients the practical importance of cooperating with the staff by fulfilling their WIN assignments. The rest of this section is concerned with the ways in which staff members developed and applied the "WIN as a job" claim. We begin by considering how they used it to define proper client conduct.

Defining Proper Client Conduct

Staff members stated that realistic and cooperative clients were persons who oriented to all aspects of the staff-client relationship as job like. For example, just as employees are expected to arrive at work on time, so WIN clients must be punctual in keeping their appointments with the staff. Staff members also stated that clients should give their appointments with WIN staff the same priority that employees gave their job responsibilities. In other words, clients should make every reasonable effort to keep their WIN appointments and could only legitimately cancel their WIN appointments under exceptional circumstances. They added that when clients could not keep their WIN appointments, clients owed staff members the same consideration that employees owe employers when they cannot come to work. Specifically, staff members stated that, when possible, both employers and staff members deserved advance notice of the times when employees and clients would be unable to fulfill their assignments.

Thus, in elaborating on their portrayal of WIN as a surrogate employer, staff members assigned practical meaning to their claim that WIN was an embodiment of the government's interest in clients. They also defined circumstances or "facts" that clients could legitimately cite in explaining and justifying their failure to fulfill their WIN assignments. Staff members treated such circumstances as matters over which clients had no control. Further, staff members' instruction of clients about organizationally approved extenuating circumstances was intended to anticipate and counter subsequent client excuses and staff-client arguments. Finally, staff members used the instruction to introduce new clients to an organizationally approved rhetoric for expressing and justifying their positions in interactions with staff members.

Consider, for example, the following explanation of WIN given by a staff member during an orientation session.

> WIN expects from you what an employer usually expects. We expect you to keep all appointments, to be on time, unless you have a good excuse. If you can't keep an appointment, you are expected to call your WIN worker in advance. A good excuse is a court appearance, illness or something like that. You are expected to accept child care, if it is needed [in order to look for jobs]. ... You are expected to faithfully look for work and if you get a job to keep your WIN worker informed if you have any problems with your job [for the first thirty days]. Should you fail to cooperate with WIN, [she explains the grievance procedure]. So, this is serious business and you must cooperate with WIN.

Most generally, this statement was a justification of an organizationally preferred client orientation to WIN which centered in treating WIN participation as "serious business." It was also a rhetorical procedure for defining the practical meaning of staff members' expectations about clients' behavior. Specifically, the staff member stated that she and other staff members expected clients to keep and be on time for WIN appointments, accept child care when needed, look for jobs, and keep their WIN workers informed about their activities and problems. Further, the staff member described organizationally approved conditions (or excuses) that would make it impossible for clients to fulfill their WIN obligations. Based on this instruction, clients could anticipate staff members' responses to their explanations of why they failed to fulfill their WIN obligations.

Staff members further stated that clients' participation in WIN was a sign and test of their behavior and attitudes on the job. That is, good clients were likely to be good employees, because clients' orientations to WIN were based on enduring attitudes having consequences for their behavior in employment settings. Staff members used this claim to anticipate and counter clients' complaints about WIN assignments. They stated that WIN, like other jobs, involved unpleasant aspects and that clients should treat them as facts of life over which they had no control. Staff members further stated that realistic clients, like realistic employees, respond to such unpleasantness by fulfilling their obligations. In this way, staff members justified client cooperation with the staff without portraying WIN participation as a pleasant experience. They also cast clients' reactions to WIN as signs and tests of their reactions to unpleasant employment circumstances.

Consider, for example, the following staff member claim made at the outset of a job search skills workshop. It was part of an exchange which began with the staff member instructing clients on the importance of being punctual to the workshops. According to the staff member, "It's very important to be here on time. It reflects your attitude." A client countered the staff member's claim by stating that there was no relationship between her attitude toward WIN activities and other aspects of her life, including jobs. Through his response, the staff member rhetorically linked clients' attitudes toward WIN and other jobs, cast punctuality as a sign of a good attitude, and defined a good attitude as something that all clients could develop. He also cast many jobs that clients were likely to get and, by implication, WIN, as unpleasant experiences.

No, it's [being punctual for WIN meetings] important though 'cause sometimes you have to take a job that you don't like. So you hafta develop a good attitude and be on time, even if you don't like the job.

Staff members also used the WIN as a surrogate employer claim to explain and justify an organizationally preferred orientation to staff-client disputes. According to the staff, such disputes were an inevitable fact of life in WIN and they did not necessarily reflect staff member incompetence or client uncooperativeness. They stated that staff-client disagreements and misunderstandings sometimes occurred even when staff members did their best to explain WIN expectations and procedures to clients and clients were committed to finding jobs. Whatever the source of staff-client disputes, staff members instructed new clients that one part of their WIN jobs involved handling the disputes in organizationally prescribed ways.

Central to proper dispute resolution in WIN was the clients' completion of their WIN assignments, even if they felt the assignments were unfair or otherwise improper. Staff members justified this requirement by portraying it as similar to that found in area factories where union members were required to complete their work assignments prior to filing grievances about them. Consider, for example, the following statement made by the WIN supervisor during an orientation session.

> Now, in the unions they have a saying, "Work then grieve." Remember that because, if you have a disagreement with your WIN worker about what you are supposed to do, you can come see me and file a grievance. We'll sit down and try to solve the problem, but you can't just file a grievance and not do anything. You have to work then grieve. That means that you have to do whatever your WIN worker tells you to do and then file your grievance with me. Remember that, work then grieve, just like in the plant [factory].

In part, the WIN supervisor used this statement to inform the clients about organizationally approved procedures for handling staff-client disputes, but it was also a justification for client acquiescence to all staff member demands. That is, proper grievance procedure involved, first, completing one's WIN assignment (acquiescence to staff demands) and then, filing a complaint about it. The supervisor anticipated and countered possible client criticisms of this procedure by portraying it as "just like in the plant," a world that many clients had experienced. Finally, the supervisor's justification of WIN grievance procedures involved the assignment of organizationally preferred identities to staff members, who were cast as similar to supervisors in a factory, and clients, who were cast as similar to factory workers.

Thus, staff members' definition of proper client conduct and justification of their right to monitor and direct clients' activities were linked. We further consider this issue in the next section, which focuses on staff members' justifications of their authority.

Justifying Staff Authority

Staff members partly justified their monitoring and directing of clients' activities by elaborating on their previous portrayals of WIN as a set of exchange relationships. They stated that the staff's efforts to hold clients accountable to WIN rules and procedures was the major way in which the government made certain that clients fulfilled their part of the exchange. Staff members used the explanation to cast their authority over clients as a fact of life that realistic clients accepted, because they had no choice. One way in which staff members explained how WIN was a fact of life for clients was by describing the negative consequences of clients' failure to fulfill WIN assignments. According to the staff, the consequences included the reduction or elimination of clients' welfare benefits and, for some clients, termination from WIN resulted in the break up of their families.

Staff members emphasized the latter consequence in their dealings with male clients classified as AFDC-UP. They stated that termination from WIN often resulted in the break up of clients' families because, with their husbands out of the household, the wives could qualify for AFDC on their own. They added that families faced with the prospect of losing their entire AFDC grants due to the husbands' inadequate WIN performances had few economic options, especially in tight area labor markets. Staff members added that sometimes termination from WIN resulted in the imprisonment of former clients because, without jobs, they could not make their court-ordered child support payments.

Staff members used such portrayals of their authority and the consequences of noncooperation to impress upon clients the importance of fulfilling their WIN assignments. Consider, for example, the following staff member description of the options available to male clients under existing WIN and AFDC policies. In describing their options, the staff member cast male clients as having no viable choices other than cooperating with the WIN staff.

> It's very peculiar situation for you men. The [welfare] grant is for your children, the check is in your wife's name, but you're responsible for earning your family's grant. If you screw up, then the whole family goes off the grant. Then you can move out of the house and your wife can file child custody against

you. When she does that you must document a job search of sixty or so contacts a week. If you don't you'll be put in that new hotel [a new jail] they're building and you'll be allowed out one day a week to look for a job. So, you're caught between a rock and a hard place.

Although staff members sometimes explained and justified their authority by emphasizing the undesired consequences of improper client conduct, they also stressed the advantages of cooperation with the staff. They did so by portraying themselves as experts at helping unemployed persons find jobs; that is, they possessed special expertise and competence at solving clients' problems. Defined in this way, WIN staff members were similar to other problem-solvers encountered by clients, who also possessed privileged knowledge about the solution of others' troubles. Staff members used this description and analogy to rhetorically cast themselves as professionals and justified client deference to their recommendations and demands. They cast client deference as a realistic and self-interested orientation to the clients' troubles and staff-client relations. In so portraying clients' troubles and the staff's expertise, staff members also justified treating clients' orientations to their WIN assignments as tests of their commitments to solving their troubles.

Specifically, staff members stated that all problem-solving occupations involved two important characteristics having consequences for their relationships with clients. First, because practitioners of these occupations possessed special knowledge, they understood their clients' troubles better than their clients. Thus, if the clients of problem-solving professionals were really serious about solving their troubles, they would acquiesce to the professionals recommendations. Second, staff members stated that solving problems is sometimes unpleasant, but the unpleasantness is necessary. In other words, acquiescence to the recommendations of professional problem-solvers is not a matter of client choice, if clients are serious about solving their troubles.

Consider the following staff member portrayal of the staff-client relationship and clients' obligations within it.

[After reviewing the staff's record in helping clients get jobs,] What that means is that you are dealing with a staff that really knows how to get people jobs. They're experts and they know what it takes to get a job. When you go to the doctor 'cause your sick, you don't question him 'cause you wanta get better, right? If you go to a garage 'cause your car's broken, you do what the mechanic says 'cause he's the one who knows about what makes cars run. Well, the same thing applies here. The staff here knows what it takes to get a job, their record shows it. That doesn't mean that you'll always like it. Sometimes the doctor prescribes medicine that doesn't taste so good goin' down, but you know you hafta take it if you're gonna get better. The same thing applies here. They're [staff members] gonna ask you to do some things that you don't wanna do and that you don't understand, but you just hafta do it. That's the way it is. You can ask if you don't understand and they'll explain it to you, but you're gonna hafta do it, whether you want to or not.

This portrayal of staff-client relations illustrates two major aspects of staff members' justifications of their authority. First, the staff member draws a parallel between the WIN staff and two other problem-solvers that clients are likely to have experienced, physicians and automobile mechanics. She uses the parallel to cast staff members as experts on clients' troubles who make assignments that are good for clients, even if the clients do not understand or want to do them. Second, the staff member portrays acquiescence to staff members' assignments as something that clients must do, it was not a matter of individual choice. Unlike in clients' relationships with physicians and automobile mechanics, then, clients cannot refuse the advice and services of the WIN staff. To do so would be to risk clients' continued receipt of AFDC benefits.

In this way, staff members anticipated and countered criticism of their actions by justifying their right to make demands on clients. They stated that, although clients had to cooperate with the staff, it was also in their best interests to do so. Staff members sometimes elaborated on this claim by portraying themselves as caring professionals who "think about you [clients] all the time, when they're here [in the WIN office] and when they're at home." The portrayal was a rhetorical procedure used by the staff to anticipate and counter clients' claims that assignments made by the staff were really intended to punish clients for being unemployed welfare recipients. It was also a procedure for anticipating and countering clients' possible future claims that the staff's inability to identify job openings for them reflected staff members' lack of concern for solving clients' troubles.

Through their use of the rhetorical procedures discussed in this section, then, staff members sought to forestall future staff-client arguments resulting from clients' "inappropriate" orientations to WIN. We next consider how staff and clients expressed and negotiated complaints about one another. In doing so, they also negotiated, defined and justified WIN purposes and procedures.

Staff-Client Negotiations About WIN Purposes and Procedures

The negotiation of WIN purposes and procedures was a potential aspect of all staff-client encounters. The negotiations partly involved staff members' and clients' efforts to link abstract organizational policies and goals to the concrete and diverse issues emergent in their everyday lives. In doing so, they assigned ideological significance to otherwise mundane issues. The negotiations also involved staff members' efforts to persuade clients to adopt a preferred orientation to WIN rules and procedures. Staff members did so by countering clients' inappropriate descriptions of WIN by emphasizing the practical advantages of orienting to WIN rules and procedures in organizationally preferred ways. In this way, staff members sought to anticipate and forestall future troubles in their relationships with clients.

Consider, for example, the following exchange which occurred in a registration and appraisal session. The client's statement was a response to the staff member's description of the ways in which WIN reimbursed clients for some of their job seeking expenses. The staff member treated the client's response as inappropriate and sought to counter it by portraying the funds as meager and getting a job as in the client's self-interests.

> Client: Oh, you mean I get paid for looking for a job?
>
> Staff Member: Well, yeah, but not much. You're better off getting a job, believe me. It's a little bit to help you with expenses.

A third circumstance associated with staff-client negotiations about WIN purposes and procedures involved complaint-making and dispute-resolution. The negotiations focused on two related issues. First, they were concerned with clients' expectations and/or desires about the WIN program. The negotiations turned on clients' complaints about WIN and staff members' responses that portrayed clients' expectations and/or desires as inappropriate. The negotiations were an aspect of routine staff-client encounters in WIN, particularly of registration and appraisal and orientation meetings. The second issue involved clients' "uncooperative" behavior. It was central to conciliation meetings at which staff members made formal complaints about clients and sought promises of future cooperation from them. The negotiations turned on clients' portrayals of their actions as necessistated by extenuating circumstances and staff members' responses intended to hold clients responsible for their past and future actions.

The rest of this section is an analysis of how staff-client negotiations about WIN purposes and procedures were organized. We begin with clients' complaints about WIN.

Negotiating Client Complaints About Staff

Client complaints focused on the fairness of WIN rules and procedures. They were responses to staff members' rejection of clients' requests for "special" treatment and criticisms of aspects of WIN. The special treatment usually sought by clients was permission to enter training or educational programs. Staff members stated that such requests involved special treatment because WIN has limited funds for supporting clients in training and educational programs and, contrary to many clients' views, only a minority of them deserved to be so treated. According to the staff, clients should first earn the right to enter training and educational programs by looking for jobs and cooperating with the staff. Clients' criticisms of WIN included complaints about specific rules and procedures, the fairness of the organization's emphasis on job seeking as the best solution to clients' troubles, and the staff's right to monitor and direct clients' activities.

Staff members responded to clients' requests and criticisms in three general ways. Most frequently, they responded by elaborating on the job seeking emphasis in WIN and the job like qualities of clients' roles and relationships, and by distinguishing their interests in clients' lives and troubles from those of other social service professionals. In so responding, staff members treated clients' complaints as normal requests and criticisms calling for staff member responses intended to clarify WIN purposes and procedures. The complaints were predictable and recurring aspects of staff members' interactions with clients.

Consider, for example, the following staff member response to a new client's request for permission to enter a training program.

> Staff Member: Part of your obligation in applying for AFDC is looking for work. We're primarily concerned with getting you a job and not training. It is part of the federal mandate.
>
> Client: Well, my social worker [official at the local welfare office] didn't say I couldn't go to school and get welfare.
>
> Staff Member: I know, but your social worker only cares about the financial aspect of your case. We're concerned with the job search aspect and you must make a sincere and honest job search if you expect to continue to receive aid. Now, at a later point, after you have made a job search, we may decide that training is appropriate, but not at this time.

The exchange illustrates how staff members routinely managed new clients' requests for permission to enter training programs. They did so by emphasizing clients' obligations to look for jobs, a responsibility that was described as part of the WIN mandate. The response was a rhetorical procedure for casting job seeking and training as contrasting approaches to the solution of clients' troubles. When the client objected to the staff member's claims, he elaborated on his initial argument by distinguishing WIN from other welfare agencies, portraying cooperation with the staff as a contingency for receiving AFDC benefits, and treating job training as a matter to be determined by staff, not the client. The response was partly an instruction to the client about how to properly interpret WIN staff members' motives in dealing with clients — motives that he describes as very different from those of welfare officials.

Staff members responded to other expected (normal) client criticisms by portraying them as unfounded and/or naive. For example, they responded to clients who complained about having to wait to see their WIN workers by telling the clients to be realistic and recognize that the staff members were overworked and, therefore, not always able to be prompt in keeping their appointments. They sought to forestall future arguments with clients by adding that clients should not use the staff's tardiness as an excuse for being late for or missing their meetings with the staff. Staff members stated that, although this circumstance could be seen as unfair, it was a practical fact of life that realistic clients accepted. Staff members also responded to normal client criticisms by treating clients' troubles with the staff as the clients' fault. In this way, the staff cast the troubles as logical consequences of clients' improper actions and their complaints as unfounded.

Consider, for example, the following staff member response to a client who had previously been terminated from WIN for failing to keep his WIN appointments. The client stated that the termination was unfair because he was in the hospital and unable to keep his appointments.

> Now, just like an employer we will understand if you are in the hospital, but if you don't call for a week and a half and you have a record of missing appointments, then we sanction you [terminate from WIN]. That's what happened to you,...right? You had a long record of missed appointments and you were on a kind of probation....The point is that keeping your appointments and keeping your caseworker informed is serious business and not something to screw around with.

The staff member's response illustrates how staff members responded to clients' portrayals of WIN practices as unfair by challenging the grounds of clients' arguments. The staff member did so by focusing on the client's record of inadequate participation in WIN. The focus undercut the client's claim to unfair treatment by highlighting the conditions that made the staff's response understandable and legitimate. That is, the staff had good reason to believe that he had improperly missed another WIN appointment. The staff member's explanation also shows how they responded to normal and expected client criticisms by undercutting clients' claims to preferred identities, such as being competent clients. Finally, the staff member instructed the client on how to properly orient to WIN participation. He stated that clients should interpret the WIN staff's actions as similar to those of employers and WIN participation as "serious business and not something to screw around with."

The second and third ways in which staff members responded to clients' complaints involved treating them as atypical and, therefore, calling for atypical explanations and justifications. These explanations and justifications did not involve elaborations of staff members' usual portrayals of WIN purposes and procedures. Rather, they focused on staff members' right to shape clients' choices and actions by implementing WIN policies and staff members' motives in doing so. One such response involved treating clients' complaints as legitimate, but concerned with matters over which the staff had no control. Staff members responded in this way to client complaints about two issues: (1) inadequate resources for supporting clients' job seeking activities and (2) some WIN rules and policies.

Staff members accomplished three practical and rhetorical ends through their responses to these issues. First, staff members cast themselves as policy-implementors (not policy-makers) and, therefore, as having no choice but to act in organizationally prescribed ways. Second, staff members morally distanced themselves from the policies and rules that they implemented and assigned responsibility for the policies to others, usually higher level WIN officials and politicians. Specifically, staff members stated that, if they were given a choice in the matters at hand, they would act differently. The response was a rhetorical procedure used by the staff to assign a preferred identity to themselves while acknowledging that their actions could be taken as evidence of alternative motives.

Finally, staff members elaborated on their response by instructing and encouraging clients to "do something about" the problem. The response was a rhetorical procedure for assigning shared political interests to staff and clients as well as justifying client mobilization to pursue their common interests. For example, staff members told clients who complained about inadequate resources to write to area politicians and newspapers to protest cuts in WIN funding and inform others on the ways in which WIN helped clients. They justified the recommendations by stating that many of the problems faced by staff and clients were based on politicians' and the public's lack of concern for and ignorance about the WIN program and its effectiveness in solving clients' troubles.

In addition to client complaints about inadequate resources, staff members also responded in this way to client requests to waive selected WIN rules and policies. For example, they responded in this way to requests by client couples that the WIN policy classifying husbands as heads of their households be waived. The policy required husbands to participate in WIN while their wives were free to volunteer for WIN or devote their full-time attention to caring for their families. Client couples who asked that the policy be waived explained that they wished to reverse their roles and responsibilities; the wives would enroll in WIN and look for jobs while the husbands took care of their children. Staff members responded to the requests by stating that they had no choice but to enforce the rule even though they disagreed with it.

In so responding, staff members justified their actions, cast themselves as policy-implementors, and countered others' efforts to hold them accountable for the rules that they enforced. They also elaborated on their initial response by encouraging clients to take legal action in order to overturn the rule. Consider, for example, the following exchange involving two staff members, a client and his wife. The meeting was about the wife's request to jointly participate in WIN with her husband, including sitting in on her husband's meetings with the staff member. She responded to the staff member's denial of the request by stating that WIN and AFDC policies were unfair because "they put all the responsibility on the man [husband]. Why shouldn't the woman [wife] be responsible too?"

> Staff Member 1: Of course, you're right. We both agree with you. We [indicating the entire staff] talk about this all the time. We think it's a sexist policy.
>
> Staff Member 2: In fact, we'd really like to see a court case on this, 'cause we think it's illegal. I mean, if you or somebody else wanted to go to court over this, you'd probable win and do us a favor. We don't like to hafta do things this way.
>
> Staff Member 1: But, that's the point, we hafta do it. It's not up to us. The man has to enroll in WIN and look for a job. If you wanna volunteer for the program, that's a different matter. Both of you could look for work, but he has to be in the program.

The third way in which staff members responded to clients' complaints involved treating them as illegitimate challenges to staff members' authority and the legitimacy of WIN purposes. The response was associated with client complaints about the staff's right to monitor and direct clients' activities. Staff members treated such complaints as confrontations calling for stern responses that emphasized the staff's right to hold clients accountable to WIN rules and policies. They generally responded by challenging clients' social competence and moral right to complain about WIN. Staff members' responses emphasized clients' economic dependence on the government and the obligations that accompany such dependence. In this way, staff members justified WIN and sought to undercut complaining clients' claims to preferred identities. Specifically, staff members responded by portraying complaining clients as unrealistic and ungrateful recipients of government assistance.

Consider, for example, the following staff-client exchanges concerned with client complaints about the fairness and legitimacy of WIN. The first occurred in a staff-client meeting about the client's failure to fulfill all of his WIN assignments. The second occurred in an orientation meeting in which WIN rules and expectations were described. The staff members responded to both complaints by casting the complaints as improper and justifying their right to monitor and direct clients' activities. The exchanges also show how staff members responded to clients' complaints by assigning devalued identities and statuses to the clients.

> Client [objecting to the staff member's warning that if he does not begin fulfilling his WIN assignments, he will be referred to a conciliation meeting]: ...this really isn't fair, nobody cares about our [WIN clients'] problems.
>
> Staff Member: Why should it be fair? You're on welfare, you're getting charity. Charity isn't supposed to be fair.
>
> Client [in response to the staff member's description of the conditions under which clients could be required to take jobs]: Sounds like communism to me, you have these people workin' for the government who say you [clients] hafta take a job whether you want to or not.
>
> Staff Member: Well, somebody said that to me the other day too and the only thing I can say to that is that it's more communistic to be livin' off the government. You know, there are some responsibilities that go with being supported by the state.

We next consider how staff members expressed and negotiated complaints about clients.

Negotiating Staff Complaints About Clients

Although staff members complained about clients' activities and orientations in their regular staff-client meetings concerned with clients' WIN assignments, they treated conciliation meetings as the major occasions for expressing complaints about clients. In most conciliation meetings staff members formally accused clients of acting in improper and unacceptable ways, sought promises from clients that they would cooperate in the future, and established records of client misconduct that staff could subsequently use to justify termination of clients from WIN, should the clients fail to keep their promises to cooperate. The referral of clients to conciliation meetings was a significant event for the staff members because it signalled their orientation to such clients as serious troublemakers and their willingness to take severe action to manage them.

Conciliation meetings began with a staff member asking clients if they knew why the meetings were being held. Regardless of the clients' responses, the question framed the meetings as one of complaint-making and client accountability because clients were asked to explain and justify their actions. The complaints were usually formulated as a problem of clients not fulfilling their obligations to look for jobs, but they sometimes involved related activities assigned by staff members, such as attendance at the Alternative Education Center or obtaining physicians' verifications of claimed illness and disabilities. Whatever the activities in question, staff members treated clients' failure to adequately fulfill their assignments as signs of uncooperativeness.

Consider, for example, the following staff-client exchanges which occurred at the outset of conciliation meetings.

Staff Member: Do you know why you are here?

Client: No.

Staff Member: You haven't been cooperating. You're supposed to go to the [Alternative Education Center] and you don't go. You don't keep appointments. You know that, don't you?

Staff Member: You know why you are here don't you?

Client: No.

Staff Member You know you are here...because you have not been cooperating. You say you are sick, but you have no medical excuse [letter from a physically documenting illness.]

These exchanges show how conciliation meetings began as confrontations centered in staff member complaints and accusations. Staff members also used their initial interactional turns to cast the issues at hand as matters of client culpability and accountability. Further, much of the complaint-making process centered on the documentation of staff and client claims. The critical documents for substantiating staff claims were the clients' files, which indicated when clients had failed to keep appointments with the staff and to fulfill other WIN assignments. Staff members treated clients' files as objective and accurate records of the most important aspects of clients' WIN participation. Documenting client claims was more difficult because clients did not routinely keep official documents, although they were required to keep a record of all employment contacts and return it to their WIN workers. Also, they sometimes obtained documents from physicians, teachers at the Alternative Education Center and other institutional officials to substantiate their claims. In a few cases, clients' spouses appeared to verify the clients' claims, but in most cases clients appeared alone and with no institutionally recognized verification or documentation to counter the staff's claims.

The following exchanges illustrate how staff members emphasized and used organizational documents in making complaints against clients. Specifically, they used client files to explain and justify their complaints and demanded that clients document their claims to having fulfilled their WIN obligations.

> Staff Member: Do you know why you are here?
>
> Client: Because I don't come in on Tuesday mornings.
>
> Staff Member [reading from the client's file]: He was in [date], right after I gave him a [warning that he had to keep all subsequent appointments or be referred to a conciliation meeting], and then he missed next time.

> Staff Member: Do you know why you are here?
>
> Client: Yes, 'cause you say I ain't looking for no jobs.
>
> Staff Member: Have you?
>
> Client: Yes.
>
> Staff Member: Can you prove it? Do you have a piece of paper to show it.?
>
> Client: No.
>
> Staff Member: Then, how can I believe you?

Taken together, these features of the complaint-making process constituted the working definition of client cooperation used by staff during conciliation meetings. That is, cooperation was defined as fulfilling the demands of WIN staff in documentable ways. For staff members, full client accountability required that clients meet both features of their definition of cooperation. Clients countered staff members' complaints by offering alternative understandings of their actions and records. Clients' responses emphasized how their actions were shaped by extenuating circumstances which they portrayed as conditions making them only partly responsible for their uncooperative actions. If accepted by the staff, the clients' responses forestalled their being dropped from the program.

Although clients appealed with a variety of extenuating circumstances their claims can be generally categorized into four types:

1. "I didn't know or understand the requirements of the program";
2. "I have overriding family and personal problems";
3. "I am trying as best I can"; and
4. "WIN is unfair."

The first response involved a claim of ignorance. For example, clients stated that the staff did not fully or properly inform them of their WIN responsibilities or that postal carriers did not deliver notices of WIN meetings. A related response involved acknowledging fault in meeting specific requirements. The clients explained, however, that because they did not understand the purposes of WIN or of the assignments made by staff they failed to fulfill their assignments. Implicit in the latter response was the claim that client cooperation hinged on a full understanding of WIN.

The second response was the most common. It focused on how features of clients' lives made cooperation difficult, if not impossible. Clients used the responses to counter staff members' portrayals of their uncooperative behavior as intentional. The factors most frequently described by clients as extenuating circumstances were baby sitting and related child-rearing problems, interpersonal problems in clients' households, housing problems, lack of money to buy gas to search for jobs, clients' physical and emotional problems, and personal habits that clients portrayed as beyond their control, such as forgetfulness or sleeping late.

Staff members responded to such claims to extenuating circumstances by instructing clients on their obligations to fulfill their WIN assignments and follow other WIN rules. One such rule was that money provided by WIN to reimburse clients' expenses must be used to cover current job seeking expenses. Consider, for example, the following staff-client exchanges concerned with the reasons for the client's failure to look for jobs.

> Client: I have been [looking for jobs] but I got a new car and it broke down. Besides, I don't have enough money for gas. You can't drive without gas. I need the [WIN reimbursement] money for other things, living expenses.
>
> Staff Member: That's not what the money is for. It's for gas and other job search expenses.

Staff members also responded to such client claims by instructing clients on the staff's right to know about problems in clients' lives that kept them from fulfilling their WIN assignments. Staff members justified the demand by emphasizing clients' economic dependence on the government, the government as clients' surrogate employer, and describing themselves as clients' supervisors. As in the following staff-client exchange, staff members also justified their interest in clients' problems by stating that they could help clients manage them.

> Client: I don't have no baby sitter....I need a baby sitter.
>
> Staff Member 1: Didn't tell me that....
>
> Client: It's not your problem. It's mine, I can take care of it.
>
> Staff Member 2: No,...it's our problem too. If you can't go to the Alternative Education Center, we need to know why. The government is giving you money and we have a right to know. If you work for somebody, they have a right to know why you're not coming to work. We can help you.

The third response emphasized clients' efforts to cooperate with WIN staff, even if staff members did not recognize or appreciate clients' efforts. Sometimes clients did so by pointing to their recently improved WIN records and, other times, they emphasized their efforts to deal with problems that might interfere with getting jobs, such as enrollment in drug or alcohol treatment programs. A variation on this response and one that was frequently combined with other responses was the "I really want a job" claim. In this way, clients cast their intentions as consistent with the WIN philosophy even if their behavior was not always consistent with it. As in the following staff-client exchanges, staff members responded to such client claims by stating that they weren't doing enough. They stated that clients were obligated to *fully* cooperate with the WIN staff.

> Client: I know I haven't cooperated. [Pointing to his WIN file] I have a bad record, I know. But I've been doing better since I talked to [the WIN counsellor]]. I've only missed one appointment [since them] and I have started to really look for a job. I even got my hair cut. I've always had it long and when [his WIN worker] told me I should cut it, I looked in the mirror and decided it didn't look that good on a thirty four year old man. [pause] I have been better.
>
> Staff Member: You're right, you have been better, but it's not good enough. You're being paid by the government to keep *all* your WIN appointments, not just some of 'em. You can't decide to come in one day and not come another.

> [The client explains that she has been looking for jobs, although she has not been keeping her WIN appointments. She lists the places where she has sought jobs.]
>
> Staff Member: I hear you saying that you are making an honest effort to find a job and that's good. You're a bright person and you can understand the problem you're in. Even if you look for work, if you don't let [the WIN staff] know, then you're not cooperating with the WIN program. [We] need to document your activities.

Finally, clients stated that WIN staff and/or the requirements of the program were unjust. For example, one client claimed she was being discriminated against because all clients were not required to report to their WIN workers at 7:45 every morning. Others argued that their WIN workers did not like them, that staff had a bad attitude toward the poor, and that their travel expense reimbursements were too small or late in arriving. In one case a client claimed that the documentation and complaint-making methods of WIN staff were unfair. The client noted that many of the examples of non-cooperation cited in the conciliation session took place while she was a voluntary client and therefore free to ignore the requests of her WIN worker.

Staff members responded to these claims by stating that the clients were not being treated differently than others, staff members' seeming "bad" attitudes were expressions of their concern for making certain that clients fulfilled their WIN obligations, and all aspects of clients' WIN records were relevant for conciliation meetings. Consider, for example, the following staff-client exchanges concerned with these matters.

> Client: Well, I know a lot of people on welfare and they don't come in here early in the morning. They have kids and they don't have to come in....It's not fair. Other people with kids don't hafta come in. I feel like I'm being picked on.
>
> Staff Member: You're not alone. If you'd come in in the morning, you'd see that you're not alone. There are other people having to do this.
>
> [Staff member reads from the client's record, noting the times when she missed her WIN appointments.]
>
> Client: What does all this have to do with what's going on here. I was [a] voluntary [client] then, I didn't have to come in then. I'm mandatory now.
>
> Staff Member: Well, they're relevant because there is a pattern, if you see a pattern going over several years, it is important. You have a long record of missed appointments.

For the most part, then, clients' responses to staff members' complaints explained why clients were not meeting the requirements of the program. By appealing to ignorance, family and personal problems, improved cooperation or intentions to cooperate, and the inequities of the program, clients offered alternative interpretations of their obligations to the program. Few clients addressed the issue of documentation and the staff's treatment of client files as an accurate and unbiased rendering of their involvement in the program. When clients did challenge staff's documentation of their actions, they usually offered additional documents to be added to their files. Because clients focused on extenuating circumstances, staff responses were primarily directed at the legitimacy of the circumstances. In negotiating this issue, staff and clients also distinguished between acceptable and unacceptable excuses.

Conciliation sessions ended with either an agreement between the staff and client remedying the problem or an irreconcilable disagreement, in which case the client was dropped from the program. The latter meetings were preceeded by staff member discussions and agreements that the clients were serious problems and deserved more severe responses than others. Staff members refused to honor such clients' explanations and justifications during conciliation meetings. They responded to clients' statements by emphasizing the clients' responsibilities to fully cooperate with the staff, the ways in which clients had created their problems, and the many "second" chances staff members had given the clients. The responses were rhetorical procedures for casting clients' appeals to extenuating circumstances as excuses and unacceptable explanations of their circumstances and motives.

In most cases, however, staff members honored one or more of the clients' appeals to extenuating circumstances. They did so by linking their actions to clients' promises to cooperate in the future or else face termination from WIN. Further, the promises sought by the staff focused on concrete client behaviors, not general and unenforceable agreements to cooperate with the staff. Consider, for example, the following staff-client exchange in which cooperation was defined as the clients' keeping her early morning WIN appointments and making five job contacts per day.

> Client: I thought I was supposed to go out and look for jobs then.
>
> Staff Member: No, it was explained to you that you were to come here.
>
> Client: I didn't know that.
>
> Staff Member: Are you prepared to cooperate now?
>
> Client: Yes.
>
> Staff Member: Will you come in every day at 7:45 in the morning?
>
> Client: Yes.
>
> Staff Member: And look for five jobs a day?
>
> Client: Yes.

In so producing clients promises to cooperate, staff members undermined client's future appeals to extenuating circumstances. They also frequently elaborated on their portrayals of WIN as a job and formulated new understandings of the program for clients. One way in which staff members elaborated on their portrayals of WIN as a job was by claiming that there was not conflict of interest between clients' obligations to WIN and their families. Consider, for example, the following staff member-client exchange.

> Client: Well, all I can say is my kids come first, I'm gonna feed them before I go lookin' for a job.
>
> Staff Member 1: What'll your kids do for food if you lose your grant? You will, you know, if you don't look for work.
>
> Staff Member 2: This is a job...it's your job, and like any other job, if you don't go to work, you'll get fired. Look at it that way.... All I'm saying is that you're being paid to cooperate, that's what your [AFDC] grant is, and so this is your job, to keep appointments and look for work.

Based on the rhetorical practices discussed above, participants in conciliation meetings negotiated the practical meaning of cooperation and WIN purposes. The definition and negotiation of adequate WIN participation was also an aspect of staff-staff relationships and interactions. We turn to these relationships next.

Negotiating Proper Staff Performance

Although each of the staff members who monitored clients' activities maintained separate caseloads and were somewhat autonomous professionals, they were still accountable to others. In part, they were accountable because the WIN supervisor observed and evaluated all aspects of their work. Specifically, the supervisor. read and commented on their case files, set annual performance goals for each staff member, met with staff members to assess their past work performance, and heard client complaints about staff members. Staff members were also accountable to one another in meetings about how best to respond to clients' troubles and actions, such as registration and appraisal and conciliation meetings. The meetings involved producing jointly agreeable responses to clients' troubles. More generally, however, staff members held each other accountable by observing one another's daily work practices and complaining about those which they assessed as inadequate and/or inconsistent with WIN purposes.

Initially, the complaint-making involved accusing others of acting in opposition to organizational purposes and procedures. Complainants took a strict orientation to the issues at hand and portrayed others as overly lenient. Although staff members sometimes directly accused other staff of acting in improper ways, they frequently voiced their complaints to the WIN supervisor. In doing so, they sought official sanction for the complaints as well as intervention intended to hold accused staff accountable for their actions and orientations. Consider, for example, the following complaint made to the supervisor about a new staff member.

> You've really gotta do something about [the new staff member]. He's letting clients do anything they want. He buys every excuse they come up with [for not doing their WIN assignments]. They're walking all over him. You've gotta talk to him or somethin'. Explain to him how we do things here.

In general, such complaint-making involved treating otherwise discrete aspects of everyday life as indicators of underlying patterns of improper activity and orientation. It also called into question other staff members' commitments to the WIN philosophy and assigned a preferred identity to the complainant. Specifically, staff members cast themselves as responsible professionals and their complaints as expressions of their commitment to achieving WIN goals. Each of these claims was subject to assessment by and negotiation with others, however; particularly, by staff members accused of acting improperly and the WIN supervisor to whom many of the complaints were directed. The assessments and responses focused on two questions: (1) Does the claimed pattern of improper action really exist and (2) Are the recommended responses justified?

In responding positively to both questions, other staff members and the WIN supervisor cast the complaints as legitimate and justified taking actions intended to hold accused staff accountable to organizational purposes and rules. Consider the following exchange occurring in a staff meeting concerned with the actions and orientation of a staff member absent from the meeting. The exchange began with the initial complainant stating that "something has to be done about" the absent staff member. The complainant explained and justified his recommendation by citing a recent incident in which the staff member advised a new client to consider seeking funds to enroll in a training program. The advice was treated as both a violation of typical organizational practice and a sign of the staff member's overly lenient orientation. Others expressed support for and elaborated on the accusation by portraying other incidents as aspects of a problematic pattern of behavior and orientation about which something had to be done.

> WIN Supervisor: You know, I think he has gotten worse since [he won a dispute with other staff members regarding a client].
>
> Staff Member: That's right, I think so. He told me to put [a client] in [a special WIN program] and I said "No way." He thought the guy was appropriate for [the program], can you believe that? And he told [another staff member] how to handle [one of her cases] too. [Another staff member states that the social worker "has gotten so bad" about advocating for clients that she tries to avoid working with him.]
>
> WIN Supervisor: [Begins making notes.] When has he interfered, what cases? [Others note occasions when the social worker has acted in "improper" ways.] Anybody else, we need documentation on something like this.

Thus, one way in which the WIN supervisor and staff responded to complaints about others' work performances and orientations was to express support for and elaborate on the complaints. It involved treating a variety of events as signs of other staff members' inadequate work performance and overly lenient orientations. The WIN supervisor recorded the events and later cited them in explaining and justifying her subsequent actions. The actions ranged from advising accused staff members on the importance of acting in organizationally approved ways and on how they could improve their work performances to making formal complaints intended to punish staff members for their improper actions and orientations. The records were treated as evidence of a pattern of action that necessitated the supervisor's actions and were used to cast the supervisor's actions as based on more than personal differences of opinion about how WIN policies should be implemented. According to the supervisor, such records left her with no choice in responding to troublesome staff members; they had to be held accountable for their actions.

Most staff complaints were not so treated, however. Rather, the WIN supervisor and/or other staff members countered most complaints by offering alternative explanations of the actions and events in questions. The explanations recast the events and actions as signs of appropriate professional behavior. Staff members also used their alternative explanations to question the empirical and logical grounds for complainants' accusations and recommendations. Most obviously, they signalled the need for complainants to substantiate their accusations and show why the recommended responses were justified. Perhaps less obvious were the ways in which others' alternative explanations altered the conditions of subsequent exchanges.

Specifically, respondents portrayed the actions in question as consistent with (1) the general intent or spirit of WIN policies or (2) written rules, procedures and/or purposes. Responses focusing on the spirit of WIN cast others' accusations within a broad social and interpretive context. They called for complaint elaboration showing how the actions in question were contrary to the general and, to some extent, unrecorded purposes of the organization. Responses focusing on documentary aspects of WIN narrowed subsequent interaction by calling for the citation of specific written rules, procedures and/or purposes that substantiated the claimants' accusations and recommendations.

The rest of this section is concerned with the ways in which staff members negotiated and defined others' actions. The definitions involved portraying staff members' actions as consistent with the spirit of WIN or its rules.[1] In doing so, the staff members treated the spirit of WIN and WIN rules as justifications.

The Spirit of WIN as a Justification

Responses focusing on the relationship between staff member actions and the spirit of WIN cast WIN purposes as complex and including a diversity of actions and orientations. Respondents stated that a diversity of staff member work orientations was a necessary and realistic response to the range of practical problems encountered by the staff in their work. They also stated that complainants were advocating overly strict and intolerant orientations to the purposes of WIN and others' work performance. Although it was expressed differently in each circumstance, both staff members accused of acting in improper ways and the WIN supervisor responded in this way to complaints. In doing so, they challenged the grounds of the complaints and complainants' portrayals of themselves as more committed to WIN purposes that others.

Staff-staff negotiations about proper work performance were part of social interactions concerned with developing joint responses to practical issues, such as clients' requests to enroll in vocational training programs. In the interactions, a staff member would recommend a course of action to which others responded. One way in which others explained and justified their rejection of the recommendation was to portray it as a reflection of the recommenders' overly lenient work orientations. Staff members so accused responded by portraying themselves as committed to the purposes of WIN, although acting from different orientations than those preferred by their accusers. The respondents stated that their orientations were equally legitimate and consistent with the purpose of WIN as were those of their accusers.

Staff members accused of holding overly lenient orientations displayed their commitment to holding clients accountable by acquiescing to the recommendations of complainants. However, in acquiescing, they pointed to conditions justifying their recommendations. For example, in the following exchange, the staff member accused of being overly lenient stated that clients sometimes changed their attitudes toward WIN and getting jobs. She also pointed to aspects of the client's life that might be taken as signs of change. The exchange began with Staff Member 1 recommending that a long-term client with a record of uncooperative behavior be allowed to enter a training program. Staff Member 2 rejected the recommendation by portraying Staff Member 1 as overly lenient and an advocate for clients.

Staff Member 1: An advocate, is that what I am? Yeah, I guess I am. Well, I don't know. You know what I try to do. I try to sit down with a client and find out what he or she really wants, then we can work from there, but I have to know what they want. I suppose I take their side a lot, but not all the time. I mean, I can be tough on 'em too, but the key thing is that you hafta know what they really want. I think a lot of [the client's] problem is that she doesn't know what she wants.... You know, too, I think a lot of these [clients] don't understand what [WIN is] about. I mean, [other staff] explain and so do I, but it doesn't get through.

Staff Member 2: [The client] understands the system. She's been in it a long time. She was in [WIN] in [another city] and

she always had a job. Maybe they were tougher on her up
there.
[Discussion turns to the reasons for the client's recent record
of "uncooperative" behavior.]

Staff Member 1: Well, okay, maybe we should start by having
her follow through on something and I'll talk to her next time
about the importance of WIN. You know, I do stress that they
cooperate...I tell 'em that it's the law and they don't have any
choice. But don't you think people change? I mean she got rid
of her husband and now maybe she's ready to change. People
do sometimes realize what's going on and turn their lives
around, you know.

Complaints expressed to the WIN supervisor emphasized
the supervisor's responsibility to hold other staff members
accountable for their improper activities and orientations. The
supervisor responded by portraying the purposes of WIN and
problems with which the staff dealt as complex. She stated
that the practical circumstances of the staff's work necessitated the development of a variety of staff member work styles.
The supervisor elaborated by linking organizational needs and
purposes to the work styles and strengths of individual staff
members. In this way, she cast the actions and orientations of
staff accused of being overly lenient as professionally proper
and complainants as having inadequate understanding of the
purposes of WIN. She also portrayed complainants as holding
intolerant attitudes toward other staff members' proper work
orientations and performances.

Consider, for example, the following supervisor response to
a complaint and recommendation that she admonish a staff
member.

Well,...I really don't think that's necessary. I know what you
are saying and for what you do [the kinds of clients with
whom the complaining staff member typically dealt], they are
too lenient, but we don't all do the same thing. Look at [a staff
member], she's not very good with troublemakers, but she's
outstanding with other clients. You know, the job ready
[employable] ones. I mean, she shows them how to write
resumes and how to handle [job] interviews. A lot of clients
need that and she really helps them get jobs. [The supervisor
notes the strengths and weaknesses of other staff.] You see,
we're all different. We have our own styles and we don't all
hafta be as strict as you are.

In part, the supervisor's response was an explanation and justification of her refusal to act in recommended ways. It also recast the terms of subsequent interaction by requiring that complainants show how the work orientations of other staff members were inappropriate and/or inadequate for the types of clients with whom they typically dealt. The response was also rhetorically significant because all complainants acquiesced to the supervisor's portrayal of others' actions as consistent with the spirit of WIN. However, she responded differently to complaints about her own work performance. We consider this response next.

WIN Rules and Justifications

The supervisor responded to complaints about her own work performance by treating written organizational rules and procedures as constraints on her choices and actions. Specifically, she stated that she was rule-bound and had no choice in responding to the matters at hand. The explanation was expressed in anticipation of and/or to counter others' portrayals of her actions as based on personal preference. The response challenged complainants to show that the supervisor was not rule-bound and she gained complainant acquiescence by citing written rules and procedures which complainants took as proof of the supervisor's rule-boundedness. The negotiations involved one or both of the following rhetorical procedures.

First, the supervisor pointed to written rules and procedures in the WIN manual which could be taken by complainants as evidence of her rule-boundedness. Complainants countered by portraying the rules and procedures as inapplicable to the issues at hand. Complainants acquiesced to the supervisor's claims by ceasing to counter her portrayal of selected rules and procedures as relevant to the issues at hand and as constraints on her decisions and actions. Second, the supervisor explained and justified her response by distinguishing her actions from her attitude toward the issues at hand. Specifically, she stated that although the actions in question were necessary, they were not her preferred response. The supervisor also distanced herself from her actions by declaring moral alignment with complainants.

Consider, for example, the following staff member–supervisor exchange about a client who has requested a meeting with the supervisor to complain about her WIN worker.

Staff Member: Why are you letting her come in? She doesn't have a case. You're too easy.

WIN Supervisor: They [clients] can complain about anything they want. I can't turn 'em down.

Staff Member: Oh, yes you can.

WIN Supervisor: Look at the Rights and Responsibilities [statement given to clients outlining their rights and responsibilities in the program].

Staff Member: Okay [reads a passage indicating that clients may complain about discrimination]. This case doesn't involve prejudice or discrimination, she just doesn't want to cooperate. You shouldn't let people like that come in...

WIN Supervisor [looking through the WIN manual]: Okay, here. [She reads a passage stating that clients can complain about anything involving their relationship with WIN.] See, I don't have a choice, 'cause this involves her relationship with WIN....

Staff Member: Well, I guess so, but I get tired of this kind of shit.

WIN Supervisor: I know, so do I.

The exchange shows how the WIN supervisor justified her decisions and actions by describing herself as rule-bound. She substantiated her claim by strategically using aspects of the WIN manual to counter alternative interpretations and claims. The exchange also illustrates how complainants invited declarations of moral alignment from the WIN supervisor while acquiescing to her position. They did so by portraying the supervisor's actions as unfortunate and undesirable. The supervisor declared her alignment with the complainant by agreeing with his portrayal of her actions.

Conclusion

This chapter has focused on the ways in which WIN staff members rhetorically defined and justified WIN purposes and procedures. They did so by treating otherwise mundane events as politically significant and related to WIN purposes. Their portrayals of the WIN philosophy and its implications for themselves and clients were also rhetorical procedures for highlighting and prioritizing the various policies associated with the program. For example, the "WIN as a job" portrayal was a procedure for prioritizing policies and rules by casting some (those that were joblike) as more central to the WIN philosophy than others. Further, because they used their portrayals of the WIN philosophy to instruct others on how to "properly" orient to WIN and justify complaints against them, the portrayals may be analyzed as aspects of professionally advocated codes of conduct (Goffman, 1963). Staff members used the codes to assess the appropriateness of their own and others' actions and assign identities to themselves and others, including assigning differing levels of social competence and worth to clients and other staff members.

We next consider how staff members defined and implemented the WIN philosophy as they described the sources of their own and clients' troubles.

5

Defining Troubles in WIN

Troubles were defined in WIN based on typical organizational expectations about proper client and staff member activities. The expectations and procedures were partly routine ways of managing the various practical issues emergent in staff members' work activities and relationships, but they were also orientations to the issues and others. That is, they were organizationally preferred ways of understanding and responding to clients' and staff members' troubles and organizational roles. For example, the organizationally preferred understanding of and response to clients' troubles involved treating them as employment problems calling for a job seeking response. This understanding and response was associated with a staff member orientation to clients and their troubles which emphasized individual responsibility and accountability.

The "clients as responsible for their troubles" definition and orientation may be contrasted with other understandings and responses that emphasize how employment opportunities are shaped by institutional forces beyond WIN clients' control, such as the demand for the goods and services produced in local industries. Such understandings call for organizational responses and staff-client interactions that de-emphasize client culpability and accountability. For example, persons taking this orientation to clients' troubles might argue that because typical WIN expectations and procedures are based on the assumption that job openings exist for clients, they should not be applied in recessionary economies. They might ask, "What is the point of having clients look for jobs that don't exist?"

The trouble definition process in WIN, then, also involved taking a position on the legitimacy of typical organizational expectations and procedures. Most of the time, staff members argued that the expectations and procedures were appropriate and, consequently, they and their clients should be held accountable to them. Specifically, staff members treated typical organizational expectations and procedures as "facts of life" which they and their clients must accept, regardless of their personal feelings about them. They portrayed persons who did so as realistic and those who did not as both unrealistic and sources of trouble. Staff members sought to convey this image of WIN to clients in all staff-client interactions, ranging from initial registration and appraisal meetings to meetings with former clients who had been terminated from WIN for being uncooperative.

The latter meetings were concerned with the reasons for former clients' termination from WIN and conditions that the former clients would have to meet in order to be reaccepted into the program. Staff members emphasized two major rhetorical goals in the meetings. First, they sought to counter the former clients' claims that they were terminated from WIN for reasons other than their failure to follow typical organizational procedures and fulfill their obligations in the program. Second, staff members stated that they did not have to reaccept former clients into the program and would not do so until the former clients had demonstrated (documented) that they were willing to accept and abide by typical organizational expectations and procedures.

Consider, for example, the following staff member response and instruction of a former client who claimed that the "real" reason he was terminated from WIN was because his mother-in-law complained to the WIN staff about him. He stated that his mother-in-law's complaint was a lie and an attempt to "get even" with him for their long-standing disagreements and animosities.

> You can believe that your mother-in-law got you deregistered [terminated from WIN] if you want to, but that's not what happened. This is a logical consequence of your actions. You refused to cooperate with the staff [in the special program to which he was assigned] and you were deregistered. If you want to reapply, then, you had better document, and I *mean* really document, that you will cooperate. That's why I think you should [apply for another welfare program which involved doing public service work]. Then you will have a clear, documented work record.... You have got to realize that you are responsible for your behavior. If you don't provide documenta-

tion, we don't have to take you back. We can cut you off [of AFDC] forever if we want.

The rest of this chapter considers how troubles were rhetorically defined, negotiated and justified by WIN staff, clients and state officials. We first consider how definitions of clients' troubles were socially produced and negotiated in WIN. Later sections focus on two major definitions of trouble: (1) clients' attitudes toward employment, welfare and WIN and (2) the impact of the recessionary area economy on the staff's work and clients' efforts to find jobs. The definitions involved different orientations to the causes and proper solutions to troubles as well as the appropriateness of typical organizational expectations and procedures for persons' troubles.

Defining Clients' Troubles

Initially, staff members defined clients' troubles by assigning them to WIN statuses. The statuses were both organizationally useful classifications of clients' troubles and orientations to clients, which ranged from treating clients and their troubles as typical and appropriate for WIN to treating them as atypical and totally inappropriate. Staff members used the latter classification to justify their recommendations that some clients be exempted from WIN participation. Staff members' initial definitions and classification of clients' troubles were always potentially subject to reconsideration and change, however, because they tested and reconsidered their initial classifications of clients and their troubles in subsequent interactions. They did so by considering new information about clients' troubles and circumstances and reassessing the meaning of previously known information in light of clients' participation in WIN.

Consider, for example, the case of a young female client who was referred to WIN as a mandatory youth. Clients were defined and classified as mandatory youths if they were of school age, not enrolled in school, and economically dependent on another person who received AFDC. The staff members who enrolled the client in WIN described her as an appropriate referral and assigned her to a typical WIN status requiring that she look for jobs. However this definition and categorization of the client and her troubles changed at the subsequent meeting when the client stated that she was also the mother of an infant. The staff member supervising the client treated the statement as new information justifying his reassessment of her WIN status.

The staff member's reassessment partly involved treating the conditions initially used to classify the client as an appropriate referral as irrelevant to the "real" issues at stake in the case. Specifically, the staff member stated that, as the mother of a child, the client qualified for AFDC support in her own right and instructed her on the procedures for applying for such aid. He added that because the client's child was under school age, she could not be compelled to participate in WIN. He also cited this circumstance and the client's desire to no longer participate in WIN in explaining his termination of the client from the program.

More generally, staff members defined clients' troubles by treating aspects of clients' life circumstances as facts and classifying them as typical or atypical. Typical troubles were produced by treating the relevant facts or circumstances associated with an issue as expected, normal and, therefore, unproblematic. Staff members responded to troubles defined as typical by assigning clients to organizational categories involving job seeking or other activities intended to help then get jobs. In doing so, they responded to clients' troubles in expected and organizationally preferred ways. In the case discussed above, for example, the client's circumstances were initially treated as normal and unproblematic because they met the conditions needed to classify her as a mandatory youth and assign her to a preferred WIN status involving job seeking.

On the other hand, staff members defined clients' troubles as atypical and justified organizationally dispreferred responses to them by treating the relevant facts associated with the troubles as extraordinary and extenuating. They further portrayed the facts as matters which could not be ignored and their recommended responses as necessary and professionally proper. In the above case, for example, the staff member treated the client's status as an unemployed mother of an infant as a relevant and overriding fact justifying his exemption of her from the WIN program. The action was atypical because staff members treated exemption of clients from WIN as a last-resort response to their clients' troubles. They also stated, however, that the staff member's actions were justified because clients with children under school age had a legal right to choose not to participate in WIN.

Further, trouble definition in WIN was organized as a rhetorical process centered in staff members' and others' justifications of their orientations to clients' troubles. The justifications were responses to anticipated and stated criticisms of others to their decisions and actions. This concern was central to the staff members' orientation to their case files which included written assessments of the sources and relevant contexts of clients' troubles, and explanations of staff members' responses to the troubles. The files were periodically reviewed by the WIN supervisor, who used them to evaluate the staff members' work performances. The evaluations included making suggestions and criticizing staff members' decisions and actions based on information contained in the files.

Thus, although staff members usually wrote their case descriptions in a perfunctory style, the descriptions were nonetheless intended to justify their actions and persuade the supervisor that they were competent professionals. Consider, for example, the following case description explaining a staff members' decision to terminate a client.

Failed to report or call. Has been in thirty day conciliation. This client has had a poor record according to WIN standards that we must abide by. Turned folder over to [the staff member who handles the termination of clients from WIN].

This description emphasizes aspects of the client's involvement in WIN which justify the staff member's action. Specifically, the staff member notes that the client failed to keep his most recent WIN appointment, was already on probation for being uncooperative (thirty day conciliation), and had a poor record in WIN. The staff member also casts her actions as necessary and professionally proper by stating that the client has violated organizational standards to which all WIN staff and clients were accountable. In this and similar ways, staff members used case descriptions to justify their actions and assign preferred identities to themselves and others by emphasizing selected aspects of their clients' life circumstances and the staff-client relationship.

Staff members also voiced justifications of their decisions and actions which were partly intended to counter criticisms of organizational superiors, but were also directed toward potentially troublesome clients and staff members. Consider, for example, the following staff member justifications (expressed during staff meetings) of their definitions of new clients' troubles as atypical and assignment of the clients to WIN statuses involving no job seeking. In both cases speakers justified their actions by portraying the clients as inappropriate referrals to WIN because the clients were not job ready.

> Why should I waste my time with an old woman, dragging her in here, when I have all these other cases that are more serious. It's a waste of my time and her's.

> What am I gonna do with this guy [client]? He shouldn't have been sent [from the welfare department]....I can't do anything for him....Who's gonna hire [this] guy with that thing, brace, on his arm? They [employers] spot him six blocks away. Employers go, "Oh, you have a disability and a [pending] Workman's Comp [Compensation] [law]suit [against a former employer] too." They don't want him. Injured on the job, they think maybe he's accident prone. He probably isn't, just a guy who had an accident. They [employers] go, "Well, he'll probably slip and hurt himself and he's lawsuit happy too."

These statements illustrate how staff members emphasized selected aspects of clients' life circumstances in portraying them as inappropriate candidates for WIN. The first statement emphasizes the client's age and the second treats the client's physical disability as an extenuating circumstance making the client unlikely to find jobs or benefit from WIN services. The second statement is rhetorically significant for, at least, two additional reasons. First, the staff member explains that the client is an inappropriate referral because there is nothing that he can "do for" the client. In this way, the staff member casts helping clients as a central aspect of the staff-client relationship and clients' abilities to benefit from staff member help as a criterion for distinguishing appropriate from inappropriate referrals.

Second, the staff member justifies his portrayal of the client as an inappropriate referral by describing how area employers would respond to him. The portrayal is one way in which staff members used altercasting to achieve their rhetorical ends. It involved constructing a typical employer's perspective by describing how employers would assess and respond to clients in job seeking situations. According to the staff member, employers would be negatively impressed by the client because of his disability (employers want healthy workers), the circumstances surrounding his disability (he was injured on the job and, therefore, might be accident prone), and a pending lawsuit against the employer for whom he was working when he got injured (employers do not want employees who are likely to sue them when they get hurt on the job). The staff member used his portrayal of the typical employer's probable assessment and response to the client to cast the client as unemployable and, therefore, an inappropriate referral to WIN.

Because staff members sometimes changed their definitions of and orientations to clients' troubles, however, their case descriptions and verbal portrayals of the troubles also changed. Indeed, the same general circumstances were sometimes cited to justify new and different responses to clients' troubles. One way in which staff members explained and justified their new orientations was by treating others' understandings of clients' troubles and recommendations for remedying them as new sources of information. Staff members used the information to recast known, but previously ignored, circumstances as relevant facts and social conditions calling for new responses. Indeed they sometimes portrayed their previous definitions of and responses to clients' troubles as mistakes which their new orientations were intended to rectify.

Consider, for example, the case of a client who was initially assigned to a WIN status requiring no job seeking. The staff member justified the assignment by noting the clients' many family and health problems, including a conflict with her ex-husband over custody of one of their children and serious dental problems. The staff member concluded her initial case description by stating, "Because of this, limited [job seeking] is appropriate for [the client] at this time." Sometime later, however, the staff member changed her orientation to the proper solution to the client's troubles, stating that it would be good for the client to get out of the house and focus her attention on something other than her family and health problems.

The staff member used a conversation with an official in another social service agency to justify her reassignment of the client to an organizational category involving intensive job seeking. In doing so, the staff member cast the official's recommendation as a new source of information and facts justifying a change in her orientation to the client and the client's troubles. She explained and justified the change by writing the following entry in the client's WIN file:

[An official from another social service agency] called to inform me of [the client's] situation with her daughter. Her daughter was recently picked up for [committing a crime]. [The official] thinks it would be good for [the client] to start work[ing] to get her out of the house. Placed in [job seeking category] today.

Thus, staff members cited clients' family problems to sometimes justify requiring clients to look for jobs and other times to exempt them from job seeking. More generally, the cases discussed in this section illustrate some of the complexities of the process through which staff members defined and responded to clients' troubles. The process involved ongoing assessments of aspects of clients' lives and the staff-client relationship in light of typical organizational expectations and procedures. It also sometimes involved staff members' reconsideration of the relevance and appropriateness of typical organizational expectations and procedures for properly responding to clients' troubles.

Staff members reconsidered typical organizational expectations and procedures near the end of the research period and used their discussions to justify their redefinition of the concept of client job readiness. They stated that cuts in staff positions and increases in the number of new clients made it impossible for them to adequately monitor and direct clients' job seeking activities. According to staff members, these circumstances required that they reconsider which clients should get their attention and help. In doing so, staff members redefined the concept of job readiness to include clients who were both willing and able to find and hold jobs. Previously, they had defined job readiness to include all clients who were physically and emotionally able to hold jobs, regardless of their desires.

Staff members used the new definition of job readiness to justify reclassifying troublesome clients as not job ready. Consider, for example, the following instructions given to staff members by WIN supervisor about the reclassification of clients in response to these circumstances.

We can only work with those who are job ready, y'know? We'll put them in [a job search category], but all the others in [a category requiring little or no job searching]. They should really be job ready, I mean, if they give us a bad time, mouth off, fight bein' in WIN, ya know, let's put 'em in [the non job-search category]. We'll just concentrate our efforts on those we can help and who want a job. Okay?

Go through your files and see if you can remember who is job ready. Put them in [a job search category]. Only those who are really job ready in [the job search category], you know, those with skills, those who'll show up, I mean show up to look for work. Put all the others in [the non job-search category] and we won't deal with them.

One way in which clients' troubles were initially defined and sometimes reassessed was in negotiations between staff members and others in their work world. The negotiations turned on the presence of extraordinary and extenuating circumstances that made typical organizational expectations and procedures inappropriate. We next consider how such negotiations were organized.

Negotiating Definitions of Clients' Trouble

Staff members' negotiations about the proper definition of clients' troubles were practical interactions focused on how best to solve the troubles. They were organized as claim–counter claim sequences in which one party recommended a solution to the troubles and another responded by countering it. The interactions involved a party who argued that the typical organizational response to clients' troubles was appropriate and another who claimed that a dispreferred response was most appropriate. Although the negotiations sometimes involved recommendations that clients be exempted from WIN, many were concerned with responses which the staff treated as less extreme and dispreferred, such as recommendations that clients be allowed to enter training programs or be temporarily excused from job seeking in order to get help with problems which were keeping them from getting jobs.

Further, in staff meetings and other interactions organized to select a single response to a practical issue, the interactants treated their recommendations as opposed orientations to the issue. In doing so, the interactants cast the interactions as arguments calling for rhetoric intended to gain argumentative victory by persuading others to acquiesce to their claims and recommendations. The staff members' rhetoric was intended to counter others' portrayals of the meanings, contexts and proper solutions to the issues a hand and justify their preferred orientations to them. Consider, for example, the following exchange concerned with the proper definition and response to a new client's troubles. The issue in question involved whether the client was job ready.

> [Staff Member 2 initiated the exchange by stating that the client "might not be job ready" because he was unable to get a job prior to enrolling in WIN. She added that the client might be appropriate for a special program involving no job seeking.]
>
> Staff Member 1: He was gettin' $166 a week from Unemployment [Compensation]. He wasn't looking for a job.
>
> Staff Member 2: You don't know that....Things are tough out there. How can you say that?
>
> Staff Member 1: I know it....I know it because I've had lots of experience. I've had lots of experience with these people. They don't look [for jobs] unless they're pushed a little.
>
> Staff Member 2: Do you think he's ready to get a job? I mean his appearance, age and all that stuff.
>
> Staff Member 1: Yeah, he could be....He could be job ready if he needed to be. There's nothing wrong with him.

This exchange shows how the client's long period of unemployment prior to enrolling in WIN and aspects of his appearance were differently portrayed by staff members taking opposed orientations to the client's troubles. For Staff Member 2, who argued that the client was not job ready, the client's inability to get a job and his appearance signified his shortcomings as a job seeker. The staff member used the portrayal to justify her recommendation to place the client in a program intended to make him job ready. On the other hand, Staff Member 1 argued that the client was job ready and that his extended period of unemployment and appearance reflected his lack of commitment to finding a job, not an extenuating circumstance justifying an atypical response. Staff Member 1 justified his orientation and "won" the argument by offering an explanation to which Staff Member 2 ultimately acquiesced. The explanation was an alternative understanding of the reasons for the client's extended period of unemployment (he was receiving financial aid prior to enrolling in WIN) and justification of the staff members's orientation to the case (it was based on many years on experience in dealing with such clients.).

In sum, staff member negotiations about how to properly define and respond to clients' troubles were organized as rhetorical contests centered in interactants' opposed orientations to clients and their troubles. The orientations were expressed as competing and mutually exclusive categories involving different understandings and responses to clients and their troubles. For example, in the above exchange, the contest turned on whether the client was job ready. The issue was formulated as a mutually exclusive contrast, the client was either job ready (and, therefore, job seeking was an appropriate remedy to his troubles) or not job ready (and, therefore, a less preferred remedy was appropriate). In formulating the issue in this way, the staff members cast their interaction as an argument in which one category and orientation had to prevail over the other.

The above exchange also displays how extended staff member negotiations and arguments were usually resolved in WIN. Specifically, if both interactants persisted in making claims and counter claims, the party arguing for the less preferred response eventually acquiesced. They did so in several ways, ranging from statements that the typical response should be tried and tested to see if it would "really work" to statements that the party arguing for the typical response had the power to impose his or her will on the party arguing for the atypical response. The latter response was a procedure for describing the negotiations as unequal and acquiescing to others' greater power without making them exercise it. In this way, staff members and clients cast their acquiescence as realistic responses to political circumstances, not to the correctness or persuasiveness of others' arguments.

However persons explained their acquiescence, in granting it they agreed to treat typical organizational expectations and procedures as appropriate to clients' troubles and circumstances. One effect of this argumentation pattern was to maintain the established hierarchy of definitions and remedies making up WIN policies and programs as well as the organizational practices intended to implement them. This is not to say, however, that persons arguing for atypical and less preferred responses always acquiesced. Rather, the argumentation pattern associated with the selection of less preferred responses was different. Specifically, such negotiations involved fewer claims and counter claims. Persons who argued for organizationally preferred responses acquiesced to others' claims and recommendations right away or not at all.

Also, in such negotiations, persons who argued for less preferred responses anticipated others' objections and answered them before the objections could be raised. One way in which they sought to anticipate and counter others' objections was by presenting the rationales of their arguments before stating their conclusions and recommendations. In doing so, they sought to persuade others that the clients and troubles at hand were atypical and, therefore, less preferred responses to them were appropriate. Consider, for example, the following exchange which occurred prior to a conciliation meeting. The staff member who argued for termination of the client from WIN anticipated and countered others' possible objections to his recommendation by requesting a staff meeting immediately prior to their meeting with the client. The request signalled the seriousness of the staff member's concern because such meetings were not held for most clients referred to conciliation sessions.

Further, the staff member used the staff meeting to make a case for his recommendation that the client be terminated from WIN. He did so by selectively reading from the client's file, noting her record of "uncooperative" behavior and "bizarre requests." The staff member's review of the client's file included the following items: a number of missed WIN appointments, insolence in dealing with the WIN staff, continuing failure to obtain medical verification for her claim to a disability, a pattern of applying for jobs at the same employers in a nearby city where relatives lived, a claim to having applied for four jobs on a major holiday, and a request for travel reimbursement for an "unreasonable" amount of miles. The staff member concluded by recommending a resolution to the matter to which the other staff member involved in the meeting acquiesced.

Staff Member 1: I don't want this one getting a medical [exemption]. The most we can do for her is to give her two weeks to take a new checkup, and if she doesn't then she's off the grant.

Staff Member 2: I'm not gonna fight ya. I'm just gonna have trouble not laughing during this, its a comedy.

Thus, staff members' negotiations about how to properly define and respond to clients' troubles centered in rhetoric and argumentation. Through their negotiations, staff members and others in their work world produced and justified practical understandings and responses to clients' troubles.

Two major issues emergent in staff members' interactions involved the impact of clients' attitudes and of the recessionary area economy on clients' and staff members' efforts to achieve organizational goals. The issues were significant because staff members and others used them to justify differing orientations to clients' troubles and their proper solution. Persons who portrayed clients' troubles as attitude problems emphasized the ways in which clients' orientations to work, WIN and welfare caused and/or perpetuated their troubles. The portrayal was partly used to justify treating clients' troubles as typical and, therefore, solvable through typical organizational procedures. On the other hand, persons who defined clients' troubles as economic problems emphasized the ways in which the recessionary area economy restricted clients' and others' efforts to fulfill organizational expectations. The definition and portrayal was a major way in which staff members and clients justified treating clients' troubles as atypical and cast typical organizational expectations as inappropriate.

The rest of this chapter is concerned with how these issues were rhetorically formulated and used in staff members' interactions with clients, state officials and each other. We first consider how the clients and staff members portrayed the recessionary area economy as an extenuating circumstance.

Clients' Troubles as Attitude Problems

For the WIN staff, assessment of clients' attitudes was a partial solution to a practical problem. The problem involved distinguishing between clients who were cooperating with the staff and those who were not. The staff members stated that the distinction was important because part of their professional responsibility in WIN involved holding uncooperative clients accountable for their actions. They also stated, however, that the practical constraints of their work circumstance made it difficult for the staff to distinguish between clients who were "really trying to get jobs" and those who were not. The major way in which the staff solved this problem was by classifying clients within contrasting categories made up of clients with good and bad attitudes toward welfare, WIN and employment.

The staff stated that clients with good attitudes wished to get off of welfare as soon as possible by finding jobs, and that such clients recognized that the best way to achieve this goal was to fulfill the assignments made by the WIN staff. On the other hand, the staff stated that clients with bad attitudes were uncommitted and sometimes opposed to getting off welfare, finding jobs or fulfilling their WIN assignments. Described in this way, clients' attitudes towards welfare, WIN and employment were aspects of an enduring disposition toward responsible and irresponsible behavior having consequences for the solution to clients' economic troubles. In so orienting to their clients' attitudes, the WIN staff also justified treating staff-client interactions as signs and tests of clients' orientations toward employment and job seeking.

One way in which staff members used their assessments and classifications of clients' attitudes was to explain clients' past employment problems. They portrayed the problems as most obviously caused by clients' improper actions on the job, but "really" based on clients' improper orientations to employment, particularly their value to employers. Staff members stated that a frequent problem involved clients' unrealistically high evaluation of their value to employers. According to the staff, such clients were often arrogant employees who acted as if many of the "realistic" demands made on them by employers were unreasonable, demeaning and/or "beneath them." Staff members stated that another source of clients' improper behavior on the job was their unrealistic devaluation of their social and occupational worth.

According to the staff, such clients got in trouble on the job because they sometimes responded to otherwise small and insignificant problems by getting defensive, obstinate and/or angry. Consider, for example, the following staff-client exchange concerned with the "real" reasons for the client's past employment troubles. Early in the interaction, the staff member described the client as "having a chip on his shoulder." The staff member uses the rest of the interaction to produce signs and causes of the client's attitude and link it to the client's employment problems.

Staff Member: You know what I think? I think part of your problem is that you don't think very much of yourself. You're down on yourself. The clue is here [in the client's WIN file] where you put down [on a registration and appraisal form] that you don't have any special skills....I don't believe that you don't have any special skills.... But I also think that part of your problems at work are related to you being down on yourself. If somebody says something, then you fly off the handle 'cause you don't think you have anything special to offer.

[The client describes the circumstances associated with his employment problems.]

Staff Member: But the point is that if you didn't have a chip on your shoulder, you wouldn't get so angry.

Further, the process of defining clients' attitudes was open-ended and provisional because the staff sometimes used new sources of information about the circumstances of clients' lives and new understandings of clients' past activities to redefine the sources and solutions to clients' troubles. Sometimes the new assessments were explained as necessary because the staff had initially misinterpreted clients' motives and problems and other times because clients had changed their attitudes. Whatever the explanation, such reassessments had practical consequences for clients' lives, and their relationships with the WIN staff, because staff members used their assessments of clients' attitudes to organize and justify their orientations to the causes of and solutions to clients' troubles. The orientation ranged from treating clients portrayed as having good attitudes as trustworthy and even deserving of participation in special WIN programs (such as vocational training programs) to recommending that clients assessed as having especially bad attitudes be terminated from WIN.

The next two sections are concerned with the ways in which the WIN staff members assessed their clients' attitudes and responded to clients assessed as acting from bad attitudes. We begin with the social organization of attitude assessment in WIN.

Attitude Assessment in WIN

Staff members' assessments of clients' attitudes began with the initial definition of clients' troubles during the registration and appraisal of new clients. One source for the assessments was the application form completed by new applicants and reviewed by the staff immediately prior to their first meetings. The staff members conducting the sessions noted and discussed the clients' responses that they deemed professionally significant, such as unclear or contradictory responses and work experiences that made the clients especially employable or unlikely to get jobs. At these times, staff members also discussed aspects of the application form as signs of client attitude. One such sign was whether new clients were "mandatory youths,"meaning that they had quit school but were still economically dependent on an AFDC recipient.

Staff members treated all mandatory youths as potential sources of trouble and likely to have bad attitudes toward WIN and employment. A staff member explained and justified his orientation to mandatory youths in the following way:

> There's nothing you can do with them. They don't do anything [fulfill their WIN assignments]. Nobody wants them. Their parents can't control 'em.

Staff members also treated other aspects of the WIN application form as signs of bad attitudes. For example, they sometimes portrayed clients who misspelled words that the staff stated everyone should know how to spell, or used incorrect grammar, as possible sources of trouble and having bad attitudes. Two other indicators of attitude frequently used by the staff were the clients' employment records (a work history involving several short-term jobs was treated as a sign of a possible bad attitude) and preferred wage (a high wage was treated as a sign of possible bad attitude.). Consider, for example, the following statement made by a staff member prior to a registration and appraisal meeting with a new client.

> We might have a problem here. [The client] quit a job two years ago at [a local factory]. She was makin' $3.15 an hour and she quit 'cause [reading from the client's application card] "It didn't pay enough to live on." She's been on welfare ever since. She could be a problem right away.

Thus, an initial assessment of client attitudes was sometimes made prior to any face-to-face contact with clients, although it was frequently modified at subsequent meetings. Sometimes the modifications resulted from direct questioning of clients about problematic answers on the application form. But clients' general demeanor during the meetings and their responses to the routine questions that made up the registration and appraisal process were also used to justify the modification of initial assessments. For example, the staff treated clients' answers to questions concerned with the types of jobs for which clients wished to apply, and the circumstances in clients' lives which might interfere with their efforts to find and keep jobs, as indicators of client attitude.

Staff members' initial assessments of their clients' attitudes were subject to further reconsideration and modification in all subsequent staff-client interactions. In this way, staff members treated subsequent staff-client interactions as tests of clients' attitudes toward WIN and employment. Clients who fulfilled their WIN assignments were treated as having good attitudes (or as having passed the test) and those who did not as having bad attitudes (or as having failed the test). Indeed, staff members sometimes explicitly portrayed future staff-client meetings as tests of clients' attitudes and of staff members' initial assessments of the attitudes. Consider, for example, the following staff-staff exchange which occurred after the registration and appraisal of a new client who had cancelled her first meeting, claiming that her car was inoperable.

> Staff Member 1: She looks like a good kid, interested in training.
>
> Staff Member 2: Yeah, she put down [on her WIN application form] that she'll go for training no matter what, even if we don't pay her for it. That's what it takes.
>
> Staff Member 1: That's right.
>
> Staff Member 2: I don't think we'll see her again though. Bet her car breaks down again. She'll want an exemption [from job seeking]. At least she'll say it [the car] broke. That's the way it goes, they say the car isn't running, then it is, then it isn't.
>
> Staff Member 1: I know, but maybe not this time. We'll see if she makes it [to her WIN appointment] next time. That'll tell us a lot.

This exchange also illustrates the variety of factors which the WIN staff used to assess new clients' attitudes. Indeed, the large number of factors the staff members treated as relevant to clients' attitudes made staff assessment of attitudes complex and problematic. They also made all staff members' assessments of clients' attitudes potentially vulnerable to challenge from others who advocated different assessments of clients' attitudes. The challenges and alternative assessments could be justified by citing factors that staff members had ignored or de-emphasized in their initial portrayals of clients' attitudes. As in the above exchange, staff members sometimes even challenged their own initial assessments by considering new aspects of clients' lives as signs of clients' "real" attitudes.

Specifically, Staff Member 1 cited the client's interest in training as a sign that she was a "good kid" and Staff Member 2 elaborated on the portrayal by stating that the client was willing to do "what it takes" to get a job and be successful. But Staff Member 2 countered his initial portrayal and assessment of the client by noting that the client had missed her initial registration and appraisal meeting, and predicting that the client would not cooperate. He justified his prediction by treating the client's cancellation of the meeting as part of a general pattern of behavior that is characteristic of many troublesome clients. Staff Member 1 sought to resolve the dilemma by portraying the next staff-client meeting as a sign and a test of the client's attitude. It was a practical solution to an otherwise unsolvable problem.

Although staff members assessed their clients' attitudes as changing in a positive direction, their major concern in staff-client interactions was in identifying signs of clients' emerging bad attitudes. They justified their concern by stating that part of their professional responsibility involved anticipating client uncooperativeness and taking actions intended to counter it. Thus, bad attitude was honored by the WIN staff members to explain the nature and causes of their clients' troubles. The assessment was also used to identify and justify responses to clients' troubles. Further, the staff distinguished between clients assessed as having different kinds of bad attitudes.

Classifying Clients' Bad Attitudes

Staff members stated that one type of client and attitude called for special staff member concern and treatment while the other called for the stern denial of all special treatment and privileges. The staff members treated the first type of bad attitude as a product of human weakness. More specifically, they treated some clients' bad attitudes as caused by frustration with their attempts to find jobs. Staff members stated that such clients were partly a problem because they had "stopped fighting for themselves." That is, they had lost all hope for getting jobs and no longer cared about being self sufficient. Staff members added that these clients sometimes acted in hostile ways toward the WIN staff, but that their "true" attitudes became apparent when the staff confronted the clients with their WIN responsibilities.

Consider, for example, the following staff member portrayal of an initially hostile staff-client interaction.

> That guy that was in here before. He was hostile and [another staff member] confronted him. He settled down. When it was over and he got ready to leave, I shook his hand. He held it out [staff member holds his hand in a limp manner] and I shook it. I could have done anything with it. There was no resistance. He has nothing inside.

Staff members responded to clients assessed as having this type of bad attitude by impressing upon them the importance of continuing to look for jobs. Consider, for example, the following response to a client with a record of cooperative behavior in WIN. During a regular meeting with his WIN worker, the client expressed frustration over his lack of success in finding a job. The staff member responded by telling the client that finding a job in a recessionary area economy was difficult, but that he must continue looking for a job. She justified the demand by stating that the client would never find a job if he quit looking "just because [he was] frustrated." After the client left the WIN office, the staff member portrayed the client as having an attitude problem and justified the definition in the following way:

> Staff Member: He has an attitude problem.
>
> Observer: What do you mean, he seems to be cooperating, isn't he?
>
> Staff Member: Well, yeah, but he doesn't like looking for work. I could tell that by the way he was talking. I'll have to stay on him to keep him looking. I just won't give him too much to do, 'cause he might get discouraged and give up, but I'll have to keep pushing him.

The staff portrayed clients classified as having the second type of bad attitude as manipulators and con artists who were solely motivated by their short-term interest in remaining on welfare by avoiding employment. According to the staff, such clients were totally untrustworthy and any special requests that they made were treated by the staff with suspicion. Indeed, staff members stated that one of their major professional responsibilities involved identifying such clients and making certain that the clients did not avoid their WIN responsibilities. Staff members justified their portrayals of clients as intentionally uncooperative by citing aspects of clients' WIN records as evidence of their bad attitudes.

Consider, for example, the following staff-staff interaction concerned with a client's request for funding to enter a vocational training program. The staff member supervising the client (Staff Member 1) portrayed the client as a "leaker" and likely candidate for disciplinary action because the client was known to be a manipulator who did not complete her WIN assignments. Nonetheless, Staff Member 2 recommended that the client be allowed to take a series of tests intended to assess persons' vocational aptitudes.

Staff Member 1: Well, [the client] is not going to go into training.

Staff Member 2: I know you don't like the idea, but I think she should have the [vocational] tests and then we can see.

Staff Member 1 [reading from the client's WIN file]: She has already missed a meeting with me [since her recent registration in WIN]. She was twenty minutes late so I gave her an unexcused absence. Before me [prior enrollments in WIN], let's see, she was asked to go to...for tests on [reads a date] and on [reads a date] she hadn't. That was two months, that's plenty of time.

Staff Member 2: But that was when she was getting married. [Smiling.] You know when a woman is in love she doesn't do anything else. That's all she thinks about. You're too tough, have a heart.

Staff Member 1: She doesn't have a good record. She doesn't do what she is supposed to do.

Staff Member 2: Well, okay, maybe we should start by having her follow through on something and I'll talk to her next time about the importance of WIN.... But don't you think people can change? I mean she got rid of her husband and now maybe she's ready to change. People do sometimes realize what's going on and turn their lives around, ya know.

This exchange illustrates how staff members treated aspects of clients' records in WIN as signs of clients' attitudes and used the records to justify practical decisions about how to respond to clients' troubles. It also shows how staff members who recommended "special" treatment for clients sought to discount others' uses of clients' WIN records to predict clients' future behavior and to assess clients' deservingness for special treatment. Specifically, Staff Member 1 justified her rejection of Staff Member 2's recommendation by citing aspects of the client's WIN file which were treated as documentary evidence of the client's bad attitude. Staff Member 2 countered this portrayal of the client and justified her recommendation that the client be considered for the grant by portraying the client's past bad attitude as a product of extenuating circumstances that no longer existed. Staff Member 2 ultimately acquiesced to Staff Member 1, who persisted in portraying the client as unreliable and uncooperative. In doing so, Staff Member 2 agreed to respond to the client and her troubles in the organizationally typical and preferred way, while continuing to claim that her general position was legitimate.

Staff Member Decision Making and Attitude Assessment

In dealing with any particular client's attitude and troubles, WIN staff addressed two related questions: (1) Does the client really have a bad attitude, and if so, what kind? and (2) What is the significance of this attitude for the work of the WIN staff? The questions were often raised during staff meetings and informal staff interactions concerned with making decisions about clients and their problems. In the exchanges, the staff negotiated and developed explanations of clients' "true" attitudes and differentiated between clients with different types of bad attitudes. They also assessed and negotiated the practical relevance of clients' attitudes for the issues at hand. Indeed, staff members sometimes claimed that the circumstances associated with the issues made clients' attitudes irrelevant. The claim was one way in which staff members justified granting special privileges to clients assessed as having bad attitudes.

For example, the staff members' concern for distinguishing between types of clients and bad attitudes was evident in their deliberations about which clients to recommend to employers who requested the names of candidates for job openings. Frequently, WIN staff eliminated clients with bad attitudes on the grounds that they would be undependable and irresponsible workers. But sometimes, bad attitude was assessed as irrelevant to the practical realities of particular jobs. That is, the circumstances associated with some jobs were assessed as extenuating circumstances justifying atypical actions. The assessment was rhetorically produced and justified by staff members who argued that some jobs do not require a good attitude. Consider, for example, the following exchange regarding a client under consideration for a welding job.

> [After several staff members have noted the client's bad attitude and record in WIN, as well as his unstable work history.]
>
> Staff Member 1: Well, I know [he has a bad attitude], but he's supposed to be a really good welder. At least, that's what he says. He said that of all the people at [the client's former place of employment], he was one of the top three.
>
> Staff Member 2: I think he is very good.
>
> Staff Member 3: Maybe he should be referred, I mean welders are kinda, uh, [pause] strange. [Others laugh.] I don't know, they seem to jump around a lot and it doesn't seem to matter....I don't think it's a good job. It's hot and dirty.
>
> Staff Member 4: A lot of these guys are real good welders, they really like to do it. They aren't much otherwise, but they're good welders.

Thus, the process of assessing and responding to clients with bad attitudes was complex. The complexity partly involved assessing whether clients had good or bad attitudes, but it also involved assessing the causes of clients' bad attitudes and relevance of their attitudes for the world outside the WIN office. Usually, however, the WIN staff treated clients' bad attitudes as indicators of potentially troublesome patterns of behavior with consequences for clients' performances in WIN and on the job. The orientation was central to the staff's treatment of clients' job seeking and related activities as tests of clients' commitment to finding jobs and getting off of welfare. We next consider how the WIN staff tested their clients' attitudes.

Testing for Bad Attitudes

Sometimes the test of client commitment involved a modification of the normal job seeking practices of clients, such as with the client discussed above who was classified as having a bad attitude because he did not like looking for work. At his next meeting with his WIN worker, the client was told that he did not have to contact so many employers in the future, but that he would have to get the signatures of the employers that he did contact to verify his claim that he was looking for a job. In other cases, the test of client commitment involved no change in the clients' usual WIN activities, although the clients' participation in the program was closely monitored by the staff who sought to identify signs of cooperative and uncooperative behavior and attitudes.

Regardless of the organization of the tests, the WIN staff recorded their assessments of clients' responses to the tests in clients' WIN files. The records were treated as objective reports on clients' behavior and indicators of clients' attitudes toward WIN and employment. One possible outcome of the usual staff response to clients assessed as having bad attitudes, then, was the creation of a bureaucratic record that confirmed the staff's initial definition of clients' moral character and justified a change in their status as WIN clients and welfare recipients. Indeed, the bureaucratic confirmation of the bad attitudes of clients was an important part of most conciliation sessions because the staff members usually justified their complaints by noting the clients' pattern of irresponsible behavior as recorded in the WIN files.

The following exchange is an example of how clients' attitudes and WIN records were linked and used in conciliation sessions to justify formal complaints against clients. It also shows how staff-client disputes were cast as products of clients' bad attitudes and staff members' previous actions toward clients as efforts to hold then accountable for their irresponsible attitudes and behaviors. In this way, the staff members simultaneously deflected client criticisms of themselves and WIN, and justified making formal complaints against clients.

[The client is asked why she refuses to fulfill the assignments made by her WIN worker.]

Client: He [indicating the WIN worker] has a bad attitude toward us [pause] lower-class people. He doesn't care about us, he thinks he's better than we are.

Staff Member: Well, let's see what sort of attitude you've had toward WIN. [He reads portions of her WIN record dating back several years. The emphasis is on the times when the client has missed appointments with her WIN worker and failed to complete her WIN assignments.] Now, if I have a bad attitude toward you, it may be because of your record.

However, WIN staff members' efforts to identify uncooperative clients and take actions intended to hold them accountable was made complex by their assumption that they sometimes made mistakes in assessing clients' attitudes. The assumption was significant partly because the staff members used it to justify reconsidering their previous assessments of the causes of their clients' actions and troubles.

Reassessing Clients' Bad Attitudes

Staff members' reassessments of clients' bad attitudes were initiated when the staff treated an event or client statement as new and unanticipated information. In making sense of the new information, the staff members sometimes redefined their clients' attitudes and justified new responses to the clients' troubles. Thus, a second possible outcome of the staff's routine testing of clients for bad attitudes was the redefinition of clients' troubles. In one case, for example, a client was defined as having a bad attitude at his initial registration and appraisal session. From later meetings in which the client appeared to be unenthusiastic about looking for jobs, the WIN worker "confirmed" this assessment.

Several weeks later, however, the client asked that his WIN meetings be moved to a later time in the day because his wife preferred to sleep late in the morning and he found it difficult to wake, clean, dress and feed his children before his early morning appointments. With this information, the WIN worker reconsidered her previous definition of the client's attitude and problems. The staff member explained her reconsideration in the following way, "He may have a problem in his marriage if his wife sleeps so late and he has to do all this work." Further, the WIN worker recommended that a social worker visit the home to determine the nature of the client's marital problem and to provide appropriate counselling.

A more complex and dramatic shift in the definition of the sources of client troubles involved the case of a former WIN client with a reputation for having a bad attitude. When reapplying for the WIN program, the client answered a question on the WIN application form regarding his occupational preference by stating, "I always wanted to be a politician to speak for us peasants." Staff members conducting his registration and appraisal meeting commented on this statement during their pre-meeting review of his file, treating it as another indicator of his bad attitude. Specifically, they stated that the client clearly had not "learned anything from before" (his previous WIN enrollment) or changed his attitude. The staff members elaborated on their portrayal of the client by recounting previous troublesome episodes with the client that they described as indicators of his true attitude. They concluded that they should be prepared for the client to be manipulative and should refer him to a conciliation meeting at the first sign of trouble.

The following exchange took place during the subsequent meeting with the client. It began with a staff member response to the client's request to be reassigned to the job club, an assignment usually reserved for clients assessed as having good attitudes.

> Staff Member: You're not going back to job club, I'm going to work with you. Job club won't do you any good. You have a real attitude problem. You know that? Look at this [points to the WIN application form], anyone who puts down "I always wanted to be a politician to speak for us peasants" has an attitude problem.
>
> Client: That's how I feel. That's how I am. I cut right through the bullshit and get to how it really is.
>
> Staff Member: I cut through the bullshit too and I'm telling you this is inappropriate. I have only seen you a short time here and I can see that you are angry. How do you think job interviewers see you? Part of your problem is your attitude.

This exchange also shows how staff members confronted clients with their assessments. Staff members did so by describing clients' problems as related to their bad attitudes, pointing to signs of their bad attitudes, and linking clients' attitudes to their inability to get jobs. As in the above exchange, staff members stated that employers could also see clients' bad attitudes and, consequently, would not hire them. In this way, staff members cast clients' actions in the WIN office as signs of enduring attitudes which guided clients' behavior in other settings. It was central to the staff's claim that clients with bad attitudes toward WIN were also likely to have bad attitudes toward job seeking and employment. The above exchange is also an example of how staff members sought to hold clients accountable for their attitudes and failure to find jobs by confronting them.

One part of this client's initial assignment was to take a series of diagnostic tests at the Alternative Education Center. Clients without high school diplomas were routinely required to take such tests. He returned to the WIN office two weeks later with the scores of his tests which were much higher than he or the supervising staff member had expected. The unexpectedly high test scores became the basis for the staff member's reconsidering and changing of his previous assessment of the client. The following exchange was part of the process through which the client's attitude toward WIN and employment, and the causes of his employment and other troubles, were reconsidered and recast as educational problems centered in the client's improper academic placement in grammar school. The exchange also shows how such a recasting of the client's attitude and the causes of his troubles was related to new responses to the client's employment troubles.

> Client: I never thought I could do all this.
>
> Staff Member: I know, you've got a brain. You just haven't always used it to make wise choices. [Client shakes his head in agreement.] I'll bet your problem in school was that you were bored.
>
> Client: Yeah, I was bored. About ninth grade I lost all interest.
>
> Staff Member: You didn't do the work, you acted out and you got put in the dummy group. You should have been in the gifted class or at least at the top of your group. You got in a group that didn't care and you didn't either.
>
> Client: Yeah, I'll bet that was the problem. I always liked reading and math.
>
> Staff Member: Maybe you should think about college. You could go to [a local college]. What would you like to be, an engineer?

The staff member also cited the scores of the diagnostic tests in subsequent interactions with other staff members who

expressed skepticism about his new definition of and orientation to the client's troubles. The staff member further justified
the new definition and orientation by portraying the client's
past troubles in a new light. Specifically, he stated that the
client's unstable work history was a sign of the client's bore-
dom with intellectually undemanding jobs, conflicts with the
WIN staff showed the client's desire to be independent and in
control of his life, and past criminal activities as involving
creativity and intelligence. Finally, the staff member portrayed
the case as demonstrating the importance of using objective
measures (such as the diagnostic tests) to test staff members'
subjective assessments of clients' attitudes. In doing so, the
staff member also justified typical organizational procedures,
particularly the testing of clients assessed as having bad attitudes. He stated,

> Here is an example of a gross error on my part....This just
> shows ya why we need outside input, hard data. I mean, if you
> look at the guy [client], you'd never guess he could do that
> [well on the diagnostic tests]. He did tell me that he was good
> in school, but I didn't believe him. But he probably was good.
> Well, it just goes to show ya.

The client's responses to the test scores and his expressed
desire to further his education were also treated as signs that
he was ready to change his life and orientation to work and
family. Thus, each subsequent staff-client encounter became a
test and confirmation of the new assessment of the client's
attitude. The staff member who supervised the client portrayed subsequent staff-client interactions in the following way:

> He's really changed. He's taking control of his life. It's so easy
> to work with him now....For the first time he feels like he's
> like everybody else and so he's taking over. He's doing all the
> work now. It's easy for me. I wish I could do the same thing
> with [another troublesome client].

Ultimately, the client was given financial and other aid to
attend a local college, a very different action than that predicted by the staff members based on their initial assessment
of his attitude. He was also portrayed by the staff as the "success story of the year" and the change was reported to state
WIN officials as a sign of the staff member's unique ability to

work with "troublemakers." As one staff member stated about the case: "It's so good to hear about a thing like this, where everything turns around. Their [a client's] attitude changes, you know."

Attitude Assessment and Trouble Definition in WIN

In sum, attitude was one of several defifnitions used by the WIN staff members in explaining and justifying their orientations to clients' troubles. Other definitions considered here involved treating clients' troubles as family or educational problems. The alternative definitions were partly important because staff members used them to justify orientations and responses to clients' troubles that were different from those associated with clients' troubles defined as attitude problems. Staff used the family problem definition to justify a counselling response and the education problem definition to justify helping clients enroll in educational programs.

The staff also used the family and education problem definitions to produce new understandings of clients' past actions and troubles. The actions and troubles were cast in new social contexts which justified the staff's new definition of the clients' orientations to employment, welfare and WIN, as well as new responses to the clients' employment troubles. Thus, a major issue in staff members' negotiations with others in their work world centered in whether clients' troubles were "really" attitude problems or stemmed from another source. Staff members managed this issue by negotiating short-term agreements about the sources and proper responses to clients' troubles, agreements that were always potentially open to reconsideration and change.

Another definition and orientation to clients' and staff members' troubles involved portraying them as economic problems caused by the recessionary area economy. It was a major way in which WIN staff and clients justified their claims that typical organizational expectations and procedures were inappropriate. We next consider how troubles were defined as economic problems in WIN.

Clients' Troubles as Economic Problems

One aspect of the WIN staff's everyday work involved assessing the condition of area labor markets. According to staff members, assessments were necessary because although area labor markets were generally tight, the number of job openings found within them changed from week to week. Consequently, some weeks more jobs were available for WIN clients than others. Indeed, much of the staff's concern for assessing the condition of area labor markets focused on identifying signs of economic changes having consequences for themselves and their clients. For example, the staff cited reports that some area employers had called back some laid-off workers and that other employers who had previously refused to accept any job applications were now accepting them as evidence that the local labor market was "opening up a little bit."

On other occasions, however, the staff stated that area labor markets were getting tighter. They justified this claim by noting the increased numbers of new clients with good work records and skills applying for WIN and the number of area employers who had recently laid off substantial numbers of workers. The WIN staff used their assessments and classifications of area labor markets as tightening up to justify treating their clients' troubles as, at least partly, economic problems. So defined and treated, clients were not held fully responsible for their troubles. Equally important, the staff used such assessments of area labor markets to justify modifications of typical client assignments and the development of new programs intended to better achieve organizational goals.

For example, they used assessments of area labor markets as tightening up to justify reductions in the number of job contacts clients had to make each day and a requirement that clients without high school diplomas attend classes intended to help them get high school equivalency certificates. The assignments were portrayed as a realistic response to tightening labor markets because clients who continually failed to find jobs might become frustrated and develop bad attitudes. Staff also stated that clients without high school diplomas were unlikely to get jobs in highly competitive markets. Finally, the staff justified the development of a series of job-search skills workshops by stating that getting jobs in ever tightening area labor markets required sophisticated job seeking skills.

The staff members' interest in assessing the impact of tight area labor markets on their clients' lives and troubles was also related to their interest in assessing clients' levels of job readiness and attitudes. Specifically, staff members stated that getting jobs in tight area labor markets was a competitive process, and many clients who might have gotten jobs when area labor markets were more open were no longer attractive to employers. That is, the recessionary economy made some clients less job ready than in the past. The staff also stated that clients intent on avoiding their responsibilities in WIN could easily use the recessionary area economy as an excuse for not looking for jobs, and other clients were likely to become frustrated by their failure to find jobs. According to the staff members, then, their normal interest in assessing clients' attitudes toward employment, welfare and WIN was increased in a recessionary economy.

The definition of clients' troubles as, at least, partly, economic problems was a potential aspect of all staff member interactions concerned with assessing and solving clients' troubles. These concerns were central to most staff-staff interactions which sometimes focused on the unique circumstances associated with individual clients' troubles and other times on the general causes of clients' troubles and staff members' difficulties in remedying them. They were also an aspect of many staff-client arguments concerned with clients' efforts to find jobs. Although different in some ways, all of these turned on two related questions: (1) Are typical organizational expectations and procedures appropriate for the issues at hand? and (2) Are staff or clients culpable for their demonstrated or anticipated inability to fulfill organizational goals?

The definition and negotiation of clients' troubles as economic problems was also an aspect of staff–state official interactions, particularly those concerned with setting agency performance goals. Staff members used this definition of clients' troubles to justify their recommendations that typical organizational expectations and procedures be suspended. They did so by portraying area labor markets as external constraints that limited their efforts to fulfill organizational expectations, including the expectation that agency goals be raised each year. Staff members also used this portrayal to assign a preferred identity to themselves which emphasized how they were victims of circumstances over which they had no control and for which they should not be held responsible.

We next consider how these questions were negotiated in the annual planning meeting intended to establish agency performance goals for the next year. Although the purpose of the meeting was to develop a plan that was mutually agreeable to local staff and state officials, it was developed by separately negotiating several different agency performance goals. The meeting and negotiations took nine hours to complete.

Negotiating Labor Market Effects in the Annual Planning Meeting

Although the local supervisor and state official generally agreed that area labor markets were tight, they portrayed the practical implications of economic conditions in opposed ways. Specifically, the local supervisor portrayed area labor markets as a *barrier* to the staff's achievement of typical organizational expectations and goals. She did so by describing area labor markets as closed or closing, and staff members as unable to respond to these conditions in the ways recommended by the state official. In this way, the supervisor defined clients' and staff members' troubles as economic problems while deflecting the state official's criticisms of the staff for past or projected failure to achieve organizational gcals.

Consider, for example, the following claim made by the WIN supervisor in response to the state official's request that the supervisor explain and justify her recommendation that one of the agency's performance goals be left unchanged.

> Well, basically, there isn't gonna be any growth in the labor market and [a major employer] is laying off. They're not gonna bring many people back [after the layoff].

The local supervisor elaborated on and extended her claim that area labor markets were a hurdle by citing other, related factors that made it difficult for staff members to fulfill organizational expectations. She stated, for example, that a large number of clients were in need of money to repair their cars in order to look for jobs, but the state WIN office had cut funds for the car repair program. The supervisor linked problems caused by cuts in funding for car repairs to the recessionary area labor markets by stating that many WIN clients' needed to seek jobs in cities some distance from the WIN office. She stated,

> A lot of our people [clients] have to go out of the area for jobs. In fact, a lot go to [another state] and those people are really going to be hurt by the cut in [car repair funds]. They need to have their cars repaired to get those jobs.

The local supervisor further justified her recommendation that the agency's performance goals be left unchanged by portraying the existing evaluation system as narrow and unfair, particularly in light of the recessionary area economy. The supervisor also offered an alternative approach that she described as more realistic, because it took account of the broad range of problems dealt with by the staff. She stated,

> ...but I don't understand why we only look at this in terms of going up [higher performance goals]. I think there are a lot of services that are important that are part of a broad program. We have to deal with a lot of [clients with] job barriers, especially now [in the recessionary area economy], and they aren't counted in this [evaluation] system. But they're part of a broad [evaluation] system. That's one of the reasons I think we may be at our maximum [performance level], 'cause we're having to deal with these problems.

These claims were countered by the state official who portrayed area labor markets as a *hurdle*. She stated that local staff members described area labor markets as a barrier in order to excuse and justify their lack of commitment to fulfilling organizational expectations and goals. According to the state official, although area labor markets were tight, they were still sufficiently open that clients could find jobs. Through her response, the state official rhetorically cast local staff members' orientations to the recessionary area economy as a measure of their commitment to meeting organizatonal expectations. She also emphasized how the problem of reduced job opportunities for clients could be overcome through extra effort by staff members and the development of better approaches to job seeking and client guidance.

According to the state official, one such approach involved encouraging clients to car pool. She stated,

> Have you tried any carpooling where several people go together [to look for jobs]? That can save money and everyone doesn't have to have a good car that way.

In this way, the state official justified an orientation to local staff members which acknowledged that they were not responsible for the tight condition of area labor markets and, on the other hand, treated them as accountable for their responses to tight area labor markets.

Justifying Typical Organizational Expectations

More specifically, the state official responded to the super-visor's portrayals of area labor markets as barriers in four related, but different ways. The responses focused on (1) the existence of evidence indicating that area labor markets were not "really" a barrier; (2) the advantaged position of the local agency (relative to other WIN agencies in the state) in over-coming the constraints of tight area labor markets; (3) the local supervisor's improper motives in refusing to acquiesce to the state official's recommendations; and (4) additional (non-market) facts that made it necessary that the local agency have higher performance goals. The first two responses were rhetorical procedures for relativizing the practical implications of the area economy on local staff and clients. They were also procedures for casting the local supervisor's portrayals of tight area labor markets as an extenuating circumstance as an excuse intended to justify the local staff's lack of commitment to organizational goals.

The first response centered in the claim that the local staff members' portrayals of area labor markets as a barrier were overstated. The state official substantiated her claim by citing evidence showing that local staff could meet organizational objectives, despite the tightness of the area economy. Specifically, the state official pointed to the local agency's past record of performance which exceeded the goals recommended by the local supervisor. Consider, for example, the following responses made by the state official to the supervisor's claims that agency performance goals should not be raised because of the recessionary area economy.

What about the past figures? You've done a lot better that that in the past, even with the economic problems.

A lot of what happened [job loss in the local economy during the past year] wasn't planned for [in the existing performance plan] and you still got...over your goal. You have to be real-istic and look at what you have done, look at the figures. You really need to raise the [recommended performance goal]. That's not enough.

The second statement is particularly significant because it shows how the state official simultaneously countered the supervisor's claim and emphasized local staff members' responsibility to try to achieve organizational goals, despite the recessionary area economy. The state official stated that economic problems could be overcome through more realistic and efficient efforts by staff members. The state office elaborated on her claims by describing how other WIN agencies had developed "creative," new programs in order to more efficiently and effectively help clients find jobs. She also reviewed and criticized the inefficient organization and operation of specialized programs in the agency.

Consider, for example, the following criticism and instruction given by the state official about the operation of the local agency's job club program.

> The job club should be full-time and [the staff member supervising the job club] shouldn't be used for other things. Job club is one of the most efficient ways of getting people jobs. It only involves one staff person and several clients. It is important that it be run properly. That person shouldn't be expected to do anything else.

The state official's second response to the local supervisor's claim that agency performance goals should not be raised centered in the claim that all local WIN agencies were not equally affected by tight area labor markets. She explained that although area labor markets were tight, they were not as tight in this area as in other parts of the state. The state official partly justified her claim by describing the circumstance in another area of the state where the largest employer was about to shut down completely. She also responded by noting that employers were centralized in area labor markets, making it easier for clients to apply for several jobs each day and increasing their chances of finding jobs. The state official contrasted this situation with that in rural areas also experiencing economic recessions.

> Yes, I know but your [recession] problem is less serious than in the [rural] Districts where people [clients] have to drive for miles just to get to the [WIN] office. They're really hurting.

When the local supervisor agreed with the state official's comparison, the state official asked, if WIN staffs in other parts of the state were willing to commit themselves to increased productivity, then shouldn't the local staff also be willing to make such a commitment?

The state official's third response focused on the local super-visor's improper motives in continuing to portray area labor markets as a barrier to achieving higher performance goals. Specifically, the state official portrayed the local supervisor's position as a game which was both unwarranted and short-sighted. She stated,

A lot of locals [local staff members] treat these planning ses-sions like a game. They want [performance] figures that they know they can exceed. They don't want the pressure from higher goals, but they don't realize that this affects funding. We're competing with [WIN programs in] other states and the better the locals [local agencies] do, the more money we will get. It's really that simple.

In so responding to the local supervisor, the state official questioned the local staff members' commitment to fulfilling their organizational responsibilities and recast the issue at hand as unrelated to the condition of area labor markets. She recast the issue by portraying the "real" reasons for raising the agency's performance goals as competition for funds with WIN programs in other states. In this way, the state official sought to make the condition of area labor markets irrelevant to the negotiations. The state official elaborated on this claim in sub-sequent exchanges in which the local supervisor continued to portray the recessionary area economy as a relevant extenuat-ing circumstance.

Specifically, the state official's fourth response emphasized the larger political and economic significance of higher perfor-mance goals for the entire WIN program. The state official noted that state and federal officials were considering the development of a number of alternative programs to WIN, includ-ing one called workfare. She stated that, if implemented, the programs would compete with and perhaps replace WIN. In so responding, the state official not only cast the condition of area labor markets as irrelevant to the interaction, but she also stated that raising the agency's performance goals was man-datory. In part she stated, "But,...we have to have higher goals than last year. We're dealing with this workfare thing and we need to look as good as we can. We have to do better."

Through this rhetorical procedure, the state official organ-ized the interaction around a new theme involving new rele-vant facts. She also justified her insistence that the agency's performance goals be raised and sought to elicit a statement of acquiescence from the local supervisor.

Acquiescing to Typical Organizational Expectations

Although their negotiation of new agency performance goals was sometimes extended, the local supervisor acquiesced to all of the state official's major recommendations and demands. In doing so, however, the local supervisor sometimes challenged the fairness of the goal-setting process. She did so by portraying state officials as unconcerned with the needs and desires of local staff and emphasizing the differences in power and influence between herself and the state official. The first response was a rhetorical procedure for casting typical organization expectations and procedures as unrealistic and counterproductive. Specifically, the local supervisor stated,

> Well, okay, fine, I'll go along with you on it [the proposed performance goal]. But you see, ... we [the local staff] think that [state officials] play games with us too. We run a good program here, but no matter how well we do, you keep raising the figures [goals] on us. I mean, it seems that you [local staff] should only do the minimum required and then you won't be asked to do so much. I already have one person [local staff member] who feels that way. She claims that if she does too much more than her quota, then she'll be asked to do a lot more.

Thus, in acquiescing to the state official's recommendation, the local supervisor also described the expectation that agency performance goals would be raised each year as a source of frustration for local staff. She states that the practical result of the expectation was that the local staff felt that it could never do enough to satisfy state officials and, the more local staff do, the more it was asked to do. Finally, the local supervisor described the expectation as a source for some of her problems in motivating local staff members.

The second way in which the local supervisor acquiesced to the state official while questioning the fairness of the negotiations involved describing her acquiesce as a realistic response to a dispute that she could not win. The response was a rhetorical procedure for casting acquiescence as the only choice available to the local supervisor and assigning a preferred identity to herself. The identity emphasized the local supervisor's sincerity in advocating for her preferred performance goal and dependence on the state official who could positively or negatively influence other state officials' reactions to the plan under negotiation. The local supervisor accomplished these rhetorical ends to the following way:

> State Official: That puts you under your present performance. I can't support anything under your projected performance [for the current year]. You propose it [to the administrators at the state WIN office] and add an addendum justifying it if you want, but I can't support it.
>
> Local Supervisor: Well, we might as well go with [the figure recommended by the state official] then.
>
> State Official: Why?
>
> Local Supervisor: Look,...you're a powerful person in [the state WIN office]. You will affect how this plan is read, I know that. I can't propose something without your support and expect it to pass. That's silly.
>
> State Official: Do you really think you won't make it?
>
> Local Supervisor: Yes, but let's go with it, if that's what you'll support.

Through their negotiations, the staff official and local supervisor produced practical understandings of the impact of the area economy on local staff members' work and of staff members' obligation to fulfill organizational expectations and goals.

Conclusion

This chapter has focused on the ways in which WIN staff members and others in their work world defined clients' troubles. It shows how WIN staff members', clients' and state officials' descriptions of the relevant facts and contexts associated with clients' troubles were more than reports on social conditions having implications for staff members' and others' choices and actions. They were rhetorical procedures for defining the issues at stake in their interactions with one another. Although staff members', clients' and state officials' positions on practical issues were different and sometimes opposed, they sought to remedy their potential arguments by persuading others that their understanding of and preferred responses to the issues at hand were logical, accurate and/or necessary.

Thus, the production of problematic social relationships and persons' efforts to rhetorically manage them were inextricably linked in WIN. We next consider how WIN staff justified organizationally preferred solutions to clients' troubles.

6

Justifying Solutions in WIN

Although their positions within them varied, the justification of organizationally preferred solutions to troubles was a central and recurring aspect of staff members' interactions with clients, each other, and state officials. In staff-client interactions, staff members argued that organizationally preferred solutions were appropriate. Whereas in staff member–state official interactions, they claimed that organizationally preferred solutions were inappropriate. Staff members took varied positions on this issue in their mutual interactions. We have already considered how solutions were negotiated in the annual planning meeting involving the local WIN supervisor and a state official. Previous chapters have also analyzed how solutions were negotiated in staff-staff interactions. Staff members did so by making and negotiating complaints about one another's work performances, negotiating whether clients were job ready, and considering clients as candidates for special programs.

Staff members generally justified organizationally preferred solutions in their mutual interactions by portraying themselves as constrained by WIN policies and procedures. In this way, they cast themselves as having no choice in responding to the matters at hand. Consider, for example, the following staff member justifications (made as a part of training committee meetings) for denying clients' requests for permission to enter long-term educational programs, an organizationally dispreferred solution to clients' troubles. The first statement was made in response to a staff member who persisted in arguing that a client should be allowed to enter an educational program.

> You don't understand. We can't do that. [State WIN officials] won't let us, we are limited by them. It's not that we wouldn't

176

want to do it if we could, but we can't. Especially, we can't have people in four year [educational] programs.

Staff Member 1: I know, but if you ask me, all of these restrictions are just stupid. I think this guy deserves training.

Staff Member 2: Well, it's not a matter of personal feelings, we have to set them aside and do what we're supposed to do.

These negotiations are also rhetorically significant because they show how staff members simultaneously justified organizationally preferred solutions and instructed others on a proper orientation to the matters at hand. The orientation centered in staff members' setting aside their personal feelings in the interest of fulfilling their organizational responsibilities. Staff members described the orientation as a necessary and professionally responsible response to their work circumstances. They also stated that they could be held accountable by organizational superiors for their orientations and responses to the proper solution of clients' troubles.

The rest of this chapter is concerned with the ways in which staff members justified organizationally preferred solutions in staff-client interactions. As in their mutual interactions, staff members justified organizationally preferred solutions by emphasizing clients' responsibilities in WIN and the importance of clients developing dispassionate orientations to the solution of their troubles. Specifically, staff members instructed clients on the practical importance of setting aside their personal desires in the interest of fulfilling their WIN obligations to make sincere efforts to find jobs. Staff members described this response as both a central part of solving clients' troubles and an organizational responsibility for which clients could be held accountable by the staff.

We first consider how staff members initially justified organizationally preferred solutions in their first encounters with new clients. Later sections analyze how staff members elaborated on their initial justifications by treating area labor markets as hurdles (not barriers) to clients' employment troubles, devaluing clients, and emphasizing the importance of taking account of employers' desires and interests in seeking jobs. Inferiorization of clients was a central aspect of staff members' instruction of clients about how best to solve their troubles.

Initial Justifications

Staff members used aspects of the registration and appraisal of new clients in WIN to introduce clients to and justify typical organizational expectations, including organizationally preferred solutions to their troubles. The introductions and justifications involved three major staff member concerns about clients and their troubles. The first concern focused on clients' employment expectations, which staff members stated were often unrealistically high. The second centered in identifying job prospects for clients that offered sufficient pay and related benefits so that, if they got the jobs, clients could realistically hope to get off of welfare. Finally, staff members used registration and appraisal meetings to impress upon new clients the importance of looking for jobs in sincere and systematic ways. According to the staff, these concerns were central to their professional roles in WIN and, in managing the concerns by justifying organizationally preferred solutions to clients' troubles, they were fulfilling one of their major professional responsibilities.

The rest of this section is concerned with the ways in which staff members managed these concerns in registration and appraisal meetings. We begin with their concern for countering clients "unrealistically high" employment expectations.

Justifying "Realistic" Client Employment Expectations

A major aspect of staff members' interest in clients' employment expectations involved clients' income expectations. According to the staff members, they were obligated to help clients get jobs that would make the clients economically self-sufficient, regardless of the wages associated with them. Staff members stated that his organizational responsibility was sometimes at odds with clients' expectations, because some clients assumed that they had a right to turn down any jobs that did not offer the same pay as their previous or preferred jobs. They explained that clients' previous or preferred jobs were often in industries which offered wages that were substantially higher than those offered by "typical" area employers. Thus, one aspect of staff members' orientation to registration and appraisal meetings was a concern for identifying clients who were likely to make unrealistically high income demands on employers.

One source used by staff in identifying such clients was the WIN application form which included a question about clients income expectations. Staff members treated clients who answered with unrealistically high wage demands as potential sources of trouble, with this response calling for staff member instruction about clients' WIN obligations to accept any jobs that would make them economically self-sufficient. Consider, for example, the following staff member response to a client's "unrealistic" answer to this question.

> [Reading from the WIN application form,] "How much will you work for? Ten dollars an hour!" Dreamer, that'll change. They have to take something [jobs] for $3.35 an hour, whether they want to or not.

Staff members also treated new clients who reported "good" job histories and/or marketable skills on their WIN application forms as perhaps having unrealistically high income expectations. Staff members used subsequent registration and appraisal meetings to confront such clients with their assessments and counter client explanations which staff members treated as excuses. Consider, for example, the following staff-client exchange which began when the staff member asked the client if he was demanding a high wage in job interviews. The client stated that he was not and asked the staff member why she asked the question.

> Staff Member [reading the client's file]: I'm trying to figure out why you don't have a job yet with this [work] history. You're highly employable even in this labor market.
>
> Client: Hey, lady, I've applied for everything [job] down to $3.75 an hour. They ain't hirin', nobody is hirin'. That's the problem.
>
> Staff Member: Yeah, well, maybe. With a record like this though, you should have a job.

Staff members also used the subsequent registration and appraisal meetings to instruct new clients on WIN expectations about job seeking, including "appropriate" wages and salaries. In doing so, they also justified the organizationally preferred solution to clients' troubles which involved, first, finding jobs that would get clients off of welfare and then looking for jobs that were more interesting or offered higher incomes. Staff members justified this solution to clients' troubles by stating that research showed that it was easier to get good jobs if the job applicant already had a job. In this way, staff members cast finding a minimally acceptable job, not clients' long-term occupational goals, as the central issue in staff-client interactions.

Consider, for example, the following exchange which began when Staff Member 1 asked the client if he would be willing to move to another community if he was offered a job that was known to be available there.

> Client: No, I don't want to do that, not for $4.25 an hour.
>
> Staff Member 2: Well,...your [AFDC] grant is for $529 a month, that means you hafta take anything over $3.60 [an hour].
>
> Staff Member 1: That's right. Take a job and then look for something better.
>
> Client: How can you so that, ya hafta spend all your time working?
>
> Staff Member 1: No, that's not true. It's easier to find a job if you have a job. You can take a day off for an interview. After you've been there [at the first job] for awhile ask for a day off. You don't have to tell 'em you're looking for work.

In so portraying the best solution to clients' troubles, then, staff members countered clients' "inappropriate" orientations to their troubles and justified requiring clients to look for jobs that paid less than clients preferred. A related aspect of staff members' concern for clients' employment expectations involved the types of jobs preferred by clients, regardless of the incomes associated with them. According to the staff, many clients did not understand that the reason that many of them were unemployed was because area businesses were cutting back on their workforces, particularly in the fields that clients most preferred. Staff members instructed clients on this "fact of life" and sought to counter their "unrealistic" expectations by instructing them on the practical consequences of the recessionary area economy on their circumstances.

Consider, for example, the following staff-client exchanges about the types of jobs that new clients would like to seek:

> Client: Well, I've always worked construction. [I would like] something like that, construction, carpentry. I can do that.
>
> Staff Member: Anything else? Construction is a little slow right now, as you know...How about material handler, that's

sort of a general [employment] category? Fork lift [operator], you've done that, right? [Client nods agreement.] General factory work? That broadens things for you.

Client: Here on this roofing thing, I just want you to know that I don't want nuthin' less that $22 a square [yard]. I'm too damn good. I've been on roofs since I was four [years old], worked with my dad.

Staff Member: Well, we'll be looking for something for you. Okay? It might not be in the roofing though. There aren't a lot of jobs in that area right now.

These exchanges illustrate how staff members initially justified organizationally preferred solutions to clients' troubles by describing clients' preferred lines of work as unavailable. They used the descriptions to justify modifying clients' lists of acceptable jobs to include jobs that clients initially treated as unacceptable, but which the staff described as both acceptable and available. Staff members described clients who were willing to so modify their job seeking lists as realistic and those who resisted their recommendations as unrealistic and uncommitted to finding jobs and getting off of welfare. Indeed, staff members sometimes confronted new clients with their assessments of clients' job preferences as unrealistic. They used the assessments to justify asking clients to "be realistic" by seeking less preferred jobs.

Consider, for example, the following staff member response to a client who stated that he would like a job similar to the one that he previously held.

Well, yeah, of course, but with [a major employer] laying off four to five hundred people in the last month and an unemployment rate in [the area] of,...what do you realistically think you can do? You know, this is the problem you are going to have to face in the future.

Finally, staff members sought to counter clients' "unrealistically high" employment expectations and justify organizationally preferred solutions in their interactions with clients whom they described as uniquely employable. As in the following staff member instruction of a new client, the staff did so by, first, describing aspects of clients' work histories as factors that made them more employable than other WIN clients. Staff members then added the caution that, despite the clients' work histories, they might still have to accept less than their preferred jobs. In this way, staff members sought to instruct clients on the practical "facts of life" associated with being a WIN client.

> You aren't as bad off as a lot of people [clients] we see here. You have experience, a nice [WIN] application. You may have to take something less than you want. You know that, don't you?

Identifying Adequate Jobs

Although a major staff member concern in registration and appraisal meetings was identifying clients with unrealistically high employment expectations, staff members also stated that some clients had unrealistically low expectations. Staff members stated that the latter clients underestimated their value and options in area labor markets. One way in which clients underestimated their value was by failing to recognize and use all of their employment related skills in identifying appropriate jobs for which to apply and in presenting themselves to employers. According to staff members, these clients were naive and incompetent job seekers who were their own worst enemies.

Staff members responded to clients with "unrealistically low" employment expectations by emphasizing skills that were de-emphasized by clients and employment opportunities that the clients should pursue, based on their previously devalued skills. Consider, for example, the following staff-client exchange which began with the staff member asked the client if he could weld, a question frequently asked of new male clients.

> Client: Well, sort of. I used to braze and do auto bodies, but not much.
>
> Staff Member: Would you like to go to [a local welding firm to apply for a job]? You can start there as a general worker and they'll teach you welding. You don't have to be trained [in welding to get a job] there as long as you know the basics. What do you think?

Staff members further explained that some clients were unrealistic because they did not fully grasp the variety of factors that competent job seekers take into account in organizing their job seeking activities. According to the staff, one such factor was pay, but an equally important factor was the availability of fringe benefits, such as health insurance. Thus, although the staff members emphasized clients' responsibilities to look for and accept jobs, they did not treat all jobs as equally desirable or appropriate for clients. Rather, they encouraged most clients (those assessed as job ready) to look for jobs that would provide adequate incomes and, where possible, fringe benefits so that clients would be self-sufficient.

Staff members did so in registration and appraisal meetings by discounting the "inadequate" jobs suggested by clients and suggesting alternative jobs that the staff described as more likely to provide for the clients' needs. Consider, for example, the following staff-client exchanges concerned with establishing clients' initial job seeking plans.

[The client stated that he would look for clerking jobs.] Well, how about general labor. I'm concerned that you can't make enough money as a clerk. They don't get paid much. How about welding? Do you know how to do that?

Client: I don't know, anything, waitress, cashier, I guess. I applied for those jobs at [lists the places where she as applied for jobs].

Staff Member: Well, how about looking at the receptionist jobs before you look for those? There are more benefits with that kind of work. You're not likely to get any benefits with those other jobs. So, lets' put those [receptionist jobs] down.

Finally, the staff stated that some clients were unrealistic because they overestimated the value of training programs as solutions to their troubles. They stated that these clients' inadequate understanding about what it takes to get good jobs was reflected in the clients' assumptions that if training programs existed, then good jobs must exist for program graduates. Staff members treated the assumption as a problem calling for a rhetorical response when clients expressed interest in entering training programs, an organizationally dispreferred solution to most new clients' troubles. Specifically, the staff responded by portraying the programs as unlikely to lead to good jobs for clients and, therefore, unrealistic and inappropriate responses to clients' troubles.

Consider, for example, the following exchange which occurred after the client was told that WIN could not provide funds to send her to X-ray technicians' school.

> Staff Member 1: You know, if you're interested in training, you should think about something else. You should get to know the [area] labor market, it's really tight.
>
> Staff Member 2: Yeah, you know the [your] accounting and secretarial skills are probably more marketable....
>
> Client: Oh, I didn't know that. I thought it was a good program.
>
> Staff Member 1: That's a program that's been around a long time.... They've turned out a lot of people [graduates].
>
> Staff Member 2: Oh, yeah, there are X-ray technicians all over the place. Your accounting is really a better bet.

In discounting training as a solution to the client's troubles, staff members simultaneously instructed the client on how to "properly" assess job training programs and justified requiring her to look for jobs calling for skills that she already possessed. Staff members sometimes elaborated on this response by describing the ways in which the WIN training committee assessed clients' requests for permission to enter training programs. The instruction emphasized the training committee's primary interest in placing clients in training programs that would result in good jobs for clients. In this way, staff members also justified de-emphasizing clients' desires in making decisions about their training requests.

Defining a Proper Job Seeker Orientation

The third way in which staff members justified organizationally preferred solutions to clients' troubles in registration and appraisal meetings involved instructing clients on a "proper" job seeker orientation. Most generally, staff members described the orientation as a serious attitude toward job seeking and commitment to getting jobs. One way in which staff members sought to instruct new clients on a proper job seeker orientation and impress upon them the importance of their responsibilities was by describing clients' previous job seeking activities as inadequate. Consider, for example, the following staff-client exchange:

> Staff Member: How many jobs have you applied for since you've been unemployed?

Client: I don't know, maybe six.

Staff Member: That's not many. You're gonna hafta look [for] more than that if you want to find a job.

Another way in which staff members instructed new clients on a proper client orientation to job seeking and WIN was by telling clients that they must look for a designated number of jobs each day. Staff members treated clients' responses to the assignments as signs of their attitudes toward employment and welfare. According to the staff, clients who objected to the assignments might have "bad" attitudes which staff members sought to manage by insisting that the clients fulfill their WIN assignments. As in the following staff-client exchange, staff members responded to clients' objections by acknowledging that the assignments involved considerable client effort but insisting that, nonetheless, clients fulfill the assignments.

Client: Five a day, you mean five [job] applications a day?...That's a lot.

Staff Member: Uh, huh, it is.

Client: Do you think that's reasonable? I hafta walk and there aren't that many jobs out there. That's twenty five a week, a hundred a month....Five a day seems unrealistic to me. I mean five a month seems more realistic...

Staff Member [interrupting the client]: Five a month? Oh, no, no way.

This exchange also shows one way in which staff members dismissed new clients' appeals to extenuating circumstances that made typical organizational expectations and solutions inappropriate for them. Specifically, the staff member dismissed the client's appeal by refusing to consider his claim that placing five job applications a month was a more realistic expectation than that proposed by the staff member. In doing so, the staff member also dismissed the clients' rationale for making the claim and recommendation, the rationale being that "there aren't that many jobs out there" and he had to walk to apply for jobs.

Another way in which the staff responded to such client appeals was by portraying WIN as a job and assessing clients' requests based on the typical expectations of employers. Frequently, staff members sought client acquiescence to their claims by asking clients how they thought a typical employer would respond to their claims and requests. Consider, for example, the following staff-client exchange concerned with a client's claim that she could not take any jobs requiring her to work during the early morning. The client stated that she was needed at home every morning to give an insulin shot to her mother-in-law.

> Staff Member 1: Well, I don't know if that is a legitimate job barrier. I mean, if you had a job and you said you couldn't come in [to work] because you have to give your mother-in-law her insulin, that wouldn't be a legitimate excuse, would it?
>
> Client: Well, no, I guess not.
>
> Staff Member 2: Well, that's how we look at it here, too. This is a job too and you'll hafta make arrangements at home so you can be here when you're supposed to.

Finally, staff members responded to new clients who expressed frustration about their inability to find jobs by instructing them on the practical "facts of life" associated with being unemployed in the recessionary area economy. The responses partly involved describing area employers as having an advantage over job seekers and, consequently, stating that clients would have to become more assertive and committed in seeking jobs. The responses were also rhetorical procedures for making clients responsible for solving their troubles and casting continued client complaints as excuses. Consider, for example, the following staff-client exchange.

> Client: I get awful tired of bein' told that they'll [employers will] call [to arrange for job interviews] and they don't. I go around and fill out applications and don't hear.
>
> Staff Member: Maybe, you hafta be a little more aggressive? [The staff member describes how the client might call employers to remind them of the need to arrange job interviews.] That's the way things are now. They don't hafta call.

Staff members reiterated and elaborated on the justifications and instructions considered in this section in subsequent staff-client interactions, ranging from orientation to conciliation meetings. We consider how they generally did so in the next section.

Elaborating on Initial Justifications

Staff members built on their initial justifications of organizationally preferred solutions to clients' troubles in two major ways. First, staff members anticipated and countered clients' criticisms of preferred solutions through instructions intended to persuade clients that the solutions were legitimate, effective and/or necessary remedies to their troubles. For the staff members, their most important instructions emphasized the need for clients to do whatever was necessary to find jobs and fulfill the assignments made by the WIN staff. They stated that the emphases were related because finding jobs in tight labor markets required that clients commit themselves to finding jobs and take advantage of the help and expertise of the WIN staff.

Consider, for example, the following staff member response to a client's question about the purposes of a job-search skills workshop.

> I believe that there are jobs out there. I'm not sayin' that there are jobs for everyone or that it will be easy. It may mean that you have to widen your search and commute or even to relocate. It may mean that you'll have to rethink what you want or can do. Maybe you have a special skill or talent that you can use to get a job that you haven't been using. That's one of the things we'll work on here.

A major part of the staff's instruction of clients in orientation meetings and job-seach skills workshops involved written exercises. Some of the exercises were intended to teach clients basic job seeking skills and an organizationally preferred orientation to job seeking. The exercises often involved critiquing fictional cases of persons' job seeking efforts. Staff members used the cases and clients' discussion of them to justify an organizationally preferred orientation to job seeking. Consider, for example, the following staff-client exchange about a fictional job seeker who was late for a job interview. Initial discussion of the case centered in whether the employment agency that arranged the job interview had given the job seeker all of the information that she needed to keep the interview.

> Staff Member: Okay, let's say that the employment agency didn't do what it was supposed to do. She's the one who's lookin' for a job and, even if it didn't do what it's supposed to,

who's still responsible for findin' out how to get to the interview and bein' there on time?

Several Clients: She is.

Staff Member: That's right, you're always responsible for
bein' at the interview.

Thus, one way which staff members used formal exercises
was to assign full responsibility for finding jobs to clients.
Other exercises were intended to assess aspects of clients' work
experiences, aptitudes and values which staff members portrayed as relevant to the solution of clients' troubles. For example, one aspect of the job-search skills workshops was a survey
of clients' values, which staff members justified by describing
it as a tool for identifying appropriate jobs for clients. Staff
members stated that different types of jobs involved different
types of values and one possible source for clients' past
employment problems was the lack of fit between their values
and those underlying their jobs. Clients identified "appropriate" jobs by comparing their values survey results with a list
of jobs and the jobs' central values which was provided by
the staff.

For the staff, then, one way in which clients could avoid
their past employment problems in the future was by assessing their values and identifying appropriate jobs to seek. Staff
members also instructed clients to be realistic about the types
of jobs that they selected as appropriate to seek. Specifically,
they stated that clients should not pick jobs that involved education or training that clients did not possess, but should focus
on jobs that they could immediately begin to seek. On occasion, the relationship between clients' values (as identified in
the values survey) and clients' assessments of appropriate jobs
became matters of staff-client negotiation. Staff members used
the negotiations to justify both the test results and their claim
that clients could find appropriate jobs without further education or training.

Consider, for example, the following staff-client exchange.
The client's values survey indicated that she was well-suited
for the medical field and the staff member suggested that she
apply for nurses' aide jobs. The client stated that she did not
think such jobs were appropriate.

Client: Well, it's not like bein' a nurse. There's no diagnosis,
I mean, there's nothing medical about it. You deal with

patients, er, as regards getting them water, changin' sheets, stuff like that. I mean, I don't think that's gross or nothing like that, I just don't think I'd like it.

Staff Member: Well, [nurses'] aides provide a lot of psychological care for patients. They spend more time with patients than [nurses] who are busy with a lot of patients and have a lot of responsibility. They don't have time to talk to patients the way an aide can. I've had people tell me that they wouldn't want to move up to be a registered nurse 'cause they don't want the responsibility, they like spending time with patients.

Client: That's right, I never thought of it like that. I guess I don't know enough about the occupation.

The second way in which staff members justified organizationally preferred solutions involved countering clients' questions about and criticisms of aspects of the program. They did so by challenging the factual accuracy of and/or motives underlying clients' questions and criticisms and offering alternative understandings of the issues in question which the staff portrayed as realistic. According to staff members, their responses were intended to counter the excuses used by clients to justify their lack of commitment to organizational goals and to persuade them to take responsibility for solving their troubles. Consider, for example, the following staff member explanation of his efforts to encourage client criticisms and questions about WIN during orientation sessions.

Of course, it helps that I've heard all these questions and complaints before, so I have answers. When you first start and you hear, something [a client complaint] for the first time, you think, "Oh my God, they're right." But you learn what they're up to. They're just trying to figure out how to get out of doing something. You have to be firm with 'em. They may be only five minutes late [to the orientation meeting], but they have got to learn that they are responsible for themselves.

The circumstances most emphasized by staff members in justifying organizationally preferred solutions to clients' troubles were tight area labor markets and clients' characteristics that reduced their chances of getting jobs. According to the staff, the circumstances were related because one consequence of the increased competitiveness of tight area labor markets was that employers could be more selective in making hiring decisions than in the past. The staff further stated that one part of a realistic client orientation to getting jobs in tight area labor markets involved taking account of the advantaged position of employers in the employer-job seeker relationship. Thus, according to the staff members, one purpose of the assignments that they made of clients was to instruct clients on the practical concerns associated with employers' assessments of them as prospective employees, particularly the ways in which they might be negatively assessed by employers.

We next consider how staff members justified requiring clients to look for jobs in the recessionary area economy.

Area Labor Markets as a Hurdle

The staff stated that persuading clients to look for jobs was made more difficult by tight area labor markets because clients used the condition of the area economy as an excuse to avoid looking for jobs. Such client excuses involved describing area labor markets as a barrier keeping them from getting jobs, despite their best efforts to fulfill their WIN assignments. Although the staff members assigned a variety of motives to clients so portraying area labor markets, they stated that one of their major professional obligations involved anticipating and countering such client excuses. They did so by portraying area labor markets as a hurdle to clients' achievement of economic self-sufficiency.

The staff stated that a basic aspect of clients' overcoming the limits imposed by tight area labor markets involved clients' taking responsibility for their lives and troubles as well as not making excuses for them. Thus, staff members' descriptions of the impact of tight area labor markets on the solution of clients' troubles was partly intended to persuade clients that job seeking and related WIN assignments were realistic responses to their troubles. They were also intended to persuade clients that solving their troubles by getting jobs was largely a matter of individual initiative and commitment. Finally, staff members used their portrayals of area labor markets as a hurdle to justify treating the inferiorization of clients as a central part of solving their troubles.

We first consider how staff members used portrayals of area labor markets as tight to cast client initiative and commitment as a solution to their troubles.

Client Initiative and Commitment as a Solution

One way in which the staff cast client initiative and commitment as a solution to their troubles was by responding to vague and general statements made by clients about their desires to find jobs and get off of welfare. The responses focused on the practical importance and meaning of having a good attitude toward finding employment. Consider, for example, the following staff member response to a client statement that he wanted to find a job and get off of welfare.

> Okay, with an attitude like that, I can assure you that you'll do alright, you'll find work. Everyone who wants a job will get one. It won't be easy. The job market isn't real good right now, but there are jobs, you hafta really look and work to find 'em. It may mean taking something less than you wanted and may mean working your way up. You may even hafta be willing to relocate someplace else, like...but you hafta be willing to do these things if you really want a job.

Thus, staff members partly sought their rhetorical goals in staff-client interactions by claiming that job openings existed in the area and WIN clients were qualified for many of them. The staff further justified the claim and the related requirement that clients look for jobs by noting that WIN records showed that clients were getting jobs "even though the labor market is bad right now." Staff members described this circumstance as a reflection of many clients' commitment to doing "whatever it takes to get jobs" and the fact that, despite the recessionary area economy, employers still needed new workers. The explanations were rhetorical procedures for justifying clients' continued job seeking. Consider, for example, the following staff member responses to clients who claimed that there were no jobs available in the area economy.

> [The client stated that "there ain't no jobs out there" and employers are "layin' off [employees] all over the place."] Yes they are, but you just hafta really look. Ya know, sometimes they're layin' some people off and hirin' in other areas. It really depends on what they need and what you can do.
>
> There are jobs out there, it's just that you hafta really look. It's tough, but the people who really want them, we have

people every month who find jobs because they really want them. It's tough though 'cause employers don't hafta advertise in the paper, if they do, they get swamped with app's [job applications]. So, you hafta really look to find the jobs now.

Staff members responded to clients who persisted in claiming that there were no jobs available to them by asking, "Where do the numbers [showing that clients had gotten jobs] come from then, if people aren't finding jobs?" In so responding, staff members sought to persuade clients that their employment troubles could be solved if they continued to look for jobs and fulfill other WIN assignments. The question was also a rhetorical procedure for casting clients' continued objections to looking for jobs as excuses. The logic of the response may be restated as: "Since there is documentary evidence that clients are getting jobs, your claims to the contrary must be justifications for your lack of commitment to finding a job and getting off of welfare." Staff members responded in this way to clients who expressed frustration about their inabilities to find jobs.

Consider, for example, the following staff member response to a client who stated that he was depressed because there were no jobs available in the area. The client responded to the staff member's claim that other clients had gotten jobs by asking how long they had been in the program prior to finding jobs and stating that he "bet that they looked for a long time before they found anything." The staff member's response was both a justification of his demand that the client continue to look for jobs and a rhetorical procedure for casting the client's claim to depression as an excuse.

> Like I said, some people are in [WIN] a week, two weeks or eight months [before they find jobs]. But the important thing is what is the common denominator they all had?...I mean they kept looking and looked at several different things [jobs]. When they couldn't find something in one area, they looked in other areas. They were willing to bring down their expectations. They didn't stop just because they got depressed.

In this way, the staff member attempted to persuade the client to continue looking for jobs while holding him accountable for this potentially bad attitude. Staff members also sought these goals in job-search skills workshops, where they instructed clients on a proper client job seeking attitude which included clients not allowing themselves to become so depressed that they stopped looking for jobs. One implication of the instruction was that although clients could do nothing about area economic conditions, they could control their attitudes toward welfare and employment. Clients could choose to overcome the constraints of the area economy by continuing to look for jobs and making sacrifices in order to get the jobs or they could choose to give up in the face of adversity. Staff members portrayed the latter choice as a negative response which would ultimately make clients' troubles worse.

One way in which staff members who conducted the job-search skills workshops instructed clients on the importance of a positive attitude toward employment was by asking clients to identify positive and negative responses to their troubles. Staff members described clients' responses as choices having different implications for the solution of clients' troubles. Consider, for example, the following staff member response to such an exercise. A client stated that his problem "is not having a job and [that] it makes me feel useless." The positive solutions noted by the client and others in the group included making better use of the local Job Service Office, attempting to improve the client's level of self-esteem and finding someone to push him so he wouldn't give up looking for jobs. The negative solutions were to stay in bed all day, purposely "blow" job interviews and "get down" on himself. The staff member concluded,

> Sure, you can get down on yourself and blame the world for your problems. You can say that it isn't my fault and everybody's out to get me. That's a real negative solution, to give up, quit trying. But it doesn't do you any good, does it? You aren't going to deal with your problem positively by looking at it that way.

WIN as a Solution

Staff members also portrayed WIN programs and activities as sources of help in overcoming the constraints of tight area labor markets. One way in which staff members did so was by describing selected WIN programs as special opportunities and privileges for clients. The descriptions were rhetorical procedures for anticipating and countering clients' questions about their assignment to the programs. As in the following staff member statement made at the outset of a job-search skills workshop, staff members sometimes sought to manage potentially troublesome clients by describing them as different from most WIN clients and, therefore, more deserving or likely to benefit from the programs to which they had been assigned. In this way, staff members sought to produce a preferred client attitude which partly involved appreciation of the staff's interest in them and their troubles.

> It's a real privilege for you people to be in this class. I hope you realize that. The fact that you are in this class means that the [WIN staff members] see a real prospect for you. Maybe this class will open some prospects for you. At least, we hope so. I hope you appreciate that.

According to the staff, a major source of help that several WIN programs and activities offered clients involved identifying client skills and experiences that clients might use to more effectively seek jobs. Staff members elaborated on and justified this claim by emphasizing the negative effect of tight area labor markets on clients' job seeking efforts. Specifically, staff members stated that getting jobs in the recessionary area economy involved developing effective job seeking skills and strategies, such as those taught in WIN programs. Consider, for example, the following staff member announcement that the participants in a job-search skills workshop would be assigned to the Job Club upon completing the workshop.

> That's an extension of what you've been doing here. You'll be doing that when you get back in [the regular] WIN [program]. You'll all be going into what's called a job club and you'll continue the search you've started here. You'll be out there interviewing strangers like you've been doing here, looking for jobs and information about jobs. That's the most effective way of finding a job 'cause about 60 to 65% of jobs are never advertised. That's cause employers don't know they have a job available. They know they have a need, but they don't know that they need a worker. By getting out there and talking to people, you can show them that they need you. That's especially important now, in this lousy job market...It's tough right now and you hafta do this kind of search, it's not enough to use the newspaper [to identify job openings] anymore.

Finally, the staff anticipated and sought to counter clients' resistance to their WIN assignments by portraying the assignments as necessary steps in getting jobs. The portrayals were one way in which the staff cast clients' participation in WIN as a test of their commitments to finding jobs and getting off of welfare. Consider, for example, the following staff member justification of an assignment concerned with the proper ways to write letters of application to prospective employers. It was given to clients in a job-search skills workshop.

> There are a couple of ways of looking at this. You can say I don't wanna do this bullshit or you can try to learn how to do it. I know, myself, I didn't wanna to do this for a long time and so when I'd see an ad in the paper for a job calling for a letter of application, I'd pass it up 'cause I didn't wanna bother with it. So I screwed myself out of a lotta jobs that way. Sure you can get a job at [a local factory] without writing a letter, but what are you gonna do? You're gonna end up sweepin' the floor or workin' on a machine, but what kind of job is that? The better jobs call for a letter of application. More and more employers are requiring letters of application.

The staff member anticipated and sought to counter client resistance to the assignment by portraying clients' responses to the assignment as signs of their orientations to job seeking and employment. Specifically, clients who resisted doing the assignments were cast as not being willing to do what it takes to get good jobs.

Inferiorization as a Solution

Much staff member instruction of clients about how to get jobs in tight area labor markets was also a justification of inferiorization as a solution to their clients' troubles. Staff members inferiorized clients by devaluing them and portraying them as marginal participants in the area economy, that is, as persons having little value and few choices in area labor markets. The staff members justified their inferiorization of clients by portraying it as an effort to get clients to face the "facts of life" associated with being unemployed, welfare recipients in a recessionary economy. For the staff, an important sign that clients had realistically faced and accepted these facts of life was their willingness to comply with the staff's demands and recommendations. In this way, staff members cast their inferiorization of clients as a source of help for clients and a professionally responsible activity.

Staff members also inferiorized clients by instructing them on a proper orientation to employer-employee relations. The staff emphasized employees' subordinate position in the relationship and the practical necessity that employees do whatever their employers asked, including tasks that they might find unpleasant or degrading. Staff members justified this orientation to employee-employer relations by portraying it as both morally proper and necessitated by tight area labor markets. Consider, for example, the following staff member claims made in a job-search skills workshop. The clients were reporting on interviews that they had done with friends and neighbors who were employed. The client reported that the interviewee stated that "the thing she liked the least about her job was being told what to do" by her bosses and being reprimanded by them for "goofing off."

> Staff Member 1: Well, that's what bosses are supposed to do. Isn't it? . . .
>
> Staff Member 2: You know, the economy is real bad right now and ya can't do that anymore. You've gotta be willing to go along with employers today or you'll be replaced. There are a lot of people out there lookin' for work.

Such instruction and inferiorization of clients was also an aspect of staff-client interactions about clients' job seeking efforts. Consider, for example, the following exchange which began when the client reported that his former employer, who had fired the client, had called to offer him a new job. The client stated that he declined because he disliked the former employer and did not want to do the tasks associated with the offered job.

> Staff Member: Ya shoulda taken it. If my boss told me to pick up a broom and go sweep the parking lot, that that was gonna be my job from now on, you'd see me out there [makes broom sweeping motions with his arms]. In this job market, ya gotta do whatever the employer wants.
>
> [The clients describes how unreasonable the former employer was in their past dealings; the client got hurt on the job because the former employer made a "bad" decision, and the boss got angry when the client suggested a better way of organizing his work. The client stated that his former employer told him that he "was not paid to think."]

Staff Member: That's too bad that you got hurt, but ya know, he [the former employer] was right. You aren't paid to think, only to do the job. It's not your responsibility if your boss makes bad decisions.

These exchanges show how staff members sought to counter clients' "improper" orientations to employment by discounting clients' and employees' interests and desires. In doing so, staff members also sought to anticipate and counter clients' excuses for their employment records and failure to find jobs.

The next two sections further consider how staff members treated inferiorization as a solution to clients' troubles. We first consider how staff members rhetorically cast WIN clients as inadequate job seekers and then how the staff instructed clients on how to positively impress employers.

WIN Clients as Inadequate Job Seekers

According to the staff members, many of their clients had inflated notions about the types of jobs that they could reasonable expect to get because they were unable and/or unwilling to objectively assess themselves as job seekers and prospective employees. The staff explained that one source for clients' unrealistic expectations and assessments was their inability to distinguish their desires from the practical circumstances of their lives and troubles which made clients' desires unrealistic. For example, the staff members stated that many of their clients did not understand that their lack of education and job skills, records of unstable employment and/or dependence on drugs and alcohol were job barriers reducing clients' chances of getting jobs. The staff also stated that such practical circumstances made it imperative that clients be willing to modify their occupational desires and expectations and otherwise accommodate themselves to the desires and interests of employers, if they wished to get jobs.

The staff sought to persuade their clients to adopt realistic orientations to their troubles by offering alternative assessments of their value in area labor markets that emphasized how selected client traits and circumstances were job barriers which clients would have to take into account and effectively manage in order to get jobs. The staff portrayed their assessments as objective evaluations and used them to devalue clients as job seekers and prospective employees. They did so by making two major claims which emphasized (1) the typical-ness of clients and their troubles and (2) local employers' nega-tive assessments of clients as prospective employees. The claims were rhetorical procedures for casting clients as inade-quate job seekers and making clients responsible for solving their own troubles.

The first claim involved treating clients and their troubles as typical of employed persons. It was one way in which staff members cast their clients as members of an anonymous social category made up of similar types of persons and trou-bles. The staff did so by identifying client traits which they portrayed as typical of unemployed persons and factors keeping them from getting jobs. Consider, for example, the following instruction given to a group of new clients during an orien-tation meeting The instruction was intended to explain and justify an exercise in which the clients identified personal and life style traits that might hinder their efforts to find jobs. The traits included: poor driving record, lack of vocational skills and training, criminal record, physical and mental health problems, poor attitude toward work, and poor personal appearance. The exercise was also a way of casting clients' unemployed status as a salient identity and selected aspects of clients' lives as signs and causes of their troubles.

> Okay, I'm gonna hand out a paper now called "Characteristics of the Unemployed." It's a list of things, problems, that a lot of unemployed people have, things that hold them back from getting a job. The list was put together by a labor market specialist in the Job Service...and it shows the most com-mon job barriers of people who come to the Job Service for help, not just WIN clients. So, go through the list and pick out the things that apply to you. Nobody will mark every one of them, at least I hope not. [laughter] Then, I want you to think about how to get rid of these problems. These are things that you and your WIN worker will have to work on if you really want a job. Okay, I'll give you a little time to look at the list. Be honest with yourself now, you know whether you have a prob-lem or not, then we can help you work on it

Thus, staff members' instruction of clients on how to prop-erly assess themselves as job seekers and prospective employ-ees emphasized clients' inadequacies and the ways in which clients were responsible for their troubles. The instruction was a major way in which the staff devalued clients and justified organizationally preferred solutions to clients' troubles. The staff partly did so by portraying the staff-client relationship as a source of help for clients wishing to overcome their inadequacies as job seekers.

The second and most frequent way in which the staff attempted to persuade clients to develop realistic orientations to the solution of their troubles involved assessing clients from the standpoint of a typical employer. The staff used the assessment to devalue clients as prospective employees and justify their claim that effective job seekers take account of the employer's perspective. One way in which the staff introduced their clients to the typical employer's perspective involved formal exercises similar to the one analyzed above. The exercises focused on clients' traits and experiences that positively and negatively affected their chances of getting jobs. The exercises required that clients cast themselves in the role of employers and then evaluate themselves as prospective employees. The staff explained that the exercises were intended to get clients to analyze themselves and their troubles from a different perspective.

Consider, for example, the following instruction given to a group of new clients during an orientation meeting.

> Okay, now we want you to think about what you have going for you in finding a job What is there about you that would make an employer hire you ahead of somebody else? You know, maybe you have good references or you can operate a machine. Something like that. And then, what is holding you back in getting a job. And don't put down the local economy. Be specific about qualities that you have that might be a problem.

The instruction is also rhetorically significant because it shows how staff members anticipated and countered possible client claims that the recessionary area economy was a job barrier. They did so by instructing clients to only consider personal qualities keeping them from getting jobs and not the area economy. In this way, the staff member cast clients' troubles as personal problems that were solvable through individual initiative and WIN participation.

Staff members also used clients' self-assessments based on the typical employer's perspective in justifying WIN assignments which did not promise to make clients economically self-sufficient. The issue involved clients whom the staff assessed as unlikely to ever be fully self-sufficient and independent from welfare. The staff stated that it was enough for such clients to hold part-time or low paying jobs, but the clients sometimes objected. The staff responded to such clients' objections by asking the clients to assess themselves from the standpoint of area employers. The assessments emphasized clients' devalued vocational characteristics and disadvantaged position in dealing with area employers. In doing so, the staff sought to persuade clients to accept partial dependence on welfare realistic and necessary.

Consider, for example, the following staff-client exchange concerned with the client's desire to find a job that would make her economically self-sufficient. To that end, the client had recently quit a job paying too little to fully support her and her family. The staff member replied that the client should have kept the job and accepted partial dependence on welfare as a fact of life. He justified his claim by stating that the job was the best one that the client was likely to get and that to think otherwise was unrealistic.

> Client: ...but I want to get off welfare.
>
> Staff Member That's an admirable goal and I'd like to see you off of welfare too, but how are you going to accomplish this? You'd need to make about twelve hundred dollars a month to go completely off of welfare. Given your skills, what employer would pay you that kind of money?
>
> Client: Well, none I guess.
>
> Staff Member: Okay, so maybe you should start by looking at lesser paying jobs to start. You may even have to start with part-time work, 'cause this labor market is tight right now.

The staff explained that such exercises and assessments were realistic and necessary because clients would not solve their economic troubles until they learned to look at themselves from a typical employer's perspective. They added that, based on the assessments, clients could develop job seeking strategies that emphasized their positive characteristics and de-emphasized those which employees treated as undesirable.

The staff justified the job seeking strategies by portraying them as rational and necessary accommodations to clients' disadvantaged position in the recessionary area economy. Put in Adam's (1978) language, this orientation to the solution of clients' troubles was centered in the assimilation of clients into employers social worlds. It was intended to make clients appear to be like employers by identifying salient aspects of the typical employer's perspective and strategically managing impressions of self to positively impress employers.

Taking Account of the Employer's Perspective

The WIN staff's instruction of clients on how to take account of the typical employer's perspective focused on how clients' appearances influenced their chances of getting jobs. The staff treated appearance as more than dress and grooming; it included any aspect of the client's presentation of self that might make a positive or negative impression on employers. Thus, their instruction of clients on how to make a proper appearance was concerned with all aspects of the job seeking process, ranging from initial telephone inquiries regarding the availability of job openings to job interviews. Basic to the staff's instruction was a concern for the ways in which employers use job seekers' appearances to assess their moral character and desirability as employees. The staff started that employers use their assessments to screen job applicants and eliminate those assessed as undependable, incompetent, or of bad moral character.

In part, such staff member instruction of clients was intended to emphasize the impersonal and arbitrary nature of employers' first impressions and how employers made important hiring decisions based on them. It was also intended to deflate clients' "unrealistic" expectations by identifying aspects of clients' appearances that the staff portrayed as job barriers. Consider, for example, the following staff member instruction of a new client which focused on the client's lack of a high school diploma.

> You left something out here,...Under employment barriers you put "None." You've got a big handicap, you don't have a high school diploma. When you fill out a job application and you put down that you only have a ninth grade education, you're at a disadvantage. Lots of times the only thing an employer sees is the application and on paper you have a

handicap. Right away your application gets tossed into a special category and you're out of a job. The employer doesn't even interview you to find out whether you're intelligent or, er, you know, that you can do the job.

This statement shows how staff members simultaneously devalued clients and cast employers as a source of uncertainty and trouble for clients. The staff member did so by, first, portraying the client as handicapped because he did not have a high school diploma and then describing the "typical" employer's orientation to job applicants with this handicap; he/she throws away their job applications. In this way, the staff member simultaneously casts area employers as arbitrary and a major source of trouble for clients and instructed the client on the "facts of life" associated with his circumstances.

According to the staff, employers use a variety of indicators in making their assessments of job applicants. For example, clients were instructed on how to properly complete job application forms which were described by the staff as the basis for employers first impression of the applicant. Applications that were incomplete, were sloppily written or contained spelling errors were described as giving an impression of incompetence, laziness and/or a bad attitude. Indeed, the staff stated that virtually any aspect of job seekers' backgrounds and conduct might be used by employers to draw unfavorable conclusions about their desirability as employees. Consider, for example, the following staff member instruction of clients about how to explain to prospective employers why they quit previous jobs.

Staff Member: Never bad mouth a former employer 'cause the guy [employer] who reads your app [job application] is gonna think you'll blame his company too [for troubles at work]. Employers don't want people with bad attitudes. Put down something else, like, uh, er...
Client: Like, "found a better position."
Staff Member: Yeah, that's good. It sounds like an advancement.

Staff members stated that such instruction was intended to impress upon clients that "getting good jobs is a serious business." They also used the instruction to justify their concern for identifying job seeking strategies intended to make a good impression on employers.

Making a Good Impression With Employers

The job seeking strategies emphasized by the staff centered in anticipating employers' negative assessments of aspects of clients' appearances and developing responses intended to counter the assessments. Staff members identified such strategies by instructing clients on how to properly seek jobs and on employers' practical concerns in assessing prospective employees. They also negotiated these issues with each other and with clients who sometimes asked how to properly assess and manage potentially troublesome aspects of their lives in light of the typical employer's perspective. Consider, for example, the following exchange which occurred in a job search skills workshop.

The clients were completing an exercise made up of "Questions That Employers Frequently Ask" during job interviews. A client asked one of the staff members directing the session if she should tell an employer that she does not get along with her family. In considering the question, the staff members conducting the session cast the client's family circumstances as a possible job barrier by asking "Don't employees want people who come from good families?" They also negotiated the practical usefulness of lying in the interest of making positive impressions on prospective employers and, ultimately, identified an alternative strategy for managing the problem.

> Staff Member 1 [to Staff Member 2]: ...how about this [question], "How do you feel about your family?" What if people come from a bad family situation, shouldn't they fudge [lie] a little bit here?
>
> Staff Member 2: Well, I don't know.
>
> Client: How about "We're not close?"
>
> Staff Member 1: Yeah, ya could, but I'm not sure if they should say that. Don't employers want people who come from good families, ya know close? If ya don't, then maybe you should fudge a little?
>
> Staff Member 2: What if the employer knows your family?
>
> Staff Member 1: Well, then you can't in that case.
>
> Staff Member 2: Well, if you're [applying for jobs] out of the [local] area, maybe you could get by with it [fudging]. Maybe a better thing to do might be to ask what they [employers] mean by the question or what they want to know about your family.

In many staff-client encounters, the staff members cast themselves in the role of employer and the clients' conduct and appearances in the WIN office were treated as indicators of their conduct and appearances in employment settings. The staff stated that the practice was justified because many clients did not know how to properly present themselves in formal settings and, for this reason, they were eliminated from many jobs. Although they did not defend the employer's perspective that they expressed, the staff's assessments focused on problematic aspects of the clients' presentations of self in the WIN office. The staff used the assessments to display for clients the logic and importance of taking account of the employer's perspective in presenting themselves in employment settings.

Consider, for example, the following exchange involving a client who came to the meeting accompanied by his children who remained in the waiting area of the WIN office while he met with two staff members. During the meeting a staff member stated that the client should not bring his children to the office in the future. The client then explained the circumstances making it necessary on this day. The staff members justified their claim by instructing the client on typical employers' negative assessments of his actions and the practical consequences of their assessments. The staff members' response was also a rhetorical procedure for casting their assessment of the clients' actions and their recommendations as an impersonal and realistic analysis of the circumstances faced by clients in dealing with employers.

> Staff Member 1: You see, the problem really isn't [with] today. We want you to understand that you shouldn't take them with you when you're looking for a job.
>
> Staff Member 2: The employer wonders, if you bring the kids in when you apply, if that will be a problem on the job [i.e. that child-care problems may keep him from coming to work everyday]. They might not hire you.

The staff generally described taking account of the employer's perspective as being positive, meaning that clients should always present themselves to employers in the best possible light. Staff members justified their instruction of clients on how to be positive by portraying job seeking as a process of selling one's self to prospective employers. They stated that employers make hiring decisions based on factors other then those listed in job advertisements and descriptions, including their subjective assessments of job applicants' sincerity in seeking jobs. Thus, one part of staff members' instruction of clients on how to take account of the typical employer's perspective involved identifying positive factors that clients could emphasize in their interactions with perspective employers.

The factors included skills and experiences that clients might emphasize in portraying themselves as qualified for jobs. They also included claims to being dependable and hard-working employees. According to the staff, the latter qualities were sometimes just as important to employers as sophisticated occupational skills and experiences. Consider, for example, the following response to a client's claim that employers only hire job applicants with extensive experience at the jobs for which they are applying.

> Well, yes, they do want people with experience but you can sell yourself in other ways too. Ya know, you can tell them that you're dependable and you work hard, that you'll be there at eight o'clock [AM] everyday. Employers want dependable employees too. You can sell yourself that way too.

According to the staff members, job interviews were especially important because they were major occasions for job applicants to sell themselves to employers. They further stated that, whenever possible, clients should avoid putting negative information on job application forms because employers might use the information to eliminate them from further consideration for jobs. According to the staff, a major problem for many clients was their lifestyles which the staff described as unlikely to positively impress employers. Staff members advised clients to avoid talking about such aspects of their lifestyles in job interviews and to focus on aspects that employers would find desirable. Consider, for example, the following staff member instruction to clients about how to properly answer a practice job interview question about how they spent their leisure time.

> Don't put down no smut, though. Don't put down smut, stuff employers don't want to hear. Like don't put down that you spend all your time drinkin'. Employers don't want to hear that. You've cost yourself a job right off the bat [if you state that you spend all your time drinking].

Staff members also recommended that clients answer "Will Discuss" to questions that they could not answer in positive ways. They justified the recommendation by stating that clients could later explain the troublesome circumstances in positive or, at least, less negative ways in job interviews. Staff members also sometimes asked clients to practice being positive and, in the process, the staff further displayed the logic of the employer's point of view to clients. The staff used the practice sessions to identify and justify impression management techniques intended to minimize the negative impressions that might be drawn from aspects of clients' biographies, and to teach clients how to positively impress employers by anticipating and addressing their unstated concerns. Consider the following staff-client exchange.

> Staff Member: Lots of times employers ask you questions [during job interviews] right from the app [job application form]. You know, they have it right in front of them and they could read it, but they ask you instead. I had a client who got mad because all the questions in the interview were from her app. She said, "Why'd I bother filling it out if he's going to ask me that? He could have just read it." Well, employers are looking for something when they ask those questions. Sure they could read your app, but they're looking for more and you need to make something positive out of it. What if the employers asks, "Are you married?" That's right there on the app, what are you going to say?
>
> Client: Well, I'd say, "Yes, I'm married and I have a little baby. He'll be fourteen months real soon."
>
> Staff Member: Okay, now you're volunteering too much. He [the employer] doesn't want to hear about your baby, he wants to know if you'll be a good worker. So, you have to turn everything back to the job. There's nothing more boring than hearing about somebody's family. So you could say, "Yes, I'm married and I want this job so that I can support my family properly." What you're saying is that you have family obligations and you'll be a dependable worker.

Justifying Taking Account of the Employer's Perspective

In so orienting to the solution of clients' troubles, the staff also attempted to persuade their clients to take responsibility for solving their troubles. Specifically, the staff stated that developing effective impression management skills was one way in which clients showed that they were willing to do whatever was necessary to get jobs. Staff members responded to clients who objected to their claims and recommendations by portraying the objections as signs and causes of clients' troubles. In so responding, the staff members sought to hold their clients accountable for their orientations toward staff members' claims and recommendations. Consider, for example, the following staff member response to a client who objected to the staff member's claim that, unlike the client, an employer would not conclude that the client was a more stable person and attractive employee since his marriage.

> Staff Member: But what I'm saying is that an employer is gonna look at your record and say, "Hey, he hasn't been working since he got married. That's been a real stabilizing influence on his life."
>
> Client: That's not right. [The client explains why he lost his last job just prior to getting married and states that there is no relationship between losing his job and getting married.]
>
> Staff Member: There you go again. You explain everything as someone else's fault. You need to present yourself differently.

Staff members also tried to persuade their clients to acquiesce to their claims and recommendations by portraying the organizationally preferred orientation as realistic. Specifically, they responded to clients stating that local employers' desires were arbitrary and unfair by stating that clients had no choice but to take account of employers' biases in the recessionary area economy. According to the staff, clients had no choice because employers enjoyed an advantaged position in their dealings with job seekers. In this way, staff members cast their clients in an inferior role in relation to employers and accommodation with employers' desires as a realistic response to the clients' disadvantaged position in the relationship. Consider, for example, the following staff member response to a client who objected to being told that he should cut his hair because "there's a rumor that some employers just throw away the apps [job applications] of men with long hair."

> Yes, of course, it's unfair, but that's the way it is. Be realistic, employers can afford to be unfair when they have some many applicants. There are a lot of people who are qualified for jobs and so lots of times they decide by whether they like a person or not and a lot of employers in...[the city] don't like men with long hair. That's the way it is.

As in most such staff-client exchanges, the staff member did not defend the typical employer's orientation. Rather, she responded by emphasizing the client's disadvantaged position in dealing with area employers, which she cast as a condition that was beyond the control of clients and staff. Specifically, the staff member explained that local employers could "afford to be unfair" because of the recessionary area economy. The staff member also portrayed the client's willingness to accommodate his desires and interests with those of area employers as a realistic orientation to the solution of the client's troubles. Finally, when the client came to his next WIN meeting with his hair cut, the staff member described it as a sign that he was serious about his WIN responsibilities and getting a job.

In sum, a major way in which the WIN staff members sought to solve their clients' troubles involved instructing clients on aspects of the typical employer's perspective and how clients could sell themselves by taking account of it. In projecting a perspective on employers and identifying ways in which clients could sell themselves to employers, WIN staff and clients sought to gain some measure of control over situations which they described as uncertain. The next section is concerned with the ways in which WIN staff and clients elaborated on their interest in taking account of the employer's perspective by producing and negotiating job seeking rules and rationales.

Negotiating Impression Management Rules and Rationales

Through their interactions with clients, the staff identified a number of idealized rules and rationales of proper job seeking; that is, universal statements about how proper job seeking should *always* be done and the standards that employers *always* use in assessing job applicants. They also glossed over alternative ways to which job seeking might be successfully organized, the various factors associated with different job seeking situations that limit the job seeker's ability to achieve the ideal, and the range of interests and motives that employers might have in assessing job applicants. The following are examples of idealized job seeking rules and rationales frequently identified by the staff.

1. Always arrive at the job interview a few minutes early because employers want employees who are

punctual. But do not arrive too early because it will disrupt the office routine and be taken as a sign that you are desperate for a job.

2. Always carry all of the supplies and other resources that you might need in applying for jobs, including extra pens for completing job application forms and the full addresses and telephone numbers of references because employers want employees who are efficient and well-organized.

3. Answer all requests for information on job application forms because employers frequently throw away applications that are not complete. But never state on a job application form that you were fired from a job; rather, put "Will Discuss" in the appropriate space and explain the circumstances of the firing in the best possible light during the interview.

4. When secretaries ask about the purpose of your telephone calls to employers state, "It's personal." Otherwise, they will end the call by stating that there are no job openings.

Frequently, however, the process of identifying universal elements of the employe's perspective and rules of proper job seeking became complex and the subject of staff-client negotiation. The major source for negotiation of staff members' claims and recommendations was questions raised by clients about the universal applicability of the impression management rules identified by the staff and/or the practical implications of aspects of the employer's perspective for their circumstances. Indeed, the issues were linked because doubts raised about how to properly present one's self in job seeking situations also involved questions about the employer's perspective and, conversely, uncertainty about salient elements of the employer's perspective created doubts about how to properly present one's self in employment settings.

Three outcomes resulted from such interactions: (1) the rejection of the client's claim, (2) the relativization of the initial rule and identification of a new universal rule and rationale, and (3) the affirmation of the initial rule based on a new rationale. The outcomes were different ways in which the staff justified the organizationally preferred orientation and solution to clients' troubles.

Rejecting Clients' Claims

The least frequent staff response to clients' questions about job seeking rules advocated by staff members was to dismiss them as irrelevant. It involved noting unique circumstances in the client's experience that made the experience an inappropriate source for judging a job seeking rule and/or understanding the perspective of the typical employer. Indeed, clients contributed to such a response by portraying their experiences and attitudes as unique. Consider the following staff-client exchange in which the staff member explained that job applicants must be careful about their dress and grooming when applying for jobs, and then turned to a client who previously worked as an assistant manager in a small business and asked:

> Staff Member: Didn't you look at people's clothes and grooming when you were working as a manager?
>
> Client: Well, yeah, I guess. I tried to see the real person though. I tried not to just see how long their hair was, but whether they were honest and sincere, you know, if they said they'd be in every day, then they'd be in. I tried not to look at them the way a fifty-year-old man would. I mean, I've worked a lot of jobs so if a rambler came in, you know, a person who'd worked a lot of jobs for not too long and moved around a lot, I'd try to see if they were honest and would come in six days a week. I might hire them even if they had a bad record. I suppose a lot of other people wouldn't hire them.
>
> Staff Member: Okay, that's what *you* did, but most employers are old men and they don't look past long hair and clothes. Right.
>
> Client: Right.

Most of the time, however, the staff responded to clients' questions by reconsidering the initial rules and rationales. One outcome of the reconsideration was the relativization of the initial rules based on the identification of a new universal rule that subsumed the initial one.

Relativization of Initial Rules

This was the typical staff member response to clients who stated that they had violated job seeking rules recommended by the staff and had still gotten jobs. Staff members never treated such client statements as irrelevant based on the clients' misunderstanding of the importance of impressions in getting jobs. Rather, staff members elaborated on their initial claims by portraying them as generally valid and important, but not appropriate for all employment settings. Staff members partly did so by identifying several types of employment settings and employer perspectives. In elaborating on the initial rules and rationales, the staff also avoided treating clients' questions as challenges to the general legitimacy of the staff's claim that successful job seekers take account of the employer's perspective. Rather, they used clients' claims and experiences to indicate the complexity of job seeking and impression management.

Two examples of this response are the following staff-client exchanges. The first exchange involved the universal appropriateness of the "do not wear jeans to job interviews" rule. The staff member relativized it by constructing a new rule declaring that job applicants should "dress appropriate for the job." Prior to doing so, however, the staff member had cast the rule as generally appropriate and had described a job seeking circumstance which justified her claim. The second exchange involved a challenge to the staff member's claim that all job interviewers prefer applicants who are assertive and ambitious. The staff member initially responded by casting the client's claim and experience as unique and citing her own experience as a justification for her recommendation. She relativized the rule by classifying job interviewers' perspectives and motives into two types reflecting the security of their jobs.

[A client stated that he regularly wore jeans to job interviews and had gotten jobs when he did so. Another asked about wearing designer jeans. The staff member replied,]

No, you shouldn't wear jeans at all. It's not a good idea. You have to remember that you're making an impression. It's not even a good idea when you just put in an app, because sometimes they [employers] review it right there and say, "Come on in for an interview." What are you going to do then, say "Wait while I go home and change by clothes?" So it's not a good idea to wear jeans. Of course, it you're applying for a factory job or something like that, then that's something else. You know, go to the interview dressed appropriate for the job.

[The staff member stated that in job interviews clients should stress their desire to get ahead because employers prefer ambitious employees. The client stated that all job interviewers do not hold such a perspective and noted that when

> he was working as an assistant manager of a small business he did not hire job applicants who said they wanted to work their way up in the business because he assumed they would try to take his job.]

> Well, yeah, I suppose it could [hurt your chances of getting a job] in cases like that. But most of the time you're being interviewed by the owner or you're dealing with a person in [the] personnel [department] and they got their jobs with a lot of training and experience, you're not going to take their jobs. When [a local company] was hiring, the interviewer told me that they were looking for people who'd say "I want your job." They thought that indicated that the person was willing to really work hard and wanted to get ahead. Of course nobody was going to get their jobs, but that's what they were looking for. You shouldn't say that to everybody though. Just say that you are willing to work hard and you want to grow with the company.

Another product of staff members' reconsideration of job seeking rules was to affirm the rules by seeking new rationales for them, rationales that questioning clients would accept.

Producing New Rationales for Job Seeking Rules

Staff members responded to clients who raised general questions about the plausibility of a rule for all job seeking situations by offering a new rationale for the rule. The staff justified the search for a new rationale as a way of helping clients understand the appropriateness and importance of the rule. In focusing on rationales that clients would accept, the staff avoided treating the clients' questions as challenges to the legitimacy of their general claims and recommendations. The search was also used by the staff to instruct clients on the variety of inferences that employers might draw for their self-presentations. For example, the same impression management mistake might be used to define a job applicant as technically unqualified and/or morally unsuited for a job.

Consider the following exchange in which two staff members described the rules of writing letters of application. One rule was to always use correct spelling and grammar. It was initially justified as a sign of technical competence and later as a sign of the job seeker's motives.

> Client: If I'm writing a letter to a manager of a bar or restaurant or something like that, what difference does spelling make?

Staff Member 1: Well, it is important to be able to spell. That's all the employer sees from you and if you can't spell, then it says something about you....You know, it was like yesterday [during another exercise] when some people [clients] couldn't spell "Job Counsellor." I mean, if you can't spell the job you're applying for, then it's like you can't spell your own name. I mean, it really looks bad. If you're applying for a job as a secretary and you can't spell, then you're not going to be a very good secretary. It's important to be able to spell, read, and write.

[The staff and clients go on to identify other reasons for the rule focusing on proper grammar and spelling as signs of the applicant's ability to do the job.[

Staff Member 2: It shows [that] you care.

Client: Okay, I can see that. It shows [that] you care. I'll buy that, sure.

Thus, although the staff sometimes modified the rules of conduct that they derived from their initial portrayals of job seeking as impression management, they continued to justify an orientation to job seeking that was centered in accommodation to the putative needs and desires of employers.

Conclusion

In sum, the justification of organizationally preferred solutions to clients' troubles was a potential aspect of all staff-client relations in WIN. Central to staff members' justifications was the inferiorization of clients which staff members treated as a practical activity intended to help clients get jobs. According to the staff, a first step in solving clients' troubles involved clients' recognition and acceptance of their devalued and dependent position in the area economy. Based on clients' acceptance of this "fact of life," staff members stated that clients could begin to develop strategies and tactics for realistically solving their troubles. In so justifying organizationally preferred solutions, staff members also cast themselves as knowledgeable and concerned professionals who could help clients, if clients fulfilled their WIN assignments and took seriously the advice and instruction offered by staff members.

We conclude by considering some of the general implications of the study for analyzing rhetoric and everyday life in WIN and other street-level bureaucracies.

7

Rhetoric, Argumentation and Acquiescence in WIN

A major goal of this study has been to develop a rhetorical approach to the work activities and relationships of the WIN staff and, more generally, street-level bureaucrats. The approach emphasizes the ways in which professionals in human service and social control organizations formulate, express and negotiate their practical interests in interactions with others in their work worlds. They do so by making claims and offering rationales intended to persuade others to acquiesce to their recommendations. WIN staff members' and others' rhetorical practices were interpretive and interactional procedures for producing a work world filled with problems. The problems centered in troublesome social relationships which staff members sought to anticipate, forestall, and manage by persuading others to act in preferred ways.

Thus, rhetorical analysis of everyday life in street-level bureaucracies highlights how organizational relationships and processes are discursively and politically organized. Indeed, discourse and politics are inextricably linked in such organizations because street-level bureaucrats' claims about social reality and the ways in which they are made, negotiated and acceded to have practical consequences for street-level bureaucrats', their clients' and others' lives. Such claims and procedures are activities for creating social worlds within which some persons' orientations to practical issues are cast as more realistic, socially responsible and/or necessary than others. Discourse and politics are also linked because acquiescence to the claims and interests of superordinate groups is situationally sought, justified and produced. It is a social accomplishment, not an inevitable result of organizational authority structures.

Although his primary concern is with governmental, not organizational, politics, Edelman (1977: 4) offers an apt summary of the relationship between language and politics in WIN:

> language is an integral facet of the political scene: not simply an instrument for describing events but itself a part of events, shaping their meaning and helping to shape the political roles officials and the general public play. In this sense, language, events, and self-conceptions are a part of the same transaction, mutually determining one another's meanings.

The purpose of this chapter is to further develop this aspect and goal of the study. It is developed by reconsidering some of the issues raised in the first chapter about street-level bureaucrats, in light of the subsequent analysis of rhetoric and everyday life in WIN. We first consider the WIN staff's and others' interest in rhetorically producing preferred versions of social reality and then how their rhetoric may be analyzed as work. Later sections analyze how acquiescence was interactionally produced in WIN and how staff members' and state officials' efforts to justify typical and organizationally preferred understandings of and responses to persons' troubles are similar to politicians' efforts to manage the public.

Rhetoric and Everyday Life in WIN

Looked at one way, the central image or metaphor underlying the rhetorical analysis of WIN and other street-level bureaucracies is that of cynical con artists seeking to manipulate others to their advantage. The image emphasizes the self-servingness of WIN staff members' claims and manipulative intent of their actions. The con artist imagery may also be used to cast WIN staff members' descriptions of WIN purposes and procedures, orientations to clients' troubles, and portrayals of the practical facts of life that they and their clients faced in fulfilling their WIN obligations as bureaucratic propaganda. As defined by Altheide and Johnson (1980), bureaucratic propaganda is rhetoric that is intended to promote organization members' self-interests by denying and/or mystifying the disparities between official depictions of organizational practices and organization members' activities.

WIN Staff Members' Rhetoric as Bureaucratic Propaganda

Bureaucratic propaganda is centered in official claims about social reality which cast organizational practices and relationships as proper enactments of idealized organizational purposes and policies. Although bureaucratic propaganda is often expressed as "factual" reports on social reality, it may be expressed in other ways, such as verbal descriptions and instructions intended to influence others' orientations to organizational interests and practices. Organization members selectively construct bureaucratic propaganda to manage diverse and problematic audiences having very different concerns and interests. They do so by modifying their reality claims in light of others' interests, including sometimes portraying social reality in contradictory ways for different audiences. Finally, Altheide and Johnson state that bureaucratic propaganda is produced in such a way that the organizational interests it is intended to serve are mystified.

Clearly, self-interest and -promotion were aspects of many of the claims made by WIN staff members in their dealings with clients, state WIN officials and each other. Staff members promoted their self-interests by defining and responding to most clients' troubles in organizationally preferred ways, portraying state officials' expectations and recommendations as unreasonable, and describing their orientations to WIN purposes as standards to which clients and staff members should be held accountable. Further, some staff member claims may be treated as contradictions because they portrayed the impact of recessionary labor markets on their clients' job seeking efforts differently in their interactions with clients and state WIN officials. Staff members' differing claims also highlight the ways in which they selectively constructed their arguments to manage others in their world and, on occasion, to justify actions which might have been interpreted by others as inconsistent with WIN goals.

Despite its obvious relevance, it is possible to overstate the usefulness of the bureaucratic propaganda perspective for this study, however. The usefulness of the perspective is partly limited because self-interest and -promotion were aspects of everyone's activities in WIN, not just those of staff members. For example, state WIN officials rhetorically explained and justified their positions in interactions with staff members by portraying their recommendations and demands as realistic and/or necessary responses to the problems faced by the state-wide WIN system. Similarly, clients' requests for permission to enter training programs and be exempted from mandatory WIN participation, as well as clients' explanations of their failure to fulfill their WIN assignments, were intended to persuade staff members and assign preferred identities to themselves. The requests and explanations may also be analyzed as self-interested and -promoting actions.

Thus, if staff members are to be viewed as cynical con artists seeking to manipulate others, clients and state officials must be viewed similarly. When the bureaucratic propaganda perspective is applied to all WIN participants, it becomes difficult to distinguish the manipulators from their victims. Indeed, one might conclude that staff members were correct when they argued that they were the "real" victims of WIN, being caught between the self-interested and manipulative activities of state officials and clients. Viewed this way, staff members' arguments were not really propaganda, but attempts to manage and survive in a problematic work world. Whatever conclusions one draws about the meaning of WIN staff members' actions and relationships with clients and state officials, it is clear that the usefulness of the bureaucratic propaganda perspective is reduced when the self-interested and -promoting aspects of clients' and state officials' actions are also considered.

A second limitation of the bureaucratic propaganda perspective is that it diverts attention from the variety of ends sought by WIN staff members in their dealings with clients, state WIN officials and each other. For example, staff members portrayed their interactions with clients as intended to simultaneously help clients face and manage their troubles and fulfill staff members' professional obligations in WIN. According to staff members, the goals were interrelated because in fulfilling their professional obligations, staff members held clients responsible for solving their problems. Staff members further explained that their actions were helpful to clients because, through them, staff members introduced clients to a realistic and proper orientation to their troubles and circumstances. Similarly, staff members stated that their efforts to keep agency performance goals as low as possible were both self-interested acts and necessary responses to the unreasonable expectations of state WIN officials. For the staff, then, their actions were partly self-interested and partly self-protective.

A third limitation of the bureaucratic propaganda perspective for this study is that much of the staff members' and state officials' rhetoric focused on the ways in which their recommendations and actions furthered organizational interests. They did not deny or mystify the relationship between their recommendations and organizational interests. In doing so, they made the definition of organizational interests a topic of negotiation and used preferred definitions of the interests to justify their recommendations and actions. For example, staff members told new clients that their WIN jobs primarily involved making certain that clients fulfilled their obligations to the government by looking for jobs. Also, the state WIN official who conducted the annual planning meeting justified her demand that the local agency increase its performance goals by portraying it as a necessary part of achieving organizational interests. Finally, staff member complaints about each others' work performances were occasions for defining organizational interests and negotiating whether persons' actions furthered them.

Thus, although the bureaucratic propaganda perspective highlights aspects of everyday life in WIN, it glosses over other important aspects of this social world. There is, however, an alternative way of conceptualizing everyday life in WIN which takes account of both its propagandistic and nonpropagandistic aspects. It involves analyzing rhetoric as a practical activity for anticipating and managing interpersonal problems.

WIN Staff as Practitioners of Everyday Life

The alternative perspective involves treating WIN staff members and others as complex social actors seeking to make sense of and influence their social worlds. They are, as Gubrium (1988) calls them, practitioners of everyday life. A practitioner of everyday life is

> one who, together with others, engages the matter of figuring the meaning of things and events in their worlds in order to conduct the latter's concrete business. Practitioners of everyday life not only interpret their worlds but do so under discernible auspices, with recognizable agendas. (Gubrium, 1988: 34)

The practitioner of everyday life image is useful because it highlights the ways in which WIN staff members and others sought to justify their positions and persuade others by selectively describing the issues at hand in their interactions and their options in responding to them. In doing so, staff members, clients and state officials formulated their practical concerns (agendas) and made them recognizable to others, who sometimes responded by acquiescing and other times by questioning the claims or offering alternatives to them. Negotiations about persons' positions in potential and actual arguments were occasions for elaborating on and sometimes modifying staff members' and others' concerns about practical issues.

WIN staff members, state officials and clients also used their descriptions to portray their concerns and positions as necessary and/or realistic. In this way, they cast their positions "under discernible auspices" which ranged from claims that speakers' preferred positions were mandated by government policies to claims that the policies were unfair and sources of injustice. Staff members and others with whom they interacted used such claims to anticipate and counter others' claims that their positions were purely self-interested or otherwise indefensible. Speakers made their positions defensible by describing them as backed by organizational and/or moral authority. Thus, one aspect of argumentation in WIN involved the negotiation of "appropriate" auspices for speakers' positions.

More generally, the practitioner of everyday life image highlights how reality construction and acquiescence were ongoing interactional accomplishments in WIN. They were generally produced and accomplished as staff members and others explained, justified and negotiated their preferred understandings of and responses to practical issues emergent in their ongoing social relationships. Viewed this way, staff members, clients and state officials were coproducers of and participants in the social world of WIN. Their mutual production of WIN was partly related to the organization of WIN roles and activities which involved varying types and degrees of interdependency between staff members, clients and state officials. For example, staff members were dependent on clients, state officials, and each other because they were seldom able or willing to remedy their troublesome relationships by terminating them.

Termination of WIN relationships involved significant costs for staff members, state officials and clients. Most obviously, termination from WIN cost clients all or a significant portion of their AFDC grants. The costs for staff members and state officials were less obvious but consequential, because the fulfillment of their WIN responsibilities depended on maintaining working relationships with others in their work world, even if the relationships involved arguing. For example, staff members could not achieve the organizational goal of finding employment for as many clients as possible if they terminated all clients who did not fully comply with WIN rules and procedures. Similarly, state WIN officials' interest in using the annual planning meetings to develop mutually agreeable performance goals for local agencies was unachievable if they or local staff members refused to negotiate and compromise their preferred goals.

Whatever the conditions associated with WIN staff members', clients' and state officials' ongoing dealings with one another, their efforts to persuade were rhetorical procedures for maintaining organizational relationships as well as producing short-term solutions to their disputes. The procedures may be further analyzed as work. We further consider this aspect of rhetoric and everyday life in the next section.

Rhetoric as Work

WIN staff members' and others' efforts to persuade may be partly analyzed as work because they were organized and recurring activities having significant consequences for WIN staff members and others in their work world. For example, rhetoric was central to the termination of clients from WIN. This action turned on staff members' abilities to persuade others that some clients were severely uncooperative and, consequently, did not deserve anymore chances to change. Rhetoric was also central to the WIN supervisor's efforts to hold staff members accountable to organizational rules and expectations. Staff members' and others' rhetorical activities may also be analyzed as work because they were productive activities. WIN staff members, clients and state officials used them to produce practical understandings of WIN policies, that is, to define the policies' implications for the concrete, practical issues toward which their everyday activities were focused.

This orientation to rhetoric as work is generally consistent with Wadel's (1979) approach to the anthropology of work. He defines work as an aspect of all social relationships and a middleground activity linking the concrete relationships of everyday life to the creation and maintenance of shared social values and institutions. It is through the interactional work occurring in concrete social relationships that such values and institutions are created and maintained. According to Wadel, his orientation to work could be the source for the development of new understandings of work as socially (not just economically) productive activity. He states, the social scientific study of work

> should include the mutual activities that go into maintaining personal and private relations and the collective activities that have to do with the maintenance of community, democracy and other valued social institutions. (Wadel, 1979: 381–382)

For Wadel, then, WIN staff members' efforts to persuade and gain acquiescence from others were work activities because they were partly ways of producing and maintaining shared social values and ideals.[1] The values and ideals were rhetorically expressed in WIN as claims and were used to justify speakers' preferred positions on practical issues. The three major values or claims produced in WIN staff members' interactions involved the work ethic, which staff members treated as the expectation and ideal that all adult heads of households be gainfully employed, the portrayal of WIN as a distinctive approach to the solution of clients' troubles, and cooperation between staff members and others as the preferred arrangement of social relations in WIN.

WIN staff members rhetorically produced and maintained the work ethic by describing and treating their clients as troubled persons because they were unemployed welfare recipients. That is, they were a social problem because they did not have jobs. Staff members elaborated on their orientation to clients' troubles by emphasizing their clients' social inadequacies, that is, by inferiorizing them. Staff members also produced and maintained employment as a value and ideal by treating staff-client interactions as occasions for changing clients' orientations to employment. Staff members partly did so by implementing organizational policies and rules that were intended to help clients by holding them responsible for their unemployed status. In these ways, staff members produced and maintained the work ethic by enforcing it.

Staff members also used staff-client interactions to describe WIN as a distinctive philosophy and approach to clients' troubles. They partly did so by portraying WIN as based on the government's interest in making certain that clients fulfilled their moral and legal obligations to look for jobs in exchange for their AFDC grants. Described in this way, the WIN philosophy centered in enforcing the work ethic. Staff members' complaints about each others' work performances were also rhetorical (work) activities for producing WIN as a social value and ideal to which they and others should be held accountable. Finally, staff members described WIN as a distinctive philosophy by contrasting the WIN approach with the approaches of other social service agencies, which they stated were based on competing values and orientations to clients' troubles.

Further, staff members' interactions with clients, state officials and clients were occasions for producing cooperative relationships. Cooperation was generally treated by staff members and state officials as the fulfillment of typical organizational expectations and acquiescence to their authority. They oriented to cooperation as a hierarchical relationship in which organizational superordinates monitored and directed the activities of organizational subordinates. State officials and staff members justified their orientation to cooperation by describing it as realistic, necessary and serving the self-interests of subordinates. They also instructed others on how to assess their actions as cooperative and uncooperative. For example, in the annual planning meeting, one way in which the state official objected to the local WIN supervisor's continuing claim that agency goals should not be raised was by describing the superior as "playing games" and instructing her on how to "properly" and "cooperatively" orient to the negotiations.

Staff members defined cooperation for clients by instructing them on WIN expectations and procedures and making formal complaints against clients assessed as "uncooperative." Staff members also sought to produce cooperative relations with clients in routine staff-client interactions concerned with registering new clients in WIN and monitoring clients' job seeking and other activities. For example, one way in which staff members sought to produce cooperative relations with clients involved developing clients' employment plans which staff members described as mutually agreeable strategies for finding jobs. They did so by asking clients about the types of jobs that clients would prefer to seek and listing the jobs in the employment plans as well as by suggesting (and justifying) other jobs that clients could and should seek.

Although it is less obvious, clients also contributed to the production and maintenance of organizationally preferred staff-client relationships. They generally did so by acceding to organizational procedures intended to produce cooperative staff-client relationships. For example, clients provided information sought by staff members, agreed to fulfill the terms of their employment plans and promised to stop acting in uncooperative ways. More specifically, clients contributed to the production of cooperative staff-client relationships by portraying themselves as committed to getting jobs and treating staff members as knowledgeable professionals whom they trusted to help them find jobs.

In sum, analysis of WIN staff members', clients' and state officials' rhetorical activities as work highlights the ways in which they all contributed to the production of WIN as a social and political world. To analyze WIN staff members' and others' actions as contributions is not to suggest that the participants in this social world acted from an enduring consensus on the issues that they negotiated or commitment to WIN purposes and policies. Rather, they contributed to the production and maintenance of WIN by participating in organizational relationships, despite their orientation to them as troublesome and unsatisfactory. Further, analysis of staff members, clients and state officials as co-producers of and co-participants in the social world of WIN does not involve treating them as equally influential in their dealings with one another.

However, such rhetorical analysis does require that we treat acquiescence as socially produced within WIN staff members', state officials' and clients' mutual interactions. It was produced as staff members used their interactional turns to justify their positions on practical issues and respond to others' claims and recommendations. We turn to this aspect of the social organization of rhetoric and work in WIN next.

Producing Acquiescence in WIN

Analysis of argumentation in WIN as turn-taking highlights

how social interactions were organized as rhetorical opportunities. Advocates of partisan positions initiated the process by using conversational turns to explain and justify their positions on practical issues. Respondents' subsequent interactional turns were opportunities for them to participate in the argumentation process and influence the content, tone and implications of emerging situations and relationships. They did so by treating potential arguments as disputes involving opposed orientations to the issues at hand (thereby transforming the interactions into arguments), maintaining ongoing arguments, seeking alternatives to argumentation (such as compromises or agreements to agree to disagree), and acquiescing to others' claims and recommendations.

Thus, acquiescence was one of several responses potentially available to WIN staff members, clients and state officials in dealing with others' claims and recommendations. The acquiescent response was sometimes selected after extensive interactions in which respondents challenged advocates to further justify and elaborate on their positions and/or offered counterclaims and recommendations. The justifications and elaborations were rhetorical procedures for portraying acquiescence as a realistic, if not necessary, response to the issues at hand. In this way, advocates of partisan positions simultaneously made the acquiescent response available to others and cast it as the preferred response. From the standpoint of the advocates, respondents demonstrated their proper understanding of the issues at hand by selecting the acquiescent response.

Whether brief or extensive, WIN staff members', clients' and state officials' potential arguments turned on interactants' positions on the appropriateness of typical and organizationally preferred responses to the problems at hand. Both the practical meaning of persons' claims and recommendations and their uses of interactional turns varied based on their orientations to this issue. Specifically, persons who argued that typical and preferred responses were appropriate used their interactional turns to cast issues as dichotomous choices involving mutually exclusive and opposed understandings of and responses to practical issues. They were formulated and expressed as contrastive pairs.

Producing Dichotomous Choices

Speakers used contrastive pairs to cast all but their preferred responses to practical issues as unacceptable and, therefore, unavailable to interactants in choosing how to manage practical problems. They also used the distinctions to anticipate and respond to others' responses to their arguments by assigning positive or negative identities to persons who acquiesced or objected to their arguments. Specifically, they portrayed persons who acquiesced to their arguments as responsible persons and questioned the motives and moral character of persons who might oppose them.

For example, staff members used the cooperative-uncooperative and good-bad attitude distinctions to describe the choices and identities available to new clients in responding to WIN expectations and procedures. Staff members used the distinction to cast the fulfillment of WIN expectations as the only realistic choice available to clients. According to the staff, the only other choice available to clients was for them to refuse to fulfill their WIN obligations and risk losing all or a significant portion of their AFDC grants — a choice that would demonstrate clients' bad attitudes toward WIN and employment and exacerbate their economic troubles.

Staff members elaborated on their portrayals of clients' choices as dichotomous by generalizing the consequences of clients' uncooperative behavior to other aspects of clients' lives. For example, staff members told clients that their uncooperative behavior in WIN could result in the break-up of their families. In this way, staff members cast clients' choices about whether to cooperate with the WIN staff as having far reaching consequences and reflecting the importance that clients placed on maintaining their families. Staff members described clients' fulfillment of their WIN assignments as signs of clients' commitment to their families. Consider, for example, the following staff-client exchange involving a new client and concerned with the consequences of the client's failure to fulfill his WIN assignments. Earlier in the interaction, the client stated that his son was "the most important thing in my life."

> Staff Member: You know, if you keep screwin' up [not cooperating with the WIN staff], you could lose your son.
>
> Client: Yeah.
>
> Staff Member: With your record [as a troublemaker in the community], no matter what your wife does, she'll get the child. So, if you really want him, you'd better take this [WIN] seriously. You almost lost him already, didn't you?

In these ways, then, staff members rhetorically used the cooperative-uncooperative and good-bad attitude distinctions to anticipate and forestall future arguments with new clients, as well as to justify future sanctioning of clients who did not adequately fulfill their WIN obligations.

Staff members and state officials also used contrastive pairs in responding to others' objections to their claims and recommendations and others' expressions of alternative orientations to practical issues. They used contrastive pairs to reformulate the issues within the organizationally preferred rhetoric of obligation, accountability and personal responsibility. In doing so, they also cast the choices available to themselves and others as dichotomous, involving realistic and unrealistic responses. For example, staff members responded to clients and wives who objected to the requirement that the husbands participate in WIN by acknowledging the moral rightness of the clients' positions and then recasting the issue as a matter of obligation (both staff and clients must follow the rules). So portrayed, the issue and choice at hand involved whether clients would cooperate by following the rules (the realistic response) or act in uncooperative ways (the unrealistic response).

In formulating and responding to issues as dichotomous choices, then, state officials and staff members glossed over, undermined and dismissed others' potential counterrhetoric and counterorientations to practical issues. For example, in recasting clients' and wives' complaints about rules requiring that husbands participate in WIN as a matter of following the rules, staff members glossed over and undermined others' formulation of the issue as a matter of allowing family members to decide how they would fulfill their WIN obligations. The response was a rhetorical procedure for casting clients' arguments as irrelevant or improper and reformulating the issues at hand as matters of client cooperativeness and choice. Staff members' reformulation of the issue was politically significant because, within the organizationally preferred rhetoric, they were required to hold clients assessed as intentionally uncooperative accountable for their actions.

Staff members also undermined and dismissed clients' potential counterrhetoric which focused on their family problems and obligations by noting that WIN provided funds and programs for managing clients' family problems while they looked for jobs. Staff members cited the existence of such funds and programs to justify their treatment of clients' claims as excuses. They also portrayed clients' use of WIN funds to pay expenses that were not directly related to job seeking as evidence of clients' bad and uncooperative attitudes toward WIN. Staff members used this portrayal of clients' motives and actions to justify making formal complaints against them and to counter clients' claims that they needed WIN funds to meet basic family expenses. Staff members' responses also challenged clients' claims that clients were primarily interested in protecting their families.

Consider, for example, the following staff-client exchange which occurred during a conciliation meeting.

> Staff Member: Are you looking for work?
>
> Client: Yeah, I have been but I got a new car and it broke down. Besides, I don't have enough money for gas. You can't drive without gas. I need the [WIN] money for other things, living expenses.
>
> Staff Member: That's not what the money is for. It's for gas and other job search expenses.
>
> Client: Well, all I can say is.my kids come first. I'm gonna feed them before I go lookin' for a job.
>
> Staff Member: What'll your kids do for food if you lose your [AFDC] grant? You will [lose the grant], if you don't look for work.

Staff members also undermined and dismissed clients' potential counterrhetoric by describing clients' requests for special treatment due to family problems and obligations as unacceptable grounds for missing work in conventional employment settings. The requests were, therefore, unacceptable excuses for failing to fulfill the terms of clients' WIN jobs.

In this and similar ways, state officials and staff members used their interactional turns to produce social conditions that made others' acquiescence to their claims and recommendations a realistic and preferred choice. Conditions so produced reduced the chances that they would have to resort to coercive measures in gaining others' acquiescence. Put differently, state officials' and staff members' reformulation of issues within the organizationally preferred rhetoric was central to their justification of cooperative organizational relationships. State officials and staff members were usually aided in their rhetorical efforts by persons who argued that typical and preferred understandings and responses were inappropriate. Their contribution centered in the ways in which they expressed their alternative claims and recommendations and, in doing so, signalled their willingness to acquiesce to others' positions.

Signalling a Willingness to Acquiesce

Staff members and clients who argued that typical understandings and responses were inappropriate did so in ways that allowed for challenges and counterclaims by others who argued that they were appropriate. They generally did so by expressing their objections and recommendations as conditional positions, not matters of fact which others had to accept. Positions so expressed allow for challenges and counterclaims by others arguing for opposed positions. In organizing and expressing their arguments in this way, staff members and clients also produced conditions making acquiescence to others' arguments a potential and available response to the issues at hand. Staff members and clients used three major rhetorical procedures to cast their objectives and recommendations as conditional positions.

First, they expressed their objections to others' positions as questions. In doing so, staff members and clients invited others taking opposed and unconditional positions to respond with challenges and counterclaims that were unequivocal. Consider, for example, the following staff-client exchange which occurred at the beginning of a job-search skills workshop. The client initiated the exchange by objecting to being assigned to the workshop because it would keep him and other workshop participants from looking for jobs. In casting his objection as a question, however, the client made it possible for the staff member to respond by simultaneously justifying the assignment and casting the client as an incompetent job seeker.

> Client: Don't you think this might hold some of us back [from getting jobs]? I mean, don't we need to get out there and look for a job?
>
> Staff Member: Well, maybe, but a lot of you [clients] have been looking for a long time. Maybe it's time to come back in and look at yourself and what you're doin' [wrong in looking for jobs]. Maybe you don't know how to fill out an application [form] quite right or how to handle an interview?

Client: Well, I don't know? If all we're gonna do is sit down here and fill out papers and listen —

Staff Member [interrupting]: Well obviously the [WIN staff members who assigned the clients to the workshop] think you need some help in learning how to do these things. You know, you don't get a job overnight. It takes time.

This exchange also shows how staff members sometimes managed clients' questions and complaints by cutting clients' interactional turns short. They did so by, first, interrupting clients' interactional turns and, then, challenging clients' right to object to typical organizational expectations and procedures. The response was one way in which staff members sought client acquiescence by placing objecting clients' claims to preferred identities at risk.

The second way in which staff members and clients signalled their willingness to acquiesce to others' arguments that typical organizational expectations and procedures should be followed was by acknowledging the possible legitimacy of others' positions while arguing for their own. In doing so, speakers indicated a lack of full commitment to their positions and invited others arguing for opposed positions to insist that typical procedures be followed. Consider, for example, the following staff member justification of her recommendation that a client be exempted from job seeking while the client received counselling for her emotional and family troubles. It was a response to another staff member's claim that the client did not need or deserve such counselling and that the client's claims to special problems were excuses intended to "con" staff members into exempting her from job seeking.

Well, yeah, some of these women, and men too, become pretty good at conning us. She may be one of those, but maybe not. Even with those people though, you hafta find out what they really want, find out why they feel [that] they hafta con you. I don't know, I just think that [this client] has a lot of problems and one of 'em is that she tries to please everybody. I wonder if there is a real person there?

The third rhetorical procedure used by staff members and clients to cast their positions as conditional involved treating their objections and/or counterrecommendations as based on idiosyncratic experience or personal assessments and preferences. For example, staff members and clients sometimes described their positions as subjective and based on their unique beliefs, feelings and experiences. Staff members also prefaced their claims that typical organizational expectations and procedures were inappropriate by stating that their positions were at odds with the WIN philosophy. Such descriptions of persons' positions create social conditions that allow others to respond by dismissing their claims and recommendations.

Consider, for example, the following exchange involving two staff members about the appropriateness of allowing some WIN clients to enroll in training program. It began with a staff member stating that he did not understand the purpose of WIN sponsored training programs.

> Staff Member 1: The idea is to give people training so they're not on welfare forever.
>
> Staff Member 2: I know that's supposed to be the purpose of it, but I don't...
>
> Staff Member 1 [interrupting]: That's not *supposed* to be the purpose [of training], that *is* the purpose of it. Would you rather have people on welfare for ten years? Before we had this [training program], I had people on my caseload for that long....
>
> Staff Member 2: Yeah, I know. It's my problem, I guess. It's a personal thing.
>
> Staff Member 1: Your problem is that you don't accept the premise of training.

The above exchange shows how staff members who disputed typical organizational procedures [Staff Member 2] initially cast their positions as, at least, partly based on personal confusion and concern. It also illustrates how staff members justified typical organizational expectations and procedures [Staff Member 1] by interrupting others and portraying their positions as factual; not matters of opinion or personal preference. Finally, the exchange shows how staff members acquiesced to others' arguments by describing the issues at hand as personal dilemmas. Issues described and defined in this way do not require the reassessment of typical organizational expectations and procedures.

WIN state officials and staff members countered such conditional claims and recommendations by portraying (1) staff members' and clients' arguments as applying only to atypical circumstances and (2) the issue at hand as a matter of fact, obligation or in some other way not a matter of individual choice. In so responding, speakers who argued that typical organizational expectations and procedures were appropriate sought to produce social conditions for discrediting alternative arguments which justified atypical understandings of and responses to practical problems. They also used the procedures to cast acquiescence to their claims and recommendations as realistic and necessary. We further consider how acquiescence to typical organizational expectations and procedures was discursively produced and justified in WIN in the next section.

WIN Rhetoric as Political Language

The WIN state officials' and staff members' concern for persuading their organizational subordinates to acquiesce to their claims and recommendations is generally similar to the problems faced by politicians in managing potentially troublesome publics. On occasion, politicians wish to activate such publics to support their programs and candidacies for public office. On other occasions, however, they seek to quiet politically organized groups and the general public. Politicians generally seek the latter goal by describing members of the public as satisfied with existing policies and/or the pressing problems of the day as matters that cannot be solved by government intervention. The descriptions are rhetorical procedures for anticipating and managing potentially troublesome publics by treating public apathy and acquiescence as a reasonable orientation to the troubles of everyday life.

According to Edelman (1964, 1971, 1977, 1988), a major way in which politicians seek to achieve their practical interests in sometimes exciting and other times quieting the public is by rhetorically manipulating the anxieties and ambiguities associated with persons' troubles. They do so by organizing and managing the types of demands that the public makes on them and citizens' expectations about the place of government in solving their troubles. Edelman further states that a central aspect of politicians' organization and management of public demands and expectations is banal language. Specifically, politicians attempt to make their positions understandable and credible to others by portraying them in routine, predictable and mundane ways. Political language is not intended to provide new and creative understandings of and orientations to public issues. Rather, it is intended to reaffirm existing understandings and orientations and, in doing so, to call forth predictable responses from the public.

Although they were not seeking public office or advocating for general public policies, WIN staff members' interactions with others in their work world involved political language. Specifically, staff members and state officials rhetorically sought to persuade (activate) potentially troublesome others to act in preferred ways as well as to anticipate and counter others' questions and criticisms (to quiet them). Part of their rhetoric was intended to instruct others on "proper" expectations about WIN, in general, and the practical issues at hand, in particular. The instructions were rhetorical procedures for classifying others' demands as legitimate and illegitimate and justifying the demands made by staff members and state officials on their organizational subordinates.

The instructions were a major way in which staff members sought to define and organize others' expectations about WIN and limit the number and types of demands made on them by troublesome others. Staff members and state officials justified the demands that they made on others by assigning preferred meanings to otherwise ambiguous issues and events. One way in which staff members and state officials did so was by organizing and defining others' anxieties and concerns about their troubles and the issues under consideration.

Organizing and Defining Others' Anxieties

Staff members and state officials generally organized and defined others' anxieties and concerns by portraying them as manageable within typical organizational procedures and relationships. The portrayal was a rhetorical procedure for casting WIN expectations and procedures as a solution to others' troubles. So cast, WIN participation should not be a source of anxiety and concern for others. For example, staff members responded to clients who expressed concern about their inabilities to get jobs by describing WIN programs and activities as solutions to clients' troubles. In so responding, staff members sought to mollify clients' anxieties and refocus their attention and concern on fulfilling their WIN obligations. The state official who conducted the annual planning session also sought to refocus the local supervisor's concerns in similar ways by describing how local staff members were already performing at levels higher than their goals.

On occasion, however, staff members made clients' concerns and anxieties matters of negotiation and instruction. They did so by describing clients' actions in the WIN office as signs of their underlying emotional states. Staff members used their portrayals to assign new meanings to clients' actions. In doing so, staff members deflected client criticism of themselves and the WIN program. They also used the portrayals to identify the "real" sources of clients' troubles and hold clients accountable for their troubles. Staff members sought the latter rhetorical goal by describing clients' troubles as inevitable consequences of their past actions and choices. Consider, for example, the following staff-client exchange that occurred in a registration and appraisal meeting.

> Staff Member: You are a very angry young man. You know that don't you?
>
> Client: Yes, but...
>
> Staff Member: [interrupting]: Don't be angry at me. I didn't cause your problems....Anger is a male thing that we can get away with. It usually covers other feelings. I think you have been very hurt. You feel hurt, sad, frustrated and other things. You let anger cover these softer feelings. Don't you?
>
> Client: Yeah.
>
> Staff Member: You made a mistake when you were young and you are still paying for it. A lot of it was your fault because you made some wrong choices. Now, your paying for that.

Staff members also used portrayals of clients' emotional states to justify their complaints about "uncooperative" clients and demands that clients change. The major way in which they sought this rhetorical goal was by reviewing uncooperative clients' records in WIN and using clients' responses to portray them as ashamed of themselves. They elaborated on the portrayals by stating that clients should feel shame and assigning full responsibility to clients for their current troubles and for changing their behavior. Consider, for example, the following exchanges that occurred in conciliation meetings.

Staff Member: How did you feel when I read your record?

Client: Like you had all the cards in your hand. Uh, er. Not very good.

Staff Member: You shouldn't, you don't have a very good record. It's your fault, you know. You are the one who has to change. You can't keep going like this.

Staff Member 1: I hear you saying that you feel shame about your record. Well, now you have to work on that, get some help. If you feel bad about yourself, you hafta get help and that's hard, to go to someone for help, but you hafta do it.

Staff Member 2: I agree with [Staff Member 1]. It's your responsibility.

While staff members and state officials generally described WIN as a solution to others' troubles, they also stated that it could be a source of new troubles, if clients and local staff members did not fulfill their WIN obligations. In so describing WIN, staff members and state officials sought to produce new concerns and anxieties for potentially troublesome others and to persuade them to acquiesce to staff members' and state officials' recommendations and demands. The new concerns and anxieties focused on others' WIN participation. For example, the state official who conducted the annual planning meeting produced such concerns and justified raising the local agency's performance goals by describing the entire WIN program as under siege from competing programs intended to more effectively respond to clients' employment troubles.

According to the state official, one possible consequence of such a development would be the termination of the WIN program and loss of jobs for local WIN staff members. Indeed, the local supervisor elaborated on the state official's scenario and justification by describing a situation in another state in which a program similar to WIN was terminated and, when the program's staff sought AFDC, they were assigned to a workfare program which required that they "earn" their AFDC grants by doing public service work. Their jobs in the new program involved supervising the public service work of their old clients but, as the local supervisor stated, "this time the government didn't hafta pay them a decent salary because they were on welfare too."

Through such claims and stories, the state official (with

the help of the local supervisor) justified treating the future of WIN as a matter of legitimate concern and anxiety. She also justified treating the local supervisor's claim that local staff members could not perform at higher levels as irrelevant to the "real" problem and issue at stake in their negotiations. Staff members also used their instruction of new clients in registration and appraisal and orientation meetings to describe clients' participation in WIN as a "serious business" involving severe and negative consequences if they failed to adequately fulfill their WIN obligations. They elaborated on the portrayal by responding to clients' complaints about staff members' past efforts to hold them or other clients accountable by describing the rationales underlying their actions and further impressing upon clients that their economic troubles would increase if they failed to fulfill their WIN obligations.

Staff members also sought to refocus clients' concerns and anxieties in subsequent staff-client interactions in which staff members reminded clients of their obligations to fulfill their WIN assignments and, sometimes, threatened to refer clients to conciliation meetings. In conciliation meetings, staff members responded to clients' objections to their WIN assignments and explanations of their "uncooperative" actions by stating that the clients' "real" problems were their inadequate participation in WIN. Consider, for example, the following staff member statement made in a conciliation meeting in response to a client's claim that he could not fulfill his WIN assignments because of pressing and overriding family problems.

> Well, you've got another problem,... 'cause you're in trouble with WIN too. You have a bad record with us and you're in danger of losing your [WIN] job here.... You've gotta start showin' up or you're gonna lose the [client's AFDC] grant and you don't need that.

Finally, staff members rhetorically organized and defined clients' anxieties through their responses to clients' criticisms of WIN and appeals to extenuating circumstances. Staff members responded by simultaneously justifying typical organizational expectations and procedures and questioning clients' motives in raising troublesome issues. In doing so, staff members produced social conditions for challenging clients' claims to being responsible adults and clients. They challenged such client claims by portraying clients' criticisms of WIN as excuses which clients used to justify their unwillingness to fulfill their WIN obligations. Staff members also countered clients' criticisms and appeals by portraying aspects of clients' WIN records as evidence of clients' uncooperative attitudes and behavior.

Both of these staff member responses were rhetorical procedures for putting clients' claims to preferred identities at risk. The responses raised the potential social and personal costs that clients faced in challenging typical organizational expectations and procedures. The responses also produced social conditions that made client acquiescence to staff members' demands realistic and state.

WIN Rhetoric as Banal and Repetitive

Staff members' and state officials' rhetoric was also banal and repetitive. They made the same claims and recommendations in virtually all their dealings with potentially troublesome others. The claims and recommendations were intended to justify typical and preferred orientations to practical issues, not to provide others with new insights into the sources of and solutions to their troubles. For example, staff members' portrayals of clients' "bad" attitudes as a sign and cause of their troubles and "good" attitudes as solutions were restatements of a widely known and shared orientation to poverty and unemployment in the United States. Indeed, critics of WIN might describe the portrayals as trite and hackneyed justifications of a program that is intended to implement policies that are based on a longstanding concern for blaming the poor for their problems (Auletta, 1982; Ryan, 1971).

However, such an analysis and critique glosses over the ways in which staff members' and state officials' use of banal language was rhetorically useful. Specifically, banal language served two major interests WIN staff members and state officials had in justifying typical and organizationally preferred orientations to clients' and others' troubles. First, it called forth and reaffirmed the typical and preferred orientations. For example, in describing WIN as a job to clients, staff members sought to produce and justify a client orientation to WIN that was similar to that associated with employment settings and relationships. It involved treating one's WIN responsibilities as matters of serious concern and giving them priority over many other concerns in one's life, such as family problems which are supposed to be handled during a person's nonwork time.

The WIN as job claim was also a rhetorical procedure for producing and justifying a preferred client orientation to their AFDC grants. The orientation emphasized clients' obligations in accepting financial support from the government, not their moral and legal right to it. Staff members elaborated on the emphasis by portraying WIN as intended to protect the government's interest in making certain that clients fulfilled their part of the welfare exchange. The portrayal was a rhetorical procedure for extending the WIN as a job claim to staff-client relations. That is, staff members were like employers and, therefore, had the right to make the same demands on clients as employers do on their employees. They also had the right and obligation to terminate (fire) clients who failed to adequately do their WIN jobs.

In sum, the practical usefulness of the WIN as a job claim for the staff was directly related to its ordinariness. It was a metaphor that clients were likely to understand and staff members could (and did) elaborate on to justify a preferred client orientation to WIN. Staff members' related portrayals of themselves as professional problem-solvers and bureaucratic functionaries were similarly banal and rhetorically useful. They called for clear-cut, simple and widely used responses to troubles emergent in staff-client interactions. Specifically, staff members used the first portrayal to cast themselves as caring and competent professionals who understood their clients' troubles better than clients do, just as physicians and auto mechanics have privileged knowledge of their clients' troubles. They elaborated on the image and claim by stating that, like other problem-solvers, WIN staff members sometimes required their clients to make sacrifices that clients don't understand or wish to make, but they must make the sacrifices if they wish to solve their problems.

Staff members cast themselves as bureaucratic functionaries by describing their professional activities as mandated by organizational superiors and policies over which they had no control. In other words, they were "only doing their jobs." In so describing themselves, staff members called for a client orientation to staff-client relationships that treated the undesired demands made by staff members on clients as unrelated to staff members' personal desires. The portrayal called for a client response to WIN assignments that emphasized quiet acceptance of and resignation to the "facts of life" that accompany being a welfare recipient. Staff members used the same claim in troublesome staff-staff interactions concerned with whether typical and preferred responses to clients' troubles were appropriate. They used the claim to call for and justify an orientation to the issue at hand that treated it as a matter of dispassionately fulfilling one's organizational obligations, not doing as one pleased.

The second way in which state officials' and staff members' use of banal language served their rhetorical interests in social interactions with potentially troublesome others involved the kinds of responses that others give to their claims. Banal language does more than cast practical issues within ordinary and predictable interpretive frameworks; it also restricts the range of counterresponses or criticisms that others may level against the initial claims. For example, in portraying clients' "bad" attitudes as signs and causes of their employment troubles, staff members produced social conditions making it necessary for clients to defend or otherwise show that their attitudes were proper and unrelated to their employment troubles. A major way which clients did so was by describing area labor markets as a barrier to finding jobs.

Given the widely acknowledged recessionary condition of the area economy, the response was reasonable, but it was also predictable. The predictability of the response is rhetorically significant because in producing conditions making the response reasonable, staff members also produced conditions that made it possible for them to anticipate and counter clients' claims by describing the area economy as a hurdle. Like the state official in the annual planning meeting, staff members were also able to document their counterclaim by using WIN records. Specifically, they used the records to show clients and the local supervisor that clients were getting jobs despite the condition of area labor markets. Staff members and the state official used the documents to simultaneously justify their recommendations and to cast the fulfillment of organizational expectations as a matter of others' attitudes.

Staff members also used the WIN as a job metaphor to restrict clients' appeals to extenuating circumstances. They did so by emphasizing how clients' appeals would be inappropriate "excuses" in employment settings. The emphasis was a rhetorical procedure for casting the staff's insistence that clients fulfill their WIN assignments as legitimate and restricting the types of justifications that clients could offer for their actions. The justifications were restricted to those that a typical employer would accept as legitimate reasons for missing work. For example, staff members used this rhetorical procedure in conciliation meetings to impress upon clients the seriousness of their complaints and to anticipate and counter clients' excuses for their "uncooperative" behavior.

One way in which they did so was by attempting to get clients to acknowledge that their behavior would result in termination in employment settings before allowing them to explain and justify their failure to fulfill their WIN assignments. Consider, for example, the following exchanges which occurred in conciliation meetings.

> Staff Member: What if you were working [at a regular job] and we were employers? Let's say we called you in to talk about your work record. We'd had you in before and you told us you'd improve your work record and then the next week you didn't show up for work? You overslept. What do you think would happen?
>
> Client: I'd be fired, I guess.
>
> Staff Member: That's right. Look, you're getting money from the [government] and we're like an employer. What would you do to a person with your record if you had to decide?
>
> Client: I'd cut 'em off, I guess.
>
> Staff Member 1 [after reviewing the client's WIN record]: What do you think would happen today if you were an employee and your employer read a record like that?
>
> Client: He'd probably yell at me, maybe let me tell my side, and fire me.
>
> Staff Member 2: Now you understand what's happening here.

The above exchanges also show how staff members used the WIN as a job claim to anticipate and counter clients' portrayals of WIN expectations and procedures as unfair. By portraying the government as clients' employer, staff members produced social conditions for assessing the fairness of WIN expectations and procedures. Staff members' definition of fairness turned on the definition of the expectations and practices of a typical employer. If WIN expectations and procedures could be shown to be consistent with those of a typical employer, then they were fair. Clients who criticized these definitions of WIN and fairness risked having their motives and moral character challenged by staff members. For example, staff members responded to client criticisms by emphasizing the responsibilities that accompany being on welfare and that "welfare doesn't have to be fair." In these ways, staff members challenged clients' moral right to criticize and assigned undesired identities to clients who did criticize WIN.

Thus, although staff members and state officials were not able to eliminate troublesome interactions, they attempted to restrict and manage the troubles that others could create for them. Central to their efforts to achieve this rhetorical goal was banal language.

Conclusion

The aspects of rhetoric and everyday life in WIN discussed in this chapter may be generalized to other street-level bureaucracies. Specifically, other studies might also consider how street-level bureaucrats and others in their work worlds rhetorically produce major social values, such as personal responsibility and cooperation. They might also analyze the ways in which street-level bureaucrats and others strategically manage interactional turns to achieve their practical interests in their dealings with others. Finally, further research needs to be done on the social organization and uses of political language in street-level bureaucracies. The research promises to provide fresh insight into the ways in which street-level bureaucracies are maintained as social worlds made up of potentially troublesome but, nonetheless, routine and predictable relationships and activities.

Whatever their concrete research interests, analysts of rhetoric and everyday life in street-level bureaucracies must base their studies on an appreciation of the practical and political significance of ordinary language. It is the resource from which social problems and their solutions are created and sustained.

Notes

Notes to Chapter 1

1. For example, this use of the term *rhetoric* may be compared and contrasted with McCloskey's (1985) use of it. He states that rhetoric refers to the ways in which speakers "pay attention" to their audiences. He elaborates on this definition by portraying rhetoric as a "way of accomplishing things with language" (McCloskey, 1985: xvii). I also treat rhetoric as a way of taking account of others and accomplishing one's practical goals. But in the cases of WIN and other street-level bureaucracies, at least, these activities are political events centered in persuasion. Thus, I emphasize the persuasive aspect of rhetoric to a much greater degree than McCloskey.

2. See Bilmes (1986), Button and Lee (1987), Gumperz (1982), Levinson (1988), Maynard (1988), Moerman (1988) and Stubbs (1983) for other definitions of and approaches to discourse and discourse analysis.

3. Similar findings are reported by McCleary (1978) about probation officers' relationships with their clients and Glaser and Strauss (1965) about nurse-patient relations.

Note to Chapter 4

1. See Dingwall and Strong (1985) for a more comprehensive statement on many of the issues that underlie this aspect of the analysis. In particular, they offer a logic and rationale for analyzing legitimations of organizations as sometimes based on appeals to organizational spirit and other times on written rules.

Note to Chapter 7

1. This orientation to work is generally consistent with ethnomethodology which also focuses on the ways in which social institutions are interactively produced and maintained. Perhaps the best analysis of this aspect of ethnomethodology is offered by Heritage (1984).

References

Adam, Barry D. 1978. *The Survival of Domination*. New York: Elsevier.

Altheide, David L. and John M. Johnson. 1980. *Bureaucratic Propaganda*. Boston: Allyn and Bacon.

Atkinson, J. Maxwell and Paul Drew. 1976. *Order in Court*. Atlantic Highlands, NJ: Humanities Press.

Atkinson, J. Maxwell. 1984a. "Public Speaking and Audience Responses." Pp. 346–369 in J. Maxwell Atkinson and John Heritage (eds.), *Structures of Social Action*. Cambridge: Cambridge University Press.

_____. 1984b. *Our Masters' Voices*. London: Methuen.

Auletta, Ken. 1982. *The Underclass*. New York: Random House.

Austin, J. L. 1962. *How to Do Things With Words*. London: Oxford University Press.

Banfield, Edward C. 1968. *The Unheavenly City Revisited*. Boston: Little, Brown and Company.

Barthes, Roland. 1964. *Elements of Semiology*. New York: Hill and Wang.

Billig, Michael. 1987. *Arguing and Thinking*. Cambridge: Cambridge University Press.

Bilmes, Jack. 1986. *Discourse and Behavior*. New York: Plenum Press.

Buckholdt, David R. and Jaber F. Gubrium. 1979. *Caretakers*. Beverly Hills, CA: Sage Publications.

Burke, Kenneth. 1950. *A Rhetoric of Motives*. New York: Prentice-Hall.

Button, Graham and John R. E. Lee. (eds.) 1987. *Talk and Social Organization*. Clevedon: Multilingual Matters Ltd.

Coudroglou, Aliki. 1982. *Work, Women and the Struggle for Self-Sufficiency*. Washington, DC: University Press of America.

Dingwall, Robert and Phil M. Strong. 1985. "The Interactional Study of Organizations." *Urban Life* 14: 205–231.

Dressell, Paula. 1984. *The Service Trap*. Springfield, IL: Charles C. Thomas.

Edelman, Murray. 1964. *The Symbolic Uses of Politics*. Urbana: University of Illinois Press.

_____. 1971. *Politics as Symbolic Action*. New York: Academic Press.

_____. 1977. *Political Language*. New York: Academic Press.

_____. 1988. *Constructing the Political Spectacle.* Chicago: University of Chicago Press.

Emerson, Robert M. 1969. *Judging Delinquents.* Chicago: Aldine Publishing Company.

_____. 1981. "On Last Resorts." *American Journal of Sociology* 86: 1–22.

Emerson, Robert M. and Sheldon L. Messinger. 1977. "The Micro-Politics of Trouble." *Social Problems* 25: 121–135.

Garfinkel, Harold. 1967. *Studies in Ethnomethodology.* Englewood Cliffs, NJ: Prentice-Hall.

Garraty, John A. 1978. *Unemployment Through History.* New York: Harper and Row, Publishers, Inc.

Glaser, Barney G. and Anselm L. Strauss. 1965. *Awareness of Dying.* Chicago: Aldine Publishing Company.

Goffman, Erving. 1963. *Stigma.* Englewood Cliffs, NJ: Prentice-Hall.

_____. 1959. *The Presentation of Self in Everyday Life.* New York: Doubleday.

Gronjberg, Kriston, David Street, and Gerald D. Suttles. 1978. *Poverty and Social Change.* Chicago: University of Chicago Press.

Gubrium, Jaber F. 1980. "Patient Exclusion in Geriatric Settings." *The Sociological Quarterly* 21: 335–348.

_____. 1988. *Analyzing Field Reality.* Beverly Hills, CA: Sage Publications.

Gumperz, John J. (ed.). 1982. *Language and Social Identity.* Cambridge: Cambridge University Press.

Hall, Peter M. and John P. Hewitt. 1970. "The Quasi-Theory of Communication and the Management of Dissent." *Social Problems* 18: 17–27.

Haug, Marie R. and Marvin Sussman. 1969a. "Professional Autonomy and the Revolt of the Client." *Social Problems* 17: 153–161.

_____. 1969b. "Professionalism and the Public." *Sociological Inquiry* 39: 57–67.

Heritage, John. 1984. *Garfinkel and Ethnomethodology.* Cambridge: Polity Press.

Hewitt, John P. and Peter M. Hall. 1973. "Social Problems, Problematic Situations, and Quasi-Theories." *American Sociological Review* 38: 367–376.

Higgins, Paul C. 1985. *The Rehabilitation Detectives.* Beverly Hills, CA: Sage Publications.

Holstein, James A. and Gale Miller. 1990. "Rethinking Victimization." *Symbolic Interaction* 13: 101–120.

Holstein, James A. 1984. "The Placement of Insanity." *Urban Life* 13: 25–52.

_____. 1987. "Producing Gender Effects in Involuntary Mental Hospitalizations." *Social Problems* 34: 301–315.

_____. 1988. "Court Ordered Incompetence." *Social Problems* 35: 458–474.

Johnson, Miriam. 1973. *Counter Point.* Salt Lake City, UT: Olympus Publishing Company.

Ker Muir, William. 1977. *Police.* Chicago: University of Chicago Press.

Levinson, Stephen C. 1988. *Pragmatics.* Cambridge: Cambridge University Press.

Lewis, Oscar. 1966a. "The Culture of Poverty." *Scientific American* 215: 19–25.

———. 1966b. *La Vida.* New York: Random House.

Lipsky, Michael. 1980. *Street-Level Bureaucracy.* New York: Russell Sage.

Macarov, David. 1980. *Work and Welfare.* Beverly Hills, CA: Sage Publications.

Manning, Peter K. 1987. *Semiotics and Fieldwork.* Newbury Park, CA: Sage Publications.

Maynard, Douglas W. 1984. *Inside Plea Bargaining.* New York: Plenum Press.

———. 1988. "Language, Interaction and Social Problems." *Social Problems* 35: 311–335.

McCleary, Richard. 1978. *Dangerous Men.* Beverly Hills, CA: Sage Publications.

McCloskey, Donald N. 1985. *The Rhetoric of Economics.* Madison, WI: University of Wisconsin Press.

Miller, Gale. 1981. *It's a Living.* New York: St. Martin's Press.

———. 1987. "Producing Family Problems." *Symbolic Interaction* 10: 245–265.

Miller, Gale and James A. Holstein. in press. "Social Problems Work in Street-Level Bureaucracies." In Gale Miller (ed.) *Studies in Organizational Sociology.* Greenwich, CT: JAI Press.

Moerman, Michael. 1988. *Talking Culture.* Philadelphia: University of Pennsylvania Press.

Paine, Robert (ed.). 1981. *Politically Speaking.* Philadelphia: ISHI.

Patterson, James T. 1981. *America's Struggle Against Poverty, 1900–1980.* Cambridge, MA: Harvard University Press.

Perelman, Chaim. 1979. *The New Rhetoric and the Humanities.* Dordrect, Holland: D. Reidel Publishing Company.

Piven, Frances Fox and Richard A. Cloward. 1971. *Regulating the Poor.* New York: Random House.

Pollner, Melvin. 1987. *Mundane Reason.* Cambridge: Cambridge University Press.

Potter, Jonathan and Margaret Wetherell. 1987. *Discourse and Social Psychology.* London: Sage Publications.

Rein, Mildred. 1974. *Work and Welfare?.* New York: Praeger.

Ryan, Michael. 1971. *Blaming the Victim.* New York: The Free Press.

Sacks, Harvey, Emmanuel A. Schegloff and Gail Jefferson. 1978. "A Simplest Systematics for the Organization of Turn Taking for Conversation. Pp. 7–56 in Jim Schenkein (ed.) *Studies in the Organization of Conversational Interaction.* New York: Academic Press.

Sanders, William B. 1977. *Detective Work*. New York: The Free Press.
_____. 1980. *Rape and Women's Identity*. Beverly Hills, CA: Sage Publications.
de Saussure, Ferdinand D. 1974. *Course in General Linguistics*. London: Fontana.
Schutz, Alfred. 1970. *On Phenomenology and Social Relations*. Helmut Wagner (ed. and trans.). Chicago: University of Chicago Press.
Schwartz, Howard and Jerry Jacobs. 1979. *Qualitative Sociology*. New York: Free Press.
Searle, J. R., F. Kiefer and M. Bierwisch (eds.). 1979. *Studies in Semantics and Pragmatics*. Dordrect, Holland: D. Reidel Publishing Company.
Segalman, Ralph and Asoke Basu. 1981. *Poverty in America*. Westport, CO: Greenwood Press.
Silverman, David. 1987. *Communication and Medical Practice*. Beverly Hills, CA: Sage Publications.
Stanton, Esther. 1970. *Clients Come Last*. Beverly Hills, CA: Sage Publications.
Stein, Bruno. 1976. *Work and Welfare in Britain and America*. New York: John Wiley.
Stojkovic, Stan. 1990. "Accounts of Prison Work." Pp. 211–230 in Gale Miller and James A. Holstein (eds.). *Perspectives on Social Problems* Vol. 2. Greenwich, CT: JAI Press.
Strong, P. M. 1979. *The Ceremonial Order of the Clinic*. London: Routledge and Kegan Paul.
Stubbs, Michael. 1983. *Discourse Analysis*. Chicago: University of Chicago Press.
Sudnow, David. 1965. "Normal Crimes." *Social Problems* 12: 257–276.
Toulmin, Stephen Edelston. 1958. *The Uses of Argument*. Cambridge: Cambridge University Press.
U.S. Congress. 1936. "Social Security Act." Pp. 620–647 in *The Statutes at Large of the United States of America Passed by the Seventy-Fourth Congress, 1935–1936*. Washington, DC: U.S. Government Printing Office.
_____. 1967. "Social Security Amendments of 1967." Pp. 1002–1019 in *United States Congressional and Administrative News*. St. Paul, MN: West Publishing.
_____. 1972. "Social Security Amendments of 1972." Pp. 4989–4994 in *United States Congressional and Administrative News*. St. Paul, MN: West Publishing.
_____. 1980. "Social Security Disability Amendments of 1930." Pp. 441–481 in *United States Congressional and Administrative News*. St. Paul, MN: West Publishing.
Wadel, Cato. 1979. "The Hidden Work of Everyday Life." Pp. 365–384 in Sandra Wallman (ed.) *Social Anthropology of Work*. New York:

Academic Press.

Warren, Carol A. B. 1982. *The Court of Last Resort.* Chicago: University of Chicago Press.

Weinstein, Eugene A. and Paul Deutschberger. 1963. "Some Dimensions of Altercasting." *Sociometry* 26: 454–466.

Willard, Charles. 1983. *Argumentation and the Social Grounds of Knowledge.* Tuscaloosa, Alabama: University of Alabama Press.

Willis, Paul. 1977. *Learning to Labor.* New York: Columbia University Press.

Wiseman, Jacqueline P. 1979. *Stations of the Lost.* Chicago: University of Chicago Press.

Zimmerman, Don H. and Melvin Pollner. 1971. "The Everyday World as a Phenomenon." Pp. 80–103 in Jack D. Douglas (ed.) *Understanding Everyday Life.* Chicago: Aldine.

Name Index

Subject Index

Acquiescence: in street-level bureaucracies 10–11, 18–19, 23, 30, 33, 35, 78, 99, 214; client acquiescence to staff members 10–11, 105–196, 113–114, 135, 148, 186, 221, 239; as interactionally produced 23, 28, 215, 219, 234, 237–238; staff member acquiescence to the WIN supervisor 30, 35, 148, 232–233; WIN supervisor acquiescence to state officials 32, 173, 232–233; production of 219, 234, 237–238; signalling a willingness to 28, 228–231

Aid to Families with Dependent Children (AFDC) 1, 35, 37, 43–45, 47–48, 70, 77–78, 86, 103–108, 112, 114, 117, 120, 129, 140–141, 153, 180, 220, 222, 226, 228, 235

Altercasting: definition of 73; as remedy 74; as inferiorization 143

Annual Planning Meeting: staff members' orientation to 96, 98; as unfair 97; justifying agency goals 97–98; staff official's orientation to 98, 218; as a game 98, 232; negotiating agency goals 167, 176, 220, 232; and the definition of clients' troubles 168–173

Argumentation: social organization of 8–9; as witcraft 23, 30; as interactional sequences 23, 30, 148, 234; and staff member orientations 69, 99, 150, 219

Arguments: definition of 7, 18, 20–22; as reality contests 8; as witcraft 23; as interactional sequences 23–24, 28–31, 67, 69, 72, 146, 148–149; 174, 216–217, 219, 234–235; staff-client interactions as potential arguments 69, 77–81, 83, 104, 109, 115, 118, 167, 235–239; staff-state official interactions as potential arguments 69, 92, 97–98, 176, 220; staff-social service official interactions as potential arguments 71–72; staff-employer interactions as potential arguments 72–75

Bureaucratic Propaganda: definition of 215; and WIN 216–218

Clients' Attitudes: bad attitude 70, 154–155, 158–159, 161; teaching attitude assessment 82–84; as solution to clients' troubles 140, 152; staff

249

Compiled by
Andrea Fechner-Butler